THE BLACK SOLDIER AND OFFICER
IN THE UNITED STATES ARMY

The Black Soldier and Officer
In the United States Army
1891–1917

Marvin Fletcher

University of Missouri Press

The substance of Chapter VI originally appeared as
"The Black Soldier Athlete in the United States Army,
1890–1916,"
in the *Canadian Journal of History of Sport and Physical
Education,* vol. 3, no. 2, December 1972.

Dedication
To
My Mother and Father

Acknowledgments

This study orginally began as a doctoral dissertation at the University of Wisconsin. I would like to thank Professor Edward M. Coffman for his guidance on the original work and on the several revisions that I have made since.

There are a number of other people who helped me in doing the research for this volume. They include librarians and archivists at the State Historical Society of Wisconsin, the New York Public Library, the National Archives, the Library of Congress, the Stanford University Library, the Chicago Historical Society, and the Ohio University Library.

I would especially like to thank the staff of the Old Military Records section of the National Archives for their assistance during the summer I spent there doing research. The personnel records, enlistment papers, muster rolls, and officer appointment and promotion papers used in this study are normally closed to researchers. The staff of the Old Military Records section granted me the use of these records, "*Provided* you agree to omit all references to names of individual officers and enlisted men."

Professor Louis Harlan of the University of Maryland was of invaluable assistance in locating pertinent items in the Booker T. Washington Papers. I would also like to thank the many officers, their descendants, and the black enlisted men who answered my questionnaires and consented to be interviewed. I would also like to acknowledge the late Brig. Gen. Benjamin O. Davis and his daughter, Mrs. James McLendon, for giving me some insight into the life of a black officer in this period.

Lastly, and most importantly, I would like to thank my wife Hilary. Her assistance in reading and correcting the many drafts of this manuscript was invaluable. In many ways this book is really a joint effort.

M. E. F.
Athens, Ohio
7 March 1974

Contents

I

AN INTRODUCTION

On 1 July 1898 a group of white and black soldiers and officers attacked the Spanish positions on San Juan Heights, outside Santiago, Cuba. The Tenth Calvary, an all-black regiment led by John J. Pershing, took part in the battle. Shortly thereafter Pershing described his reaction to that successful assault. "We officers of the Tenth Cavalry could have taken our black heroes into our arms. They had fought their way into our affections, as they have fought their way into the hearts of the American people." Five months later the same regiment was stationed in Huntsville, Alabama, when a black civilian killed two black enlisted men, Pvt. John R. Brooks and Cpl. Daniel Garrett, both of H Troop. The assassin was apparently motivated by an announcement made by unknown white civilians that there was a reward for every dead black cavalryman. Another member of the Tenth voiced his feelings about this situation in a letter to the Springfield *Illinois Record:* "Cuba was a paradise. There we expected and looked for trouble. Our enemies were there, but here it is among our supposed friends . . . that we face a more deadly enemy, an assassin who lays and waits for you at night and shoots you down without a word of warning." These two incidents exemplify the paradox that is woven through the fabric of the history of the black soldier and sailor in America. In war Blacks provided a ready and willing source of manpower and performed with bravery and loyalty; in peacetime whites either ignored their military potential, or if they reluctantly used them, subjected them to the whims of a prejudiced white society.[1]

Blacks contributed to the defense of the United States long before the Revolution, but whites excluded them from the colonial militia in peacetime. The southern colonies were particu-

1. John J. Pershing, speech, 20 November 1898, Box 369, JJP, Papers (all abbreviations and shortened expressions used in the footnotes are expanded in the list on pp. 195–96); *The Illinois Record,* 3 December 1898.

11

larly wary of arming Blacks. They feared that such a step was the fastest way to start a slave revolt. During the French and Indian War, Virginia faced the decision of whether or not to arm Blacks. After the defeat of Gen. Edward Braddock in 1755, men were needed to defend the frontier of the colony against the French and the Indians. The colonial legislature called out the militia but balked at arming Blacks, either slave or free. The legislature's solution was to allow free Blacks to enlist in the militia to fill positions that did not require firearms, such as drummers, pioneers, or manual laborers.[2]

During the American Revolution, again the military initially refused to utilize black manpower in any capacity. One of the first tasks that faced George Washington when he took over command of the American army in early July 1775 was to create policy for the recruitment and expansion of his forces. The army that he took over had a number of Blacks in it, such as Salem Poor, who had taken part in the recently concluded defense of Bunker Hill. Yet at the council of war held shortly after Washington's arrival, the decision was made not to enroll "any deserter from the Ministerial army, nor any stroller, negro, or vagabond." Shortly thereafter Edward Rutledge, a delegate from South Carolina, tried to persuade the Continental Army to discharge those Blacks already in the service, but he found little support for this idea. The question came up again in October of that year, and Washington, his staff, and Congress, agreed that no Blacks, whether slave or free, should be allowed in the Continental Army. Washington's staff issued the order to enforce this decision in November 1775: "Neither Negroes, Boys unable to bare Arms, nor old men unfit to endure the fatigues of the campaign, are to be inlisted."[3]

Washington was soon forced to modify his position. At the same time as he issued the edict barring Blacks, John Murray, Earl of Dunmore, who was royal governor of Virginia, pro-claimed "all indented servants, Negroes, or others (appertaining to Rebels), free, that are able and willing to bear arms, they joining His Majesty's Troops." The next month Washington moved to retain the allegiance of at least the free Blacks. He asked for and Congress passed a resolution to allow "the free

2. Larry G. Bowman, "Virginia's Use of Blacks in the French and Indian War," pp. 57–63.

3. Pete Maslowski, "National Policy Toward the Use of Black Troops in the Revolution," pp. 2–4.

negroes who have served faithfully in the army at Cambridge," to reenlist. Shortly thereafter, free Blacks were allowed to be recruited.[4]

As the war progressed, the need for manpower became more acute. At the same time, many Americans realized that the acceptance of slavery was not consistent with the purpose of the Revolution—to obtain freedom from tyranny. In January 1778 Gen. James Varnum of Rhode Island suggested that a battalion of black slaves be recruited and the soldiers then be given their freedom. Washington gave tacit approval to the project. The next month the state legislature of Rhode Island passed a law to carry that plan into effect. Its key provision said, "That every slave, so enlising, shall be immediately discharged from the service of his master or mistress, and be absolutely FREE." This practice was soon adopted in other states.[5]

By the summer of 1778 the Continental Army had a number of Blacks in its ranks. The typical black soldier was a private, often carried on the rolls as "A Negro Man" or "A Negro name unknown." Among their duties was serving the officers. One such black servant was Jordan Freeman, who helped defend Fort Griswold against British attack in 1781. He died along with the rest of the men in the garrison when the British refused to protect the Americans after they had surrendered. Another typical assignment was that fulfilled by Jabez Jolly, a drummer for the Seventh Massachusetts Regiment. Other Blacks served as foragers, workers, and infantrymen. Although their service was not welcomed at first, as whites' enthusiasm for the war decreased, their role became more respected and important.[6]

Blacks also contributed to the various navies that had been created by the Continental Congress and many of the states. In addition they joined the privateers, who engaged in legalized piracy. Surriname Wanton and Loushir were bondsmen of Commodore Esek Hopkins, and they sailed on one of the first ships of the new Continental Navy. However, black sailors were more readily accepted than soldiers because they had been seafarers before the war, and manpower was in shorter supply at sea than in the army. Blacks had often been employed as seamen and pilots during colonial times. During the war they

4. Ibid., pp. 4–6.

5. Leslie H. Fishel, Jr., and Benjamin Quarles, *The Black American, A Brief Documentary History*, p. 31.

6. Benjamin Quarles, *The Negro in the American Revolution*, pp. 71–78.

served as seamen, manned guns, and acted as pilots. One of the best-known pilots was Caesar, the slave of Carter Tarrant of Hampton, Virginia. He served as a pilot in the Virginia Navy during the war and fought in a number of engagements. After the war the state legislature bought Caesar from Tarrant and then gave him his freedom. Black abolitionist James Forten enlisted at age fourteen as a powder boy on the Pennsylvania ship *Royal Louis.* Shortly thereafter this ship was captured by a British warship, and Forten and the other members of the crew became prisoners. The British captain and his young son tried to convince Forten to renounce his allegiance to America, but he refused. As a result he spent seven months in a British prison ship before he was exchanged along with the other prisoners at the end of the war.[7]

During the period of peace between 1783 and 1812, the practices established at the beginning of the Revolution were reinstituted; Blacks were excluded from the navy and the small professional army that remained. The Militia Law of 1792, which established the pattern for the main line of defense of the United States, pertained only to white males. Because of the law and since there were enough whites to man the land forces, the question of enlisting Blacks was usually ignored. However, they continued to serve in the merchant marine and in the navy, when it was rebuilt in the 1790s. As tension built between the United States and the two warring powers in Europe, England and France, black sailors became involved. One of the most infamous events leading up to the War of 1812 was the *Chesapeake-Leopard* affair (1806). The *H.M.S. Leopard,* in an effort to find escaped British seamen, tried to stop the *U.S.S. Chesapeake.* When the *Chesapeake* refused to be stopped and boarded, the British opened fire. The Americans stopped and the British took four men into custody, including David Martin, a Black from Massachusetts, who had previously been impressed by the British and then escaped. The British did not release Martin until six years later.[8]

In the War of 1812 Blacks were again used in the land forces only when the situation got rough for the whites, but they had a much better status in the naval forces. They usually served as labor troops in the army. For example, James Forten, by then

7. Ibid., pp. 83–93.

8. Laura E. Wilkes, *Missing Pages in American History, Revealing the Services of Negroes in the United States of America, 1641–1815,* p. 62

on his way to becoming a very wealthy man, and twenty-five hundred other Blacks voluntarily served the city of Philadelphia by constructing fortifications. Late in the war (1814) the state of New York provided for the creation of two black regiments to be commanded by whites. If slaves enlisted, they were granted their freedom upon completion of service.[9]

Probably the most famous example of service of Blacks in the war occurred in Louisiana. In September 1812 the state legislature passed a bill including in the state militia a corps of free Blacks, each of whom had to own property of at least $300 in value. This group, which became known as the Battalion of Free Men of Color, had black officers as well as enlisted men, though the high positions of command remained in the hands of whites. By 1814 they had become a fairly well-organized unit. The governor of the state informed Gen. Andrew Jackson that the training of these black militiamen was complete. In return Jackson issued a proclamation to stimulate enlistment of more Blacks into the militia. "As sons of freedom, you are now called upon to defend our most inestimable blessing." Jackson went on to say that those who volunteered were to be given the same bounties as offered to white soldiers, $124 and 160 acres of land. The commissioned officers were to be appointed "from your white fellow citizens," while the Blacks were to be the NCOs. "As a distinct, independent battalion or regiment, pursuing the path of glory, you will, undivided, receive the applause and gratitude of your countrymen." Joseph Savary, a black man from Santo Domingo, took up the challenge and organized the second battalion of Blacks under Jackson's command. Savary attained the rank of second major, but command was still in the hands of whites.[10]

The two battalions of black troops, one of which was the former Battalion of Free Men of Color, were mustered into the service of the United States and took part in the Battle of New Orleans. One battalion took a leading part in the attack on the advancing British forces at Chalmette Plains in late December 1814. The other battalion helped prepare the fortifications that the British would attack in early January in the main battle. During the British attack on 8 January 1815 both battalions

9. Ibid., pp. 65–66.
10. Roland C. McConnell, *Negro Troops of Antebellum Louisiana: A History of the Battalion of Free Men of Color*, pp. 53, 62–63; Fishel and Quarles, *The Black American*, pp. 100–101.

held the center of the line and defended two batteries of artillery. They were scarcely touched since the British columns concentrated on the flanks. After the major part of the battle was over, Joseph Savary led a group of men to stop the British sharpshooters who were annoying parties looking for the wounded. A small skirmish ensued and the British retreated. Ten of the company were wounded in this last significant action of the battle. As General Jackson said, the black volunteers had "not disappointed the hopes that were formed of their courage and perserverance in the performance of their duty." He also said that Savory "continued to merit the highest praise."[11]

Battles at sea also involved Blacks. They again played a part on the privateers and in the United States Navy. Cyrus Tiffany was a sailor on the *U.S.S. Lawrence*, Capt. Oliver H. Perry's flagship on Lake Erie. When the ship was hit during the battle at Put-in-Bay in July 1814, Tiffany was one of the sailors who rowed Perry to the *U.S.S. Niagara*, which then became the flagship of the fleet. The British saw the movement, tried to sink the small craft, and Tiffany used himself as a human shield to protect Perry.[12]

In the years between the end of the War of 1812 and the Civil War the black soldier and sailor returned to their prewar status. Blacks were excluded from the Regular Army but used in the navy, where they served not only as cooks and stewards but also as common seamen. Blacks were so commonly employed on overseas voyages that an American traveler, Nathaniel P. Willis, recalled this conversation about American seamen among several Europeans on a journey from Trieste to Vienna. It seems that they had seen the *U.S.S. Constellation* when it was in Trieste, and one of the cutters of the vessel had been manned by an all-black crew. The four Europeans therefore assumed that all people from the United States were black.[13]

Although officials were not enthusiastic about recruiting Blacks for the army at the beginning of the Civil War, Blacks still made up a substantial part of the navy. Gideon Welles, Secretary of the Navy, decided early in the war to enlist Blacks. Throughout the war they were enlisted "under the same forms and regulations" as whites. They served on many of the vessels

11. McConnell, *Negro Troops of Antebellum Lousiana*, pp. 69–91.

12. Wilkes, *Missing Pages*, pp. 67–73.

13. Harold D. Langley, "The Negro in the Navy and Merchant Service, 1798–1860," pp. 277–79.

of the navy, which were necessarily integrated. One of the most famous seamen was Robert Smalls. He had been a slave seaman and pilot before the war. During the first two years of the conflict the Confederates used him aboard an old cotton boat, the *Planter.* In May 1862, on a night when the ship's three white officers were ashore, Smalls and sixteen other slaves took over the vessel and sailed it out of Charleston harbor and into the control of the Union forces. The vessel was used by both the navy and the army until the end of the war. Smalls was first the pilot of the vessel and later became captain.[14]

The situation was much different in the land forces. In the beginning of the war white units had no trouble recruiting up to strength. The general antipathy toward Blacks motivated the opposition to their emancipation and enlistment. For most white northerners the purpose of the war was to save the Union. Black leaders like Frederick Douglass and Martin Delaney did not meekly accept this verdict. "Though ignored by our friends and repelled by our enemies, the colored people, both north and south, have evinced the most ardent desire to serve the cause of the country." Their efforts were directed at both a change in the goals of the war and an acceptance of black soldiers. They found some supporters in the Union Army. In early 1862 Gen. David Hunter, the commander of the Department of the South, decided to free the slaves in his area and to recruit them into units under his command. The initial result was the creation of the First South Carolina Volunteer Infantry and at first the response of Blacks was enthusiastic, but Hunter's highhanded tactics of drafting unwilling Blacks soon soured the rest. President Abraham Lincoln was not yet in favor of this type of recruiting policy, and the Administration put an end to the experiment.[15]

Shortly after the end of the experiment in South Carolina, some politically astute men in Kansas and Louisiana began to organize their own units of Blacks. Sen. James Lane in Kansas and Gen. Benjamin Butler in Louisiana seized the initiative but were more tactful in their methods than Hunter had been. In addition a variety of circumstances forced the Administration to accept the Lane-Butler method of bolstering troops. In mid-

14. Dudley T. Cornish, *The Sable Arm: Negro Troops in the Union Army, 1861–1865,* pp. 17–18; Jay David and Elaine Craine, *The Black Soldier—From the American Revolution to Vietnam,* pp. 79–87.

15. Thomas R. Frazier, ed., *Afro-American History: Primary Sources,* p. 133; Cornish, *The Sable Arm,* pp. 35–40.

1862 the war was going badly, enlistments were dropping, enthusiasm for the war had generally disappeared, and although Great Britain and France remained neutral, they were giving some aid to the South. Abolitionists took advantage of the situation to bring forward their arguments to convert the war into a crusade against slavery. Lincoln's decision to change the goals of the war in mid-1862 and his announcement of the preliminary Emancipation Proclamation were but short steps to the acceptance of black soldiers.

The Administration continued the Kansas and Louisiana units and sanctioned another try in South Carolina. Gen. Rufus Saxton, already in the Department of the South, was authorized in August 1862 to reactivate the First South Carolina. He placed it under the command of Col. Thomas W. Higginson, an abolitionist from New England. The unit was a success, and Higginson used it as propaganda throughout the North. This experience helped build pressure for more such units. In early 1863, after the issuance of the final Emancipation Proclamation, the Lincoln Administration took the last step and authorized the creation of the United States Colored Troops as part of the volunteer army.

The unproven assumptions of white military leaders about the abilities of Blacks as soldiers greatly influenced the history of this section of the Union Army. They were affected by their prejudices even when they viewed the actual performance of the black troops. Colonel Higginson's views were typical. He believed that Blacks learned drill quickly. "One wants a squad of eager, active, pliant school-boys; and the more childlike these pupils are the better . . . . They are simple, docile, and affectionate almost to the point of absurdity." More than 180,000 Blacks served in the USCT units, which made up about 10 per cent of the total strength of the Union forces. They were organized into 120 infantry regiments, 7 cavalry regiments, 12 regiments of heavy artillery, and 10 batteries of light artillery. There was a difference of opinion concerning the competency of Blacks in combat; some officers felt they were cowards and would do best as labor troops. These generals, such as William T. Sherman, had the Black troops that were under their command dig ditches, build roads, move supplies, and construct fortifications. On the other hand, as the result of the performance of Black troops at such battles as Port Hudson, Fort Wagner, and Milliken's Bend, other Union generals came to believe that black soldiers did make good combat troops. After the battle of Port Hudson, when several black regiments attacked entrenched Confederate positions, Gen. Nathaniel Banks was glowing in his praise. "The severe test to which they were subjected, and the determined manner in which they encountered the enemy, leaves upon my mind no doubt to their ultimate success." [16]

Racial separation was a key policy. No one considered integrating the USCT into the rest of the Union Army or combining white and black troops into the same units. The only whites in the USCT were the officers, another result of beliefs about the Blacks' capabilities. Army officers accepted the concept that a black soldier would not follow the commands of a black officer. Therefore, out of a cadre of more than five thousand officers in the USCT, only about one hundred were black. The regiments, organized by General Butler, contained most of these officers. Even though the Federal Government had begun to organize and raise the black regiments, few of these Blacks received commissions.[17]

At the end of the war in 1865 military leaders made an effort to evaluate the performance of the black troops. Many believed that Blacks had proved they could be good soldiers. Maj. Gen. Lorenzo Thomas, organizer of the initial USCT units, said, "The blacks themselves . . . by their coolness and determination in battle fought themselves into their present high standing as soldiers." Other military observers saw the events differently. "Taken together, they were not equal to the same number of white troops." [18] The experiences of the war did make clear how reluctant the military was to use black manpower. Within a year of the end of the war Congress passed legislation incorporating several black units into the Regular Army.

The debate over the reorganization of the Regular Army took place during the first six months of 1866. It was closely tied to the emerging battle between President Andrew Johnson and the Radical Republicans and their respective plans for reconstruction. The size of the army would have to be determined by the types of tasks to which it would be assigned. Everyone felt that the army needed more troops to pacify the Indians on the

---

16. David and Crane, *The Black Soldier,* p. 61; Cornish, *The Sable Arm,* pp. 240, 143.

17. Cornish, *The Sable Arm,* pp. 214, 217.

18. Marvin E. Fletcher, "The Blacks in Blue: Negro Volunteers in Reconstruction," p. 4. .

frontier. In addition many Radical Republicans wanted a large army to carry out their highly controversial plans for the reconstruction of the South. There were many suggestions as to the strength and composition of the army. From almost the beginning, the bills included provisions for black infantry and cavalry units. The first bill introduced included a provision for one black artillery regiment, but on the advice of Ulysses S. Grant, the Commanding General, Congress deleted that section. Grant and most of the others in the military establishment assumed that Blacks were not intelligent enough for this highly technical duty. Once past this hurdle, the real work got underway.[19]

The voting lineups on the issue of the inclusion of black units in the Regular Army were closely related to the Radical Republican–Andrew Johnson split. The Radical Republicans supported the final legislation, which included six black units in a greatly expanded Regular Army; the conservatives opposed it. Many of the Radicals supported this bill because it would aid their black allies, punish the South, and increase the force they could use to implement their policies. Some historians have argued that Blacks were included mainly as the result of a need for manpower. Given the military's generally negative opinion about the capabilities of Blacks and the small number of them who actually became soldiers, it is clear that political issues were also involved in the decision. The Radical Republicans achieved their purpose, and the Regular Army reluctantly admitted the black soldiers.[20]

The new black segment of the army consisted of two cavalry regiments, the Ninth and Tenth, and four infantry regiments, the Thirty-eighth, Thirty-ninth, Fortieth, and Forty-first.

Congress had deliberately made provision to segregate the black units in the 1866 legislation, ostensibly to avoid the issue of racial superiority. Sen. James G. Blaine, a leading Republican politician from Maine, stated in a speech he made in the Senate several years later that the separation stipulated in the 1866 law was "to give the colored man the right to enlist in the Army of the United States, and not to raise unnecessarily the question of caste, and color, and prejudice in the Army." Actually, Congress was not ready to implement so great a social

19. Ibid., pp. 62–81.

20. Ibid.; Thomas D. Phillips, "The Black Regulars," in *The West of the American People*, eds. Allan G. Bogue, Thomas D. Phillips, and James E. Wright, p. 138.

change in the 1860s, and despite Blaine's disclaimer, the existence of these regiments did raise a whole variety of questions concerning the color line.[21]

In 1869 all of the infantry regiments were consolidated, and the four black units became two, the Twenty-fourth and Twenty-fifth. These four units were the only ones in the Regular Army that allowed Blacks until 1944, when the army disbanded the two cavalry regiments, and in 1950, when the army began the process of desegregation.

The process of organizing, staffing, and recruiting for the new regiments was often beset by problems. Until the end of the Indian War period (1865–1890), an officer was promoted within a regiment until he reached the rank of colonel. Many officers were reluctant to take positions in the black regiments because of the effect they believed this service might have on the rest of their careers. For example, George Custer turned down the colonelcy in one of these regiments to take a lower-ranking position in a white regiment. The officers also doubted the ability of black men to become competent soldiers and the possibility of getting skilled and literate enlisted men to fill positions of company and regimental noncommissioned officers. Despite their record in the Civil War, General Sherman said that they were a "quiet kindly peaceful race of men. Naturally not addicted to war." The need for skilled men was a real problem, and the officers often had to perform tasks that were performed by noncommissioned officers in white regiments, where a greater number of soldiers were literate. Despite the handicaps, the army needed and used the services of the new black Regulars.[22]

Because of budgetary considerations and military necessity, the general hostility toward Blacks was tempered and submerged for a time. For the first ten years of the Indian War period the army tried to keep the black regiments on the Texas frontier. Later the War Department assigned them to areas throughout the West. Though there was some talk, at several times during the Indian War period, of sending the Blacks to garrisons east of the Mississippi River, they remained on the frontier until 1891. After the first few years, the army's decisions

21. U. S., Congress, Senate, *Congressional Record,* 45th Cong., 2d sess., p. 2328.

22. Guy V. Henry, Sr., refused a commission as colonel of a black regiment after the Civil War for these reasons but later was very happy to serve with these men after they had proven themselves. Guy V. Henry, Jr., to author, 21 August 1966; NMS, 7:4699.

in the assignment of stations were not discriminatory; the vast majority of the white infantry and cavalry regiments never served east of the Mississippi either. There were very few troops to control the Indians, guard the mails, protect the railroads, and meet the other needs of the pioneers in the West. Consequently, few men could be spared to the noncritical posts in the East. In addition it was quite expensive to transfer regiments, and the army had very little money. Racial stereotypes apparently did influence the army's decisions as to which specific areas in the West Blacks were assigned. In the 1870s Q.M. Gen. Montgomery C. Meigs stated that Blacks should continue to be stationed in the warmer climates. They had, he said, a "comparative exemption from the epidemics and other diseases of the Southern coast." He believed that if they were moved to the cold climates of the Dakotas, within six months they would be of no more value "than an Army of Dormice or any hybernating animal." A study of stationing assignments indicates that these guidelines were followed more often than not.[23]

While the army may have wanted to discriminate when assigning posts, they were not able to because of the needs of the frontier, the limited number of troops, and the large number of posts that had to be manned. The posts on the frontier that were near large cities were not barred to black soldiers. The army assigned Blacks to stations near such cities as Galveston, San Antonio, Phoenix, Salt Lake City, and Minneapolis, as well as near many small frontier communities.[24]

Understandably, however, the black soldiers and the black press considered this policy of assignment discriminatory. Throughout the Indian War period, especially in the 1880s, they questioned the assignment of black soldiers to what they considered to be the most isolated and rural posts. Some soldiers and civilians were convinced that the War Department and white society wanted to hide them. They also felt that the military authorities gave in too easily to white opposition to their assignment to good stations.[25]

In other ways the hierarchy of the army also seemed to sub-

---

23. Much of the material in the following pages was obtained through the cooperation of Thomas Phillips, who lent me a draft of his dissertation. Thomas D. Phillips, "The Negro Regulars: Negro Soldiers in the United States Army, 1866–1890"; Jack D. Foner, *The United States Soldier Between Two Wars: Army Life and Reforms, 1865–1898,* pp. 133–34; NMS, 7:4710.

24. Phillips, "The Negro Regulars."

25. Ibid.

merge their real feelings. For example, the number and type of work details given the black soldiers were essentially the same as those given the white troops. In fact, since the black regiments often contained fewer skilled personnel than the white units, they were ordered to do less of this duty. Black units received the same arms and equipment as white regiments. When the army converted to the new Springfield rifle in the 1870s, the black units got theirs at about the same time as did the white units. The authorities gave both races the privilege of testing new weapons and equipment. They obtained the same quality of horses and received equal pay to assure that assigned tasks would be performed adequately.[26]

When people could safely ignore the necessities of pacifying the frontier, the underlying racial concepts surfaced. In general, whites judged the black soldiers not only by the prevailing standards of appearance, performance, and discipline but more frequently by current attitudes toward race. Evidence of this double standard appeared in the reports of army officers who had inspected the black units and in the comments of some company and regimental officers who commanded Blacks. In the early years of the four regiments, army inspectors often turned in unfavorable reports. They noted the units' poor discipline, ragged appearance, slovenly barracks, and lack of trained NCOs and clerks. By the 1880s the reports of the inspectors indicated that the Blacks were on a par with white units, but credit for this improvement went to the white officers, so whites continued to believe that black soldiers could only reach their full potential under the careful supervision of white commanders. Military leaders blamed failures on the innate inferiority of the Blacks and would not judge the black soldiers in the same way as they did whites.[27]

Another indicator of attitudes of the army toward black soldiers surfaced as the result of discussion in Congress in the mid-1870s about the elimination of those clauses in the Act of 1866 that specifically authorized the four black regiments. General Sherman had changed his mind and now regarded the black units as a "partially successful" experiment. He testified at one committee hearing that the black cavalrymen were good troops and were able to handle combat situations very well. On the other hand, Gen. Edward O. C. Ord commented frequently

26. Ibid.
27. Ibid.

that whites were much more effective than black soldiers and asked that the black soldiers assigned to him be replaced by whites. In general, most army officers indicated that they tolerated the presence of the Blacks but did not want to have more of them.[28]

Opinions in Congress concerning the clause were also divided, but for a variety of reasons. Sen. Ambrose Burnside introduced legislation to remove those clauses in the 1866 law with the view of opening up all areas of the army to Blacks. Upon the request of Senator Blaine he added an amendment specifying that Blacks were to be allowed into all branches of the service. The bill was supported by people like Sen. Blanche K. Bruce, a black Republican from Mississippi. On the other hand, it was also supported by southern Democrats like Senator Maxey of Texas, who believed that in this way Blacks would be forbidden to serve in any branch of the military. As he stated, "I believe the white man makes the best soldier." He and others of his persuasion believed that removal of the specific authorization for the four black regiments would disallow the army recruiters from accepting any more black recruits (the real desire of the army), and within several years the army would be made up only of white men. The bill was opposed by followers of Senator Blaine, who sincerely wanted to keep Blacks in the service as one means of expanding their opportunities. Sen. George F. Edmunds, Republican from Vermont, said, "I believe that the colored race are just as fit as soldiers as any other race under similar circumstances and in appropriate latitudes." This group felt that a real expansion of the opportunities for Blacks in the service could not be achieved through the Burnside bill. Their strategy was to table the bill and protect the status quo. They were successful, but for a variety of reasons. Some army officers and senators feared that Blacks would be eliminated from the military if the Burnside bill were passed; others were more concerned that this elimination would result in a reduction of the number of men in the service. There was no real consideration given to ending segregation or even to increasing the number of Blacks in the service. While these were the ostensible goals of Senator Burnside, his methods of obtaining them were questionable.[29]

Although the Government tolerated the presence of Blacks

---

28. Ibid.
29. *Congressional Record,* 45th Cong., 2d sess., pp. 2190, 2602.

within the service, citizens of the frontier communities near where Blacks were stationed did not always adopt the attitude. Shaping the interracial relations was the pervasiveness of white racism. Whites in the frontier regions, as in the rest of the country, believed that Blacks were inferior beings. Other determinants of the state of race relations included the ratio of black-white-Indian populations in a given area, the size of the town near the post at which the Blacks were stationed, the attitudes of the military and civilian law enforcement officers, and the feelings of the black soldiers. If there were many Indians in the area near the post whites would treat the Blacks fairly well. If there were more than the usual handful of black civilians, then the relationship between white civilian and black soldier would be relatively good. On the other hand, if there were few Blacks and few or no Indians, as was most common in the West, then conditions for the black soldiers could be bad. There was less resentment toward the Blacks when a post was located near a large town or city. Trouble most often occurred in the small towns with little or no permanent population, for the drifters were more prone to violence. Another factor was the attitude of military and civilian law officers, if they were present, toward civilian harassment of the soldiers. For example, John Jackson, a white settler near Fort McKavett, Texas, murdered two soldiers of F Troop, Ninth Cavalry, in early 1870. He was finally arrested and brought to trial, however, a jury quickly set him free.[30]

The black soldiers resented this sort of treatment. They were determined to defend themselves on "questions of the rights of their race." They were, according to Gen. Christopher C. Augur, "easily excited and thoroughly united on any question of insult to their race." Yet there was little they could do, as the Jackson incident illustrated. They got no assistance, for the most part, from their white comrades or officers. Their rights of citizenship, as guaranteed in the recently passed Fourteenth Amendment, were ignored by white civilians and army officers. It was quite clear that for the black soldiers service in the army did not ensure their civil rights.[31]

As the decades wore on, the desertion and reenlistment rec-

---

30. Phillips, "The Black Regulars," p. 140; Frank N. Schubert, "Black Soldiers on the White Frontier: Some Factors Influencing Race Relations," pp. 410–15; William H. Leckie, *The Buffalo Soldiers: A Narrative of the Negro Cavalry in the West,* pp. 99.

31. NMS, 7:4707–8.

ords are a testament to the growing esprit de corps of the black units. The desertion rate in the white regiments was 20–30 per cent, while in the black regiments it was usually about 5 per cent. The number of whites reenlisting for the five-year term was low compared to that of Blacks. Black soldiers must have found advantages in the army that they were denied in civilian society. Because of the high rate of retention, a large majority of NCOs and enlisted men were becoming well trained. Because the surrounding prejudice drove the soldiers together, cohesion of units was high and resulted in a good combat record.[32]

The behavior of the black soldiers in combat helped somewhat to reduce the prejudice within the service. In a number of battles during the Indian Wars the four black regiments, especially the cavalry units, showed that in most situations they were the equal of the white soldiers. However, their success confirmed the belief that Blacks would perform well in combat when under the command of whites. Blacks won a number of Medals of Honor and other citations for heroism during these battles. In approving the recommendations for commendations, the army showed no discrimination.

In September 1879 part of the Ute tribe in Colorado began to threaten trouble, and three troops of the Fifth Cavalry were sent to quell the disturbance. The Indians attacked the column, forcing it into a defensive position on the Milk River. After several days of constant attacks, a messenger was sent for help, and a troop of the Ninth Cavalry arrived, having had to ride through a force of about three hundred Indians to do so. They joined the whites in holding off the Indians for three more days. It was during this period that one of the black troopers, Sgt. Henry Johnson, won a Medal of Honor. One evening he left his rifle pit and, under tremendous fire, went down to the river and returned with a supply of water for his men. On other occasions during the siege he was exposed to heavy fire as he checked on his men's supply of ammunition. After several more days of Indian attacks, other reinforcements arrived and put an end to the fighting. By 1890 such actions had established a reputation for the black soldiers as being good fighters, but the praise was minimized by the belief that the Blacks had reached this level only through the extra efforts of their white commanders.[33]

32. Foner, *The United States Soldier Between Two Wars,* pp. 6–10.

33. Fairfax D. Downey, *Indian-Fighting Army,* pp. 266–70; Leckie, *The Buffalo Soldiers,* pp. 207–9.

It is hard to characterize the way in which the military viewed and treated Blacks. There was no official policy on the treatment of Blacks. Actions by officers, reports of inspectors, and testimony before congressional committees did, however, give a general impression of the way the army regarded Blacks. Most whites, including those in the army, viewed them as inferior soldiers who could be useful only if carefully trained, used in warm climates, and supervised by white officers. At times they were worrisome because of the conflicts they got into with white civilians. While the army probably would have preferred to replace the four black units with four white ones, or might have wanted to station the Blacks far away from any white citizens or assign them solely to labor duty or other noncombat roles they could not do so before 1890 because they needed them to perform military duties.

Likewise it is difficult to delineate the attitudes of the black soldiers toward the army. There are indicators that Blacks regarded the army as a good alternative to civilian life. The desertion and retention rates in the black units indicate that they found at least some satisfaction in a career in the military. On the other hand, the letters of black soldiers to the newspapers reflect an undercurrent of dissatisfaction. The issues raised in these letters were often related to race. These complaints included the isolation of their stations, the duration of their service at such posts, the lack of protection of their rights, and the low opinion many of the officers had about the Blacks' capabilities. They felt that their fine combat service merited better treatment than they received. Their expectations were high, and they were disappointed when the army did not meet them. The comments of General Augur indicate the sensitivity of black soldiers to infringements on their newly won rights. The black soldiers continued to be forced to accept one of two undesirable alternatives—acceptance of the racial slights because of the benefits that army service offered them, or rejection, through leaving the service or obtaining their rights through force. During the Indian War period they usually chose the former.

Conditions in the navy remained different than those in the army. Integration was practiced in the navy from the end of the Civil War until the early twentieth century. Blacks served throughout the navy and in many different enlisted ranks. Even in the Spanish-American War black enlisted men and petty officers served with whites in the ships that defeated the Spanish at Manila and Santiago. In the early twentieth century this traditional policy of integration began to change. The navy recruited Blacks only in the steward's branch, and by 1916 segregation was widespread in the navy.[34]

The situation of Blacks in the army also began to change, in a number of respects, after the end of the Indian Wars in 1890. The military establishment entered into a period of peace, which lasted until 1917. While there were a few conflicts in this period, such as the Spanish-American War and the Philippine Insurrection, they were either short in duration or conducted on a relatively small scale. These two wars resulted in the acquisition of new colonial possessions, which had to be protected by large garrisons. From 1890 to 1897 the army's strength remained at 25,000 men, the authorized size since the 1870s. Then beginning in 1898, the time of the Spanish-American War, the army began to grow. After 1900 the size of the army increased to about 70,000–80,000 men and, in the two years before American involvement in World War I, to more than 100,000 men. The army abandoned many of the smaller posts of the Indian War period. While prior to 1898 it was unusual for an entire regiment to be quartered at one post, after 1898 it was the general practice. Although some new posts were established, many more were closed. From the end of the Indian Wars until World War I the army was in a period of transition in terms of size, function, and location. All of these factors had an effect on racism within the military establishment.

In addition to the internal factors that changed after 1890, there were a number of external events that shaped the racial policies and actions of the military. Racism intensified after 1890 especially in the South, where the majority of the black population lived, but manifestations of it were present in all parts of the country.

One major aspect of this intensified racism was the legal segregation and disfranchisement of Blacks in the South. Through a variety of means, including the poll tax, grandfather clause, literacy test, and the white primary, white Southerners prevented Blacks from exercising the franchise. While some northern whites protested these practices as a violation of the

34. Dennis D. Nelson, *The Integration of the Negro into the U.S. Navy*, pp. 6–8.

spirit if not the letter of the Fifteenth Amendment, the northern public, northern congressmen, and the Supreme Court gave them little or no support. Henry Cabot Lodge, a Republican representative from Massachusetts and good friend of Theodore Roosevelt, introduced a bill in Congress in 1890 that would have set up a procedure for possible federal supervision of elections and might have ended some of the discriminatory practices that were beginning in the South. While the bill passed the House of Representatives, it failed in the Senate. Few northern Republicans supported it. In addition, the Supreme Court upheld restrictions of the franchise, in *Williams* v. *Mississippi* (1898), as long as they were not specifically directed against Blacks.[35]

In the same time period southern states set up a number of legal and social barriers that, in effect, excluded Blacks from mingling with whites except in the capacity of servants and defined Blacks' position in society. The law required separate streetcars, washrooms, drinking fountains, and areas in movie theaters, parks, and housing developments. Similar actions occurred in the North, though without any real assistance from the law. Economic conditions and social pressures forced Blacks of the North to live in certain parts of the urban areas and to take menial jobs.[36]

This climate of legalized racism found clear expression in the 1896 Supreme Court decision on segregation in transportation in the case of *Plessy* v. *Ferguson.* Through nominally deciding on the question of the constitutionality of a segregation law in Louisiana, the court enunciated a racial philosophy that was widely shared by whites in all sections of the country. "We consider the underlying fallacy of the plaintiff's argument to consist in the assumption that the enforced separation of the two races stamps the colored race with a badge of inferiority." The majority felt that this inferiority existed in the minds of the Blacks but that there were clear racial distinctions. "Legislation is powerless to eradicate racial instincts or to abolish distinctions based upon physical differences, and the attempt to do so can only result in accentuating the difficulties of the present situation." The Court decided that segregation was the best policy for both races.[37]

35. C. Vann Woodward, *The Strange Career of Jim Crow,* p. 82; Vladimir O. Key, Jr., *Southern Politics in State and Nation,* pp. 537–39.
36. Woodward, *Jim Crow,* pp. 97–102.
37. *Plessy* v. *Ferguson,* 163 U.S. 537 (1896).

Another aspect of the national racial situation was a lack of justice and due process for Blacks. Southern Blacks, both male and female, had reason to fear lynch law. Between 1893 and 1904 whites lynched an average of more than one hundred Blacks each year. While southerners claimed that these lynchings resulted from attacks on white women, studies have shown that this was not really the case. In the first fourteen years of this century, law officers had already accused about two-thirds of the victims with crimes such as homicide, robbery, and insulting white persons. The South was not the only area in which interracial violence occurred in this period. Race riots took place during the first decade of the twentieth century in New York City and Springfield, Illinois. The latter so shocked some northern white liberals that it led to the formation of the National Association for the Advancement of Colored People (NAACP). No more than a few whites manifested any concern in this organization or in the problems of black Americans.[38]

Contributing to this hostility was the belief, held by many white Americans, that Blacks were not equal to the white Anglo-Saxon. Thomas Dixon, Jr., a popular contemporary writer, built a series of novels, especially *The Clansman*, on these ideas. He described Blacks as:

half-child, half-animal, the sport of impulse, whim and conceit, "pleased with a rattle, tickled with a straw", a being who, left to his will, roams at night and sleeps in the day, whose speech knows no word of love, whose passions, once aroused, are as the fury of the tiger.

When in 1915 David W. Griffith made *The Clansman* into a film, *The Birth of a Nation*, the book and its racial stereotypes reached many new, impressionable audiences. By using numerous new techniques, such as alternating large-scale battle scenes with close-ups of individual participants, Griffith insured that the film would have a tremendous visual impact. This movie gave more credibility to the prevailing ideas about Blacks. Among those images he presented was that of a group of black soldiers, who were cowards and unable to stand up to white authority. White America became more convinced than ever that Blacks were inferior.[39]

---

38. Thomas F. Gossett, *Race: The History of an Idea in America*, pp. 269–70; John. H. Franklin, *From Slavery to Freedom*, pp. 440, 432.

39. Gossett, *Race*, p. 286; Thomas Dixon, Jr., *The Clansman: An Historical*

After the end of the Indian Wars the conditions that had previously prevented whites from expressing prejudices against Blacks in the military began to change. The abandonment of a number of posts, the movement of the army closer to the centers of population, and an increase in the size of the army brought it into closer touch with society and provided more opportunity for the racism within the military to surface. In addition, such practices became even more acceptable to civilian society. Segregation, disfranchisement, lynching, and the rhetoric of colonialism were manifestations of a more blatant racism that infected American society after 1890. The trend of these events made discriminatory treatment within the service much more likely.

Prior to 1890 racism was discouraged because of the overwhelming need for military force on the frontier. The Blacks were allowed to help fulfill this need because there were not enough whites to do so. After 1890, the need became less acute, and with it, the inducement to minimize racism.

In trying to decide whether the army did become more discriminatory after 1890 it will be necessary to adopt several approaches. The officers who made decisions concerning Blacks seldom recorded their reasons. In some cases it will be easy to label an action as discriminatory or not. In other instances the way in which a person acted may be the only evidence available.

In this study, I shall consider whether the previously established acceptance of the situation or the undercurrent of discontent became the dominant force after 1890. I shall also examine how and why prejudices developed toward Blacks in the military and how the black soldiers received and reacted to these attitudes.

Romance of the Ku Klux Klan, pp. 277, 289, 292–93; Charles F. Kellogg, *NAACP: A History of the National Association for the Advancement of Colored People,* 1: 142–45.

II

THE BLACK REGULAR
IN THE SPANISH-AMERICAN WAR

On 15 February 1898 an American warship, the *U.S.S. Maine*, was sunk in Havana harbor. Although the possibility of war with Spain had existed prior to the incident, afterwards discontent with her policies intensified rapidly. When the war broke out in April 1898, the War Department utilized those few troops it had on hand, including the four black regiments. Their service in the war was proudly acclaimed by both the black and white populations of the country.

Although in early 1898 Congress had appropriated some money to prepare the armed forces for a possible war, President William McKinley restricted the army's use of the money. As a result, the War Department could make only limited preparations. One action they did take was to shift some troops to the South. In March 1898 Maj. Gen. Nelson A. Miles, the Commanding General of the Army, recommended that the Twenty-fifth Infantry be sent to the Department of the South and that six of its eight companies be stationed at Dry Tortugas, a post very near Cuba. The decision to locate black troops there resulted from the belief that "the Negro is better able to withstand the Cuban climate than the white man." On 14 April the Ninth and Tenth cavalry regiments were ordered to Chickamauga Park, Georgia, and the Twenty-fourth Infantry to New Orleans, Louisiana.[1]

In the initial enthusiasm of the war most people forgot the color of the soldiers' skin. The black troops received hearty welcomes all along their routes. When the Twenty-fifth reached St. Paul, Minnesota, the train engine was decorated with flags and many people gathered at the station to greet the troops. It became popular to take the buttons from the soldiers' uniforms for souvenirs, and as a result many of the men of the Ninth

1. AGO 73129, NA, RG 94; *The Afro-American Sentinel* (Omaha, Nebraska), 2 April 1898; SA War Invest, 2:871.

Cavalry "had to pin our clothes on with sundry nails and sharpened bits of wood." The generally enthusiastic reception for the black soldiers was reversed when they reached the South.[2]

Upon the arrival of a regiment at Chickamauga the actual preparation for combat began. The camp commander assigned each regiment to a campground, and the men pitched their tents, chopped wood, set up camp fires, and then settled down into the camp routine of drilling, cleaning, and eating. Regiments that had been separated for long periods of time exercised together. There were also special events to break the monotony of their schedule. One of the high points of their stay was a baseball game between the Twenty-fifth Infantry and the Twelfth Infantry, a white unit. The soldiers played the game before five thousand spectators. Although the black soldiers were a good team, the white infantrymen won rather easily.[3]

Training at Chickamauga was completed at the end of April, and the regiments moved to Florida. Most of the troops assembled at Tampa, but because of overcrowding several regiments were sent to nearby Lakeland. In these two camps the preparations for war continued. Each day began with reveille at 5:30 A.M. Soldiers spent most of the morning and afternoon hours, Monday through Friday, drilling, with a break only for lunch and a short rest period. After a few days, however, drill was limited to early morning and after sunset because of the heat and dust.[4]

The next step in the war was the invasion of Cuba. The War Department's preparations and execution of the first phase of this operation did not augur well for the future. After the military leaders decided to make Tampa the port of embarkation, they learned that the two train routes into the city were inadequate to handle the necessary volume of traffic of men, supplies, and equipment. Compounding the problem, the navy had

2. *The Daily Missoulian*, 11 April 1898; for examples see *The Broad-ax*, 23 April 1898, *The Colored American*, 11 March 1899, Edward A. Johnson, *History of Negro Soldiers in the Spanish-American War, and Other Items of Interest*, p.22. *The World*, 13 April 1898; *Colored American*, 11 March 1899. For other examples of the reception in the North see *The Gazette*, 21 May 1898; Herschel V. Cashin, *Under Fire With the Tenth United States Cavalry*, p. 61; *The Gazette*, 21 May 1898. See also *The Illinois Record*, 23 April 1898.

3. John Bigelow, Jr., *Reminiscenses of the Santiago Campaign*, p. 15. *The New York Times*, 1 May 1898, Magazine Section, p. 4; 8 May 1898, Magazine Section, p. 5.

4. *Illinois Record*, 18 June 1898; Theophilus G. Steward, *The Colored Regulars in the United States Army*, p. 184.

already taken most of the suitable vessels, so there was a scarcity of good ships that could be converted for use as troop transports. Those ships that the army managed to find, usually old freighters, were converted to troop transports while on the way to Tampa. No particular officer seemed to be in command of the port, so there was great confusion when the men and supplies arrived there. Officers of individual units commandeered vessels, loaded their men and supplies on board, and defied being moved.[5]

The black regiments had been assigned, along with some white regiments, to six ships: *Miami, Alamo, Comal, Concho, City of Washington,* and *Leona.* On the *Concho,* as on the other ships, the black troops lived and slept on the lowest deck, where there was almost no light more than ten feet from the main hatch. The carpenters who had converted the ships into transports had built the bunks in four tiers and placed them so close together that the men could barely pass between them. These so-called beds were made of undressed lumber and surrounded by a rim four to six inches high. It was in this small space that the soldier had to keep all of his gear, including his rifle and ammunition. Making the situation worse for the soldiers was a scarcity of bathing and toilet facilities. On the *Concho* there was one toilet for 1,256 men.[6]

Even after the confusion of boarding was over, there were new problems for the individual soldier. The invasion fleet stayed in port for a week after the men were aboard because the navy had to track down a rumored Spanish fleet. Some black soldiers believed they were being treated inequitably. For example, several white officers had allowed their soldiers to leave their ships whenever they pleased. According to Sgt. Maj. Frank W. Pullen, Twenty-fifth Infantry, the men of his regiment were confined to the ship except for those few occasions when, a company at a time, they were taken ashore to exercise and bathe. Finally the navy found out that there was no Spanish fleet to menace the convoy, and on 14 June the invasion force left Tampa. At that time, the commander of the brigade on Sergeant Pullen's ship instituted segregation. He ordered that "the two regiments on board should not intermingle" and assigned the white regiment to the port and the Twenty-fifth to the starboard side of

5. James A. Houston, *The Sinews of War: Army Logistics, 1775–1953,* pp. 280–83.
6. Sec War 1898, p. 778; Bigelow, *Reminiscences,* p. 50; Sec War 1898, pp. 778–79.

the ship. "Still greater was the surprise of everyone when another order was issued from the same source directing that the white regiment should make coffee first, all the time." In Sergeant Pullen's view, these orders were issued to humiliate the Blacks, yet their regimental officers took no action to change the situation. "God only knows how it was we lived through those fourteen days on that miserable vessel."[7]

Although black soldiers on other vessels voiced no complaints about discrimination, living conditions were unpleasant for everyone on the ships. Soldiers found it difficult to sleep because the bunks were uncomfortable and narrow. The Government furnished no bedding, so they were forced to improvise. One black soldier used a blanket as a mattress and his haversack as his pillow. However, most soldiers spent the entire voyage on deck because the lack of ventilation in the holds made sleeping there unbearable. The officers tried to keep the soldiers occupied and ready to fight the Spanish. The daily routine involved inspections, roll call, guard mount, and fatigue duty. In their spare time, some black soldiers passed the time by gambling or in card games.[8]

The initial attempt to invade Cuba was as chaotic as the stay in Tampa. On one ship carrying some members of the Tenth Cavalry, the captain stopped his vessel further from the coast than the rest of the fleet. The soldiers thought the officer was a Spanish sympathizer and would have thrown him overboard had the other officers on board not prevented it. On 21 June 1898 the fleet anchored near Daiquirí, the initial landing site, while the navy shelled the beach. The following day the navy broke out the few small boards they had brought and debarkation began. The invasion force managed to land through the rough surf without much difficulty, but two members of the Tenth Cavalry were killed while attempting to climb onto the pier from their surf-tossed boat. After the initial landing, a small force moved down the coast to Siboney, a better harbor, where they established the headquarters of the invasion force.[9]

The battle of Las Guásimas, the first major action, began on the evening of 23 June. Maj. Gen. Joseph Wheeler decided to send the First and Tenth cavalry regiments and the First Vol-

7. Johnson, *History of Negro Soldiers,* pp. 24–25.

8. Cashin *Under Fire,* p. 74; Johnson, *History of Negro Soldiers,* p. 24; John J. Pershing, speech, 20 November 1898, Box 369, JJP, Papers, Bigelow, *Reminiscences,* p. 63.

9. *The New York Times,* 24 June 1898.

unteer Cavalry (Rough Riders) up the trail from Siboney to Sevilla. Maj. Gen. William Shafter, commander of the invasion force, placed actual control of the movement under the command of Brig. Gen. Samuel B. M. Young. The road on which the two units of the Regular Army marched ran from Siboney through a valley and then ascended to a gap in the hills called Las Guásimas. Along the eastern ridge of the valley was a trail that met the main road just past the gap. General Young assigned this trail to the Rough Riders.[10]

The troops of the Tenth had left camp at 3:30 A.M. and marched for a few hours. They only had time for a short rest before the battle began at 8 A.M. The troop leaders directed the black cavalrymen to attack two lines of shallow trenches which were strenghtened by heavy stone parapets and were the strongest position in the tough Spanish defense. The black regiment, along with the other two, charged the trenches and routed the Spanish. Because of the brush and the position of the Spanish fortifications, the Americans could not see the enemy, though the enemy could see them very well. As a result the Spanish subjected them to a "severe and heavy fire at each step, which was only rendered ineffective to a great degree by the poor marksmanship of the enemy." An additional handicap was the underbrush and a "thick, prickly weed, through which paths had always to be cut with knives and sabers."[11]

Some of the black soldiers tried to aid their comrades with Hotchkiss mountain guns, which were small pieces of artillery. This assistance was almost entirely ineffective because the smoke from the black powder of the mountain guns attracted the Spanish counterfire. Manning the guns was very difficult under these conditions. Some soldiers continued to shoot them despite the enemy fire. Corp. W. F. Johnson, B Troop, Tenth Cavalry, was praised by his commanding officer, Capt. James W. Watson, for "coolness under fire," for his battery was "a special target for the enemy's fire."[12]

Observers could not speak highly enough of the conduct of the black soldiers. For example, Stephen Bonsal, a war correspondent, wrote that they "were no braver certainly than any other men in the line, but their better training enabled them to

10. Herbert H. Sargent, *The Campaign of Santiago de Cuba*, 2:57–63.

11. Cashin, *Under Fire*, p. 257; Maj Gen 1898, pp. 337–38, 347; *The Spanish-American War: The Events of the War Described by Eye Witnesses*, p. 104.

12. Maj Gen 1898, pp. 338–39.

render more valuable services than the other troops engaged." After the battle many Blacks claimed that the Tenth had saved the Rough Riders. However, examination of the evidence in the records does not indicate that this was the case. In addition, by claiming they saved the Rough Riders they were in effect saying that they saved Theodore Roosevelt, a man who later attacked the valor of the black soldiers.[13]

The army spent the six days after the battle in moving up from Siboney to the plain below San Juan Heights. If the force could gain control of this terrain, it would be in good position to continue with the mission of the force, the invasion of Santiago. During the move it rained almost every day, and it was difficult to keep anything dry. In addition rations were issued very irregularly, so on one day a unit might receive two days' coffee, one day's bread, and three days' bacon. Despite these problems General Shafter managed to provide the troops with a few days' rations and concentrate most of his forces in front of the Spanish entrenchments. The Spanish commander brought only a few of his troops to face the American challenge.[14]

Shafter finally decided to take San Juan Heights by dividing his troops into two groups. One of them, a small force under Brig. Gen. Henry W. Lawton that included the Twenty-fifth Infantry, was to make an attack on the Spanish positions at El Caney, a few miles north of the San Juan Heights. After the successful conclusion of this brief attack, General Lawton was to march south and attack the Spanish positions at San Juan in coordination with a frontal assault by forces under the command of General Wheeler and Brig. Gen. Jacob F. Kent.

The Spanish position at El Caney consisted of four wooden blockhouses along the west and north sides of the village, a stone church that had loop holes for rifle fire, and a stone fort in a commanding position 500 yards southwest of the town. In addition there were a series of trenches, barbed wire entanglements, and rifle pits connecting the fort with the blockhouses. About 400–500 Spanish soldiers defended this strong point, and nearly 6,600 Americans were in the attacking force.[15]

The battle began at 6:30 A.M. on 1 July 1898 with an attack on the fort by most of the American troops. General Lawton

---

13. Stephen Bonsal, *The Fight for Santiago; the Story of the Soldiers in the Cuban Campaign from Tampa to the Surrender*, p. 95; *Southern Workman* 27:8 (August, 1898): 165.

14. Bigelow, *Reminiscences*, pp. 97–99.

15. Sargent, *The Campaign of Santiago de Cuba*, 2:101–8.

ordered the Twenty-fifth and several other regiments to be held in reserve. The night before the battle the black soldiers bivouacked near the road they were to take the next day. At dawn they arose, formed into line, and marched down toward the conflict. After a short hike, the regiment arrived at its post in a grove near the battlefield. At noon the black soldiers were ordered to advance. As they drew near the fighting, Spanish sharpshooters subjected the men to a constant fire. Two companies of the regiment were formed into a firing line with two others in support and the other four in reserve. As the line moved forward into the open, there were heavy casualties, and the two support companies were ordered to fill the gaps. The men advanced by rushes, crawling up streams and working their way through cactus, thick underbrush, and other obstacles, until they reached a little hollow in the hillside, where they remained because it gave them some shelter. Only the sharpshooters in the regiment were given permission by the officers to fire at the Spanish from this position. According to a story later told by the men of the regiment, this tactic was so effective that it demoralized the enemy. The soldiers in the fort that was the target of the assault began to wave a white flag, but the heavy fire from the other regiments prevented the Spanish from moving forward with it. At this point in the fighting there was a general assault up the hill by United States troops until the enemy fled.[16]

The black troops then, and the black public later, stated that it was their performance at the battle that had forced the Spanish at El Caney to surrender. While the Twenty-fifth was important in the victory, it was only one of several regiments on the scene, and all evidence should be considered in evaluating the Blacks' claims. It is understandable that the soldiers and their followers expanded the role of the Blacks, however, because of the limited opportunities they had had to prove their abilities. They had done well but not to the extent their followers claimed.[17]

There were many heroic Blacks in the battle. During the battle Conny Gray, a private of D Company, Twenty-fifth In-

16. Miles V. Lynk, *The Black Troopers, or, the Daring Heroism of the Negro Soldiers in the Spanish-American War,* p. 77; James A. Moss, *Memories of the Campaign of Santiago,* pp. 31; 33–35; *ANJ,* 22 October 1898, p. 175. Maj Gen 1898, pp. 386–87.

17. E. A. Johnson, *History of Negro Soldiers,* pp. 29–31. Lynk, *The Black Troopers,* p. 78. *ANJ,* 22 October 1898, pp. 175–76.

fantry, earned a Certificate of Merit for fearlessly helping his wounded captain while under fire and carrying him a considerable distance so that the litter bearers could reach him. Seven Blacks were killed and twenty-two wounded in the battle. Afterwards the men stripped the bark off two trees near the graves and carved the following inscription: "Roll of Honor, Twenty-fifth Regiment," and followed it with a list of the names of the deceased soldiers.[18]

While the black soldiers of the Twenty-fifth Infantry were fighting at El Caney, others were participating in the famous charge up San Juan Hill. The Spanish held positions on the top of a long ridge overlooking the San Juan River and a grassy plain, broken only by a small mound called Kettle Hill. The soldiers led by Generals Kent and Samuel S. Sumner, who took the place of the ailing General Wheeler, were posted near the village of El Poso. They were waiting there for the successful conclusion of the battle of El Caney when they would join with the forces of General Lawton in an assault on the Spanish positions. In order to reach the battlefield the soldiers were to march along the Aquadores River, ford Las Guásimas Creek and the San Juan River, and then attack the enemy by crossing a large open meadow.

The Twenty-fourth Infantry was on the extreme left of the American line in the attack on the Spanish. The night before the battle the soldiers lay awake wondering what the enemy had planned for them. J. W. Galaway, a member of the regiment, later reminisced, "I confess that at times I became melancholy and apprehensive as to my fate, but it was not from fear, but suspense."[19]

On the day of the attack camp was broken at 7:30 A.M., and the men marched off through the brush, often halting because of congestion in the road. As they neared the front, each delay became dangerous because the Spanish were shooting in their direction. The soldiers then reached the banks of the San Juan River and rested behind a knoll near the stream. Shortly thereafter they reached their assigned position. Upon orders the men arose and began to run toward the Spanish, following their officers. Although many of the soldiers and officers were exhausted by the time they reached the bottom of the hill, they found enough energy to go on. As they moved up the hill the

18. AGO 341397; SAWar Invest, 7:3120.
19. Lynk, *The Black Troopers,* pp. 55–59.

Spanish retreated, enabling the Americans to seize the enemy trenches and hold them against counterattacks. In his report of the battle, Capt. Benjamin W. Leavell, the commander of A Company, Twenty-fourth Infantry, praised his men for their desire to "do their duty, yea, more than their duty . . . . Too much can not be said of their courage, willingness, and endurance." In the battle the regiment lost six men and one officer, while fifty-six men and seven officers were wounded.[20]

The experiences of the men of the Ninth and Tenth cavalry regiments, which fought to the right on the battlefield, were quite similar to those of the men of the Twenty-fourth. In a number of incidents the black soldiers displayed their valor. Sgt. Edward L. Baker, Tenth Cavalry, won a Medal of Honor, when, under fire, he rescued a wounded soldier who was drowning. In this battle seven men and three officers from the black cavalry units were killed, while eighty-one soldiers and eleven officers were wounded.[21]

In addition to their duties as infantrymen, some Blacks acted as artillerymen. Sgt. Horace Bivens, Tenth Cavalry, was in charge of a battery of Hotchkiss guns. On the way to the front Bivens and his men had to stop many times because of the mudholes and other obstacles in the road. The battle had been going on for several hours before they arrived at the front. Looking through his fieldglasses, Bivens saw "so much game I did not know where to direct my first shot." However, after that first shot and the resulting cloud of black smoke, the battery attracted the attention of the Spanish marksmen, who wounded two of the black gunners in rapid succession. Bivens himself had a minor wound and was unconscious for a few minutes, but he recovered quickly and began firing shells into the Spanish trenches. Other soldiers of the Tenth Cavalry served as gunners in Lt. John Parker's detachment of Gatling guns. Parker complimented the Blacks, calling them "the peers of any soldier in the detachment.[22]

20. AGO 966421; Maj Gen 1898, pp. 436–37; 437–38.

21. For official reports see Maj Gen 1898, pp. 326–37, 704–11. For personal accounts see Cashin, *Under Fire,* pp. 232–39, 271–72. Bigelow, *Reminiscences,* pp. 106–25; Lynk, *The Black Troopers,* pp. 72–73; Pershing, "Diary," Box 316, and Pershing to Rosewater, 19 July 1898, Box 369, JJP, Papers; Mary Curtis, *The Black Soldier, or the Colored Boys of the United States Army,* p. 28.

22. *Southern Workman* 17:11 (November 1898):219–20; Cashin, *Under Fire,* pp. 90–94; John H. Parker, *History of the Gatling Gun Detachment, Fifth Army Corps, At Santiago,* p. 148.

The officers of the black regiments also praised their men. John Bigelow, Jr., who had been an officer in the Tenth Cavalry for many years and had felt at a disadvantage because of such service, commented, "Their conduct made me prouder than ever of being an officer in the American Army, and of wearing the insignia of the Tenth United States Cavalry." Reporters who had witnessed the black soldiers in action were also complimentary. John H. Hemment, a photographer, wrote that he could "never forget the coloured boys when they made the grand charge over the barb-wire fences and into the trenches filled with Spaniards." [23]

The campaign in Cuba did not end with the conclusion of the battles at San Juan and El Caney. The Spanish still had a strong line of trenches and blockhouses in front of Santiago and their fleet in the harbor. They tried several counterattacks on the American positions but were resisted. A truce was declared on 3 July. It remained in effect until 10 July, and from 12 July until the surrender of the Spanish on 17 July. However, during the truce the troops were not idle, for the American command had decided to completely invest Santiago.

The black soldiers took part in building trenches, and the men of the Twenty-fifth Infantry felt that they had more than their due share of it. They dug trenches for eleven straight days. As soon as they would finish one section of trench, they would be moved to a new area and their newly dug trench would be taken over by a white regiment.[24]

Conditions were more difficult during the siege than during the fighting. Almost all commodities were in short supply. About the only food that the men were supplied with was enough hard bread, bacon, and coffee to prevent starvation. They worked hard at trench building and digging gun emplacements, and several men collapsed from heat prostration. An additional problem for the soldier was a shortage of clothing. In the words of one member of the Tenth Cavalry, J. C. Pendergrass, "Now we are almost naked, no medicine, not much to eat, hot water to drink, sleeping on the bare ground and no papers of any kind." Pendergrass had lost his coat and shirt in the

---

23. Maj Gen 1898, p. 711; John C. Hemment, *Cannon and Camera: Sea and Land Battles of the Spanish-American War in Cuba; Camp Life and the Return of the Soldiers*, p. 169.

24. E. A. Johnson, *History of Negro Soldiers*, p. 31. See also Steward, *The Colored Regulars*, p. 189. Moss, *Memories of the Campaign of Santiago*, pp. 50–51.

fighting and had no replacements. In addition, he was constantly wet from wading streams, sweating, and the incessant rain; he had kept his shoes on for twenty days.[25]

Despite the hardships, the men continued their soldierly conduct. One Black from B Troop, Ninth Cavalry, won a Certificate of Merit for going up to the front, even though he had been suffering from yellow fever for two days. While there he was severely wounded in his right hand, but he went to a first aid station, was bandaged there, and then returned to the trenches. Even though constantly under fire, he remained with his troop until it was relieved.[26]

Blacks were depicted as being happy-go-lucky, musical, and humorous in the whites' stories about the siege. One officer related that his black soldiers brought out their musical instruments and played them constantly during the siege. According to Oswald G. Villard, the white progressive reformer and later a leader in the formation of the NAACP, "The officers had their usual trouble in making the men go to sleep instead of spending the night in talking, singing, and gaming."[27]

By the time of the surrender most of the men in the trenches were suffering from hunger and tropical fevers. According to a letter from a black soldier to Chaplain Theophilus G. Steward, Twenty-fifth Infantry, "The starving time was nothing to the fever time, where scores died per day." Because the field hospitals were crowded, regimental officers sent many men to Siboney, where most of the expedition's meager supply of beds and medical equipment were located. Some of the wounded and sick men could not get transportation to the hospital and had to walk, only to find upon arrival that there were no blankets for them to use. A few regiments set up their own rest areas in the hills away from Siboney, but they had even fewer supplies. In one such hospital established by the Tenth Cavalry, there were fourteen men sleeping under a single tent. The patients had to lie with their heads uphill and dig holes in the ground with their heels in order to keep from slipping down on their comrades. The roof of the tent leaked and the ends were open, providing no shelter from the daily rainstorm.[28]

25. SAWar Invest, 4:981; Cashin, *Under Fire,* p. 102; *Illinois Record,* 3 September 1898. Steward, *The Colored Regulars,* p. 226.

26. AGO 111974.

27. Oswald G. Villard, "The Negro in the Regular Army," p. 725. See also *Leslie's Weekly,* 13 October 1898, 287.

28. Pershing, "Memoir," Chap. 8, Box 380, JJP, Papers; Cashin, *Under Fire,*

The central yellow fever hospital was located at Siboney. Col. Charles R. Greenleaf, the surgeon in charge of the hospital, had a great deal of difficulty obtaining workers for the camp. Eight different regiments ignored requests for help. Finally the Twenty-fourth Infantry agreed to help. When they arrived at the fever camp on 15 July Colonel Greenleaf asked the commanding officer of the regiment to call for volunteers to work with the patients. Maj. Alfred C. Markley, the regimental commander, later commented, "This was the crucial test of the mettle of the men, and an anxious moment indeed." One company supplied fifteen volunteers and set an example for other companies. One of the men later made a claim, which was denied, that the regiment's commander had promised them one dollar a day for performing this duty.[29]

As part of their duties the black soldiers buried the dead, built tents, and burned or disinfected buildings. As a result many of them became sick. The work force diminished while the need for the workers increased, because the field hospitals had closed and sent their patients to Siboney.

By the end of July yellow fever had overrun all the hospitals . . . . All was pest camp; even separation of cases was impossible . . . . Surgeons, nurses, and hospital stewards were now among the patients; and so it continued to about August 20, when determined steps were taken to break up the place.[30]

The surgeon in charge of the camp felt that the men deserved a special commendation for their work. As reporter Stephen Bonsal said, "The battle they fought for forty days in the yellow fever hospital" was "more gallant" than their charge on the battlefield, and more costly in lives. Out of the 456 men of the Twenty-fourth who marched to Siboney, only 24 escaped sickness. On one day 241 were on sick report. To Major Markley this experience "effectually showed that colored soldiers were not more immune from Cuban fever than white." The evidence to the contrary notwithstanding, the army continued to hold the old stereotype well into the twentieth century.[31]

---

pp. 224; 105.

29. Sec War 1898, p. 733; Maj Gen 1898, p. 451; AGO 203434.

30. Maj Gen 1898, pp. 451–52; Cashin, *Under Fire,* p. 131.

31. Sec War 1898, p. 733. Maj Gen 1898, p. 452; Bonsal, *The Fight for Santiago,* p. 457; Maj Gen 1898, pp. 452–53.

While most of the action involving black Regulars occurred around Santiago, one augmented troop of the Tenth Cavalry distinguished itself in another part of the island. On 8 June 1898, 1st Lt. Carter P. Johnson, a detachment of M Troop, and some veterans from other troops of the Tenth embarked at Lakeland, Florida. They then sailed to Tampa aboard the *U.S.S. Florida.* At Tampa they picked up five companies of Cuban soldiers and a supply of ammunition, rations, and rifles. The men and equipment were transferred to several other small transports. The purpose of this flotilla was to assist the Cuban partisans with men and supplies.[32]

After arriving at the southwestern coast of Cuba, they made their first attempt to land at the mouth of the San Juan River. When they failed, they proceeded down the coast to Tunas de Zaza. One of the transports, the *Florida,* ran aground at this point, so a detachment of Cubans and several Americans rowed ashore to make contact with the Cuban forces and survey the enemy's positions. Without warning a Spanish force fired on the small group, pinning them down. They attempted to retreat back to their boats but found they had been destroyed by Spanish artillery fire. Meanwhile the crew on the grounded ship had managed to get it afloat, but then the men ashore were in a precarious situation. Lieutenant Johnson, after sending several unsuccessful rescue parties of Cuban soldiers, asked four men of the Tenth, Pvts. Dennis Bell, Fitz Lee, William H. Thompkins, and George H. Wanton, to try their luck. The four privates quietly rowed to the shore, but as they landed, the Spanish opened fire. After the shooting ceased, the black soldiers found the stranded group. Then the Spanish located them again and began to attack. Two of the Blacks remained behind to cover the retreat to the boat, and after everyone else was aboard they got in. Despite a hail of fire from the shore, all arrived back at the transport unharmed. The four black soldiers received the Medal of Honor for their heroic actions. Shortly thereafter the detachment received orders to land. They spent several months fighting with the Cubans. Eventually the navy picked them up, and they joined the rest of the Cuban invasion force at Montauk Point, Long Island, for rest and recuperation. During their serveral months stay in Cuba they had lost only one man.[33]

32. Cashin, *Under Fire,* p. 175.

33. Maj Gen 1898, p. 325; Irvin H. Lee, *Negro Medal of Honor Men,* pp. 90–93; Lynk, *The Black Troopers,* pp. 52–53.

While at Montauk Point the press, military leaders, and the public showered the four black regiments with praise. United States newspapers featured stories about the black soldiers and praised them in editorials. The *Baltimore Morning Herald* wrote that even the racially prejudiced could not ignore the fact that "the colored citizen makes an admirable soldier in many respects." Similarly, *Leslie's Weekly,* a national magazine, said that the black soldiers were "heroes as good as any in the land." Black newspapers were also very proud of the contribution of their brothers, though they believed the soldiers had been slighted by not having been awarded commissions.[34]

In accounts of the war, the writers of the period heaped praise upon the black soldiers. A number of novels published in 1898 and 1899 dealt with the war, and in all instances their portrait of the black soldiers was very favorable. Historical accounts of the war were also full of compliments about the conduct of the Blacks, especially their performance at the battle of San Juan Heights. Richard Harding Davis wrote, "The Negro soldiers established themselves as fighting men that morning." In another account of the war, correspondent George Kennan said that all who observed the actions of the black soldiers under fire believed that "they fought with the utmost courage, coolness, and determination."[35]

For a brief period even the leaders of the army complimented their performance. Shortly after the battle at San Juan, Theodore Roosevelt personally commended the men of the Tenth Cavalry. When the Rough Riders were mustered out while at Montauk Point, they presented Roosevelt with a souvenir designed by Frederic Remington. Roosevelt thanked his men and the other soldiers, including some Blacks, who had gathered for the ceremony. He described the Blacks as "an excellent breed of Yankees," and said that "between these two cavalry regiments and ours" there was a tie "which we trust will never be broken." He then shook the hands of his men and of the black soldiers who were present. Hassam Enver Pasha, military

---

34. *Baltimore Morning Herald,* n.d., as quoted in Hiram M. Thweatt, *What the Newspapers Say of the Negro Soldier in the Spanish-American War,* p. 8; *Leslie's Weekly,* 13 October 1898, p. 287; *The Savannah Tribune,* 13 August 1898, 18 March 1899. See also *World,* 16 August 1898.

35. Perry E. Gianakos, "The Spanish-American War and the Double Paradox of the Negro American," p. 39; Richard H. Davis, *The Cuban and Porto Rican Campaigns,* p. 244; George Kennan, *Campaigning in Cuba,* p. 144.

attaché of Turkey, after his stay in Cuba, reported that the black soldiers "showed great bravery." As evidence of this, the army presented five Medals of Honor and more than twenty Certificates of Merit to the soldiers for their actions in the Cuban campaign.[36]

The public also praised the black soldiers and honored them with parades, luncheons, and gifts. The Tenth Cavalry, on its way to camp in Huntsville, Alabama, stopped in Washington, marched down Pennsylvania Avenue before many cheering citizens, and finally was reviewed by President McKinley. After the parade the men were given a reception hosted by Maj. Charles R. Douglas and Mrs. Charles Ayres, the wife of a captain in the regiment. At about the same time Philadelphia held a Peace Jubilee and requested that all four of the black regiments be allowed to attend. The War Department replied that only the Tenth Cavalry was close enough to be able to participate, and the committee agreed to pay for the travel of four troops of the regiment. Their appearance in the parade was the occasion for cheers that, according to the correspondent of the *Army and Navy Journal*, were "almost deafening, and lasted until the last of the soldiers disappeared." Other groups of citizens around the country, in a period of several months after the war, honored the black soldiers at special luncheons and presented them with decorated regimental flags or medals.[37]

Soon after the initial burst of enthusiasm, however, whites began to have doubts about the ability of the black soldiers and began to question their conduct. Col. Theodore Roosevelt praised them only half-heartedly in his account of the Cuban campaign. He said that they had performed their duties well, "but they are . . . peculiarly dependent upon their white officers." Roosevelt's conclusions were influenced by his assumptions about the limited abilities of the negro race, but he also cited an incident that occurred on the evening after the battle at San Juan Heights. He claimed that he had had to use a

---

36. *ANJ*, 18 February 1905, p. 656; *The New York Times*, 14 September 1898. See also Elting E. Morison, ed., *The Letters of Theodore Roosevelt*, 2:1351. Elizabeth Burt, "Forty Years an Army Wife" (manuscript), Burt, Papers, Manuscript Division, p. 289; *World*, 24 July 1898; *ANJ*, 22 April 1899, p. 805.

37. *ANJ*, 15 October 1898, p. 156; *Colored American*, 29 October 1898. *The Gazette*, 15 October 1898; *ANR*, 15 October 1898, p. 235; AGO 142376; *ANJ*, 29 October 1898, p. 202; for examples see AGO 129885, 130905, 196540. *The Gazette*, 22 October 1898. *ANJ*, 23 February 1899, p. 504; 18 February 1899, p. 588.

revolver to restrain a number of leaderless Blacks who were heading to the rear.[38]

Roosevelt's story of black cowardice did not go unchallenged. Presley Holliday, a member of B Troop, Tenth Cavalry, had a different version of the events. In a long letter to the *New York Age,* one of the leading black newspapers of the day, he pointed out that at the time both whites and Blacks were going to the rear to get ammunition and supplies. According to Holliday, Roosevelt neglected to ask the Blacks why they were leaving the front. He acted on the assumption that they were retreating. "Everyone who saw the incident knew the Colonel [Roosevelt] was mistaken about our men trying to shirk duty." Holliday then went on to attack Roosevelt's assumption that the soldiers performed well only under the command of whites. He cited several specific examples when his troop was ably led by black NCOs who substituted for disabled or lost white officers. Roosevelt was not convinced by Holliday's account. He continued to believe that the soldiers of the Tenth acted in a cowardly way, and the reason for their behavior was that they were black. This change in his opinion reflected a regression to the traditional view.[39] Army officers judged the black soldiers not on any real military standard, but on a racial one. Despite their heroic efforts in Cuba, white army officers were not convinced that Blacks would make good soldiers. They continued to give all the credit for the skills of black soldiers to the white officers who trained them.

For the black soldiers and the black community as a whole, the campaign in Cuba provided an esprit de corps that was to encourage them in some of the hard times of the future. Many black civilians looked upon the black soldiers with a great deal of pride. A large number of homes of Blacks contained a picture of the two black calvary units charging up San Juna Hill.[40]

These two diametrically differing opinions on the fighting capabilities of Blacks were to be tested again soon in combat in the Philippines.

38. Theodore Roosevelt, *The Rough Riders,* pp. 94–96.

39. *New York Age,* 11 May 1899, as quoted in Willard B. Gatewood, Jr., *"Smoked Yankees" and the Struggle for Empire: Letters from Negro Soldiers, 1898–1902,* pp. 92–97; Morison, *The Letters of Theodore Roosevelt,* 2:1304–6.

40. AGO 1374702; Rayford W. Logan, *The Betrayal of the Negro,* p. 335.

III

COMBAT
PHILIPPINES, MEXICO

Shortly after the Spanish-American War, the War Department was again forced to decide whether to assign Blacks to combat. In 1899, the United States needed troops to put down a native revolt in the Philippines, and in 1916, Mexican rebels were causing disturbances on the United States border.

Although Adm. George Dewey won control of Manila Bay on 1 May 1898, he did not have enough troops to drive the Spanish out of the city of Manila. When the United States Government began to plan a campaign against the Spanish they counted on the assistance of the Filipino natives. It soon became clear that Emilio Aguinaldo, the head of the native group, would not submit to United States control. With the knowledge that the United States forces would have to compensate for the lack of support among the natives, the Government sent a large contingent of troops. After the fall of Manila and the collapse of Spanish power, the insurgents decided to set up their own government with Aguinaldo as dictator. Shortly thereafter they decided to attack the Americans in Manila. The fighting began on 4 February 1899, and the Filipinos were defeated. The Americans then captured the capital the insurgents had established at Malolos. After this defeat the Aguinaldo regime disintegrated. Army reinforcements, including parts of all four black regiments, began to arrive in the islands. By August 1899 the constant pressure of the American army turned the struggle into a guerrilla war. The Americans tried to put an end to the fighting by capturing Aguinaldo, but the rebel leader managed to elude them. Finally in March 1901 Brig. Gen. Frederick Funston captured Aguinaldo, and for all intents and purposes the insurrection was over.[1]

A controversy raged in the black press over whether the black

1. John R. M. Taylor, "The Philippine Insurrection Against the United States," Chaps. 3–4; NA, RG 94.

soldier should support the United States' effort to stop the Filipinos' war for independence. Some compared the aspirations of the Filipinos with their own, for both, according to *The Colored American* (Washington, D.C.), were "struggling for the right of liberty and the pursuit of happiness." On the other hand, there was much more support for the position held by *The Freeman* (Indianapolis, Indiana) that "the enemy of the country is a common enemy and . . . the color of the face has nothing to do with it." It was the black soldiers' duty, the supporters of this view said, to fight beside "his white brother" wherever it was necessary. The insurgents tried to capitalize on black opposition to the war. They published leaflets pointing out the ties between the Blacks' struggle for freedom and that of the Filipinos. Anti-imperialists in the United States spread the rumor that black soldiers had accepted this argument and deserted in large numbers. According to the War Department records, however, only about five Blacks, out of the several thousand black soldiers who were sent to the Philippines, took up the cause of the insurgents.[2]

All four of the black units played a role in a variety of operations against the insurgents. Upon arrival in the islands the Blacks trained briefly in the recently freed areas around Manila and then went off to the scene of operations against Aguinaldo. On 7 October 1899, for example, the Twenty-fourth Infantry participated in an engagement at San Augustin; the men had to wade through waist-deep mud in order to reach some of the enemy's outposts. After firing a few volleys the insurrectos fled. Several days later the same regiment attacked enemy positions near Arayat and again succeeded in driving the natives from their trenches, with only one casualty in the Twenty-fourth. The other regiments performed similar duties through central and northern Luzon.[3]

One unusual operation took place in November and December 1899. Several companies of the Twenty-fourth under the command of Capt. Joseph B. Batchelor marched over the mountains in central Luzon and into an area where few non-Filipinos had ever been. The force of about 350 men consisted of H and F companies and detachments of A and K, supple-

2. *The Colored American*, 13 May 1899; *The Freeman*, 1 July 1899; *The Colored American*, 16 September 1899; 24 March 1900; AGO 335956.

3. Lawton Report, pp. 29–30. For examples see also Otis Report, pp. 215, 229. *The Gazette*, 2 December 1899; Maj Gen 1899, 3:591. *The Richmond Planet*, 16 December 1899.

mented with some native scouts under the command of Lt. Joseph C. Castner. They left Cabatuan and reported to General Lawton at Tayug on 23 November 1899. Batchelor got the impression at the meeting that he was to take his command and cross over the nearby mountains into the valley of thd Cagayan River and prevent Aguinaldo from heading in that direction.[4]

The first part of the march from Tayug was through poorly mapped, mountainous country. All of the available horses were used for an impromptu pack train. For the next few days the command marched through the mountains. They had to climb cliffs, "hardly any of them surmountable except by zigzag paths cut on shelves from a foot to 18 inches wide." The marchers were sometimes without water and had little to eat other than rice and green coffee. Once they met a group of natives who gave them baskets of sweet potatoes. One black soldier, Pvt. Bruce Williams, wrote that "of course the potatoes were relished though cooked by barbarians." Batchelor and his men celebrated Thanksgiving during this part of the march, and their menu consisted mainly of rice. Private Williams commented that they had "eaten so much rice that we are ashamed to look at it. I, for one, am sick of it." [5]

At Bayombong they learned that Aguinaldo had prepared to enter the valley over the mountains to the north of them. Batchelor felt it was his duty to take possession of the rest of the valley and did so by journeying down river to Aparri on the coast. They met enemy forces several times but usually succeeded in scaring them off without any bloodshed. Their fight against the terrain was more difficult than the one against the insurrectos. Most of the trails were covered with high grass that cut the men's hands and legs, especially since many of the soldiers had worn out their trousers.[6]

By this time Batchelor's immediate superiors became worried and sent out a messenger to stop him. They ordered him to remain in Bayombong "unless . . . acting under orders received from the division commander." Batchelor replied that he felt that he was following orders and that he could not stop because he was pursuing a beaten force. Interpreting his orders to suit his needs, he continued toward the coast.[7]

4. Lawton Report, p. 373.

5. Ibid., pp. 373–74; *Paris Republican* (Illinois), n.d., as quoted in *The Recorder,* 17 March 1900.

6. Lawton Report, pp. 374–75.

7. Ibid., p. 375.

Ignorant of the official disapproval, Batchelor and his command continued their march. They crossed from the Rio Negat to the Cagayan and then marched down that larger stream toward Naguilian, where they heard an enemy force was awaiting them. When they arrived there they found the enemy entrenched on a bluff across the river. The black soldiers moved up to the river bank and fired at the insurrectos but were unable to dislodge them. Batchelor then decided to send a force across the river and flank the position. It proved to be quite hard to find any material to construct a raft. Eventually they did find a native hut, which they tore down and brought to the river bank. At the same time one of the officers and four enlisted men swam naked across the river. Corp. John H. Johnson drowned "not asking help lest it should prevent the crossing of the others." After they reached the other side, the four survivors constructed a little raft, and the three enlisted men came back to get some rifles. At the same time the first group finished their raft, constructed out of a few bamboos, canteen straps, and some shelter tents torn into strips. Swimming and using the raft a few men got across, mounted an attack, and drove the insurgents off. Captain Batchelor commented:

To see 9 men, the officers in their drawers and the privates naked, cross such a stream by such means, and drive an intrenched force not less than ten times their number, in broad daylight where their number must soon become known, is something not soon to be forgotten.[8]

After this action Batchelor and his command encountered little opposition, and they continued their march unimpeded. On 7 December Gen. Daniel Tirona, the commander of the Filipino forces in the area, surrendered to them. The Americans then collected some native canoes, and on 12 December they made camp at Tuguegarao, capital of the province of Cagayan. By 17 December all but one company, which was to remain there as a garrison, moved on to Aparri to rest and receive supplies, including the much-needed new clothing. Captain Bachelor summed up the mission by saying that his force of 350 men marched over 300 miles without any guides in an unknown territory, following trails that were "just passable through chilling nights and sweltering days; made 123 deep fords; . . . crossed 80 miles of precipitous mountains in five days . . .; lived

8. Ibid., pp. 376–77.

three weeks on unaccustomed and insufficient food;" and in the end forced the surrender of more than 1,000 men without mistreating anyone. The people were left, according to Batchelor, "enthusiastic advocates of American supremacy." High-ranking officers, after their initial displeasure, agreed that Batchelor's effort was commendable. Gen. Elwell S. Otis felt that the march would remain "memorable on account of the celerity of its execution, the difficulties encountered, and the discomforts suffered by the troops."[9]

Though the fighting died down in the months after Batchelor's march, the duties of the men increased. In order to maintain control of the islands the army had to station small detachments in the important towns of each province. These garrisons brought order to the towns and allowed the functioning of the civil government. The detachments supervised local elections and performed civil governmental functions. In Bamban they had to serve as the local police because the presence of the garrison in the town had prevented much of the native population from returning and thus there were not enough people on whom to levy a tax to pay for the police. Other duties during this period included the maintenance of telegraph lines. In early 1900 the provincial commander stationed several companies of the Twenty-fifth Infantry in the coastal towns of Subig, Iban, and Santa Cruz in Luzon and assigned them the task of protecting their telegraph lines. The insurrectos made this job quite difficult. As fast as the Americans put them up, the rebels would tear them down. In order to trap the bothersom Filipinos, the commander of the detachment authorized a combined land and sea operation. He ordered part of the Twenty-fifth to advance along the coast; then the remainder of the detachment would be landed at the rear of the enemy. Unfortunately, when the trap was closed, the rebels had disappeared. [10]

Regular patrols were equally as necessary, as arduous, and usually as unsuccessful. One of these patrols was assigned to K Company, Twenty-fifth Infantry, in late 1899. The men arose at 2 A.M., ate breakfast, and left the camp at 4 A.M. The path they followed ran through forests and rice fields, both of which made

9. For examples see Lawton Report, pp. 377–80. Otis Report, p. 310.

10. U.S., Congress, House of Representatives, *Report of Operations of Second Division, Eighth Army Corps, 1899–1900,* House Document 2, vol. 1, pt. 8, 56th Cong., 2d sess., 1900–1901, pp. 374, 361; AGO 1247237; *ANJ,* 12 May 1900, p. 879.

traveling very difficult for the flankers. The march continued all day, but they never did spot any insurrectos.[11]

The black units continued to perform this type of duty until the army ordered them home in 1902. They had again upheld their tradition of being good combat units. They had performed the same duties as white soldiers; they acted as civil governors and carried on guerrilla warfare, in addition to performing the more conventional combat patrols. Combat in the islands also demonstrated that black soldiers placed their allegiance to the nation above race and their own grievances. Though they logically might have sympathized with the Filipinos' struggle for independence, the vast majority did not.

Ten years later disturbances occurred along the United States–Mexico border, and the War Department was again compelled to depend on black troops. Beginning in 1912 the government of President Victoriano Huerta came under attack from several different groups of rebels, some of whom were under the command of Gov. Venustiano Carranza. The fighting in Mexico often led to border incidents and violations of American neutrality. In retaliation the army increased the number of troops along the boundary. Among those sent were the Ninth Cavalry, ordered to Douglas, Arizona, in 1912, and the Tenth Cavalry, to Fort Huachuca, Arizona, in 1914. One of the duties of the regiments was to patrol the border. This job was thankless, usually consisting of monotonous rides along arid, treeless trails. Ordinarily there was no fighting, but soldiers had to be alert because of the possibility of encountering hostile Mexicans, as a patrol of the Ninth did in March 1913. About fifty Yaqui Indians and Mexicans fired upon the patrol near Douglas, and though the group of American soldiers retreated, the firing continued. The regimental commander ordered reinforcements to the area and returned the Mexican fire, killing at least one of the attackers. As a result of this incident the War Department advised the officer to take the greatest precautions not to allow such fights "to complicate [the] present situation." Yet he was also responsible for protecting American lives and property. This advice made an already complex situation even more difficult.[12]

The situation began to change in 1913, when the United

11. *Richmond Planet*, 11 November 1899.
12. *ANJ*, 5 October 1912, p. 137; AGO 2008188.

States Government decided that it would support the Carranza forces. As a result it lifted its arms embargo. Within a year Huerta was overthrown, and Carranza was victorious. Unfortunately, this victory did not stabilize the situation because Pancho Villa, originally one of Carranza's supporters, attempted to depose him and take over the government. Carranza retreated to Vera Cruz, and the fighting began again. In April 1915 Villa was soundly defeated at the battle of Celaya, and he retreated north to his bastion in Chihuahua, immediately south of New Mexico and Texas. Villa blamed his defeats on the United States and determined to exact revenge. He decided to involve the United States in a war with Mexico. His first step was to take sixteen American miners off a train near Santa Ysabel and shoot them. When the American Government did not react, in March 1916 Villa raided the border town of Columbus, New Mexico. The American garrison managed to drive the Mexicans off, pursuing them into Mexico for a short distance.[13]

There was a strong reaction to the raid, and many Americans immediately demanded that Villa be captured and punished. On 10 March, President Woodrow Wilson decided that the best policy would be to send an expedition into Mexico to capture Villa and destroy his group. Brig. Gen. John J. Pershing was placed in charge of the Punitive Expedition. His mission was twofold: to break up the Villa bands but to avoid offending the Mexican government—a task that was practically impossible.[14]

Pershing decided the expedition should enter Mexico in two columns. One started from Columbus and consisted of the Thirteenth Cavalry, the Eleventh Cavalry, Battery C-Sixth Field Artillery, one company of Engineers, and the First Aero Squadron. The other column, which was faster, started from Hachita, New Mexico, to the west of Columbus. It was composed of the Seventh Cavalry, the Tenth Cavalry, and Battery B-Sixth Field Artillery. Both columns crossed the border on 15 March 1916 and joined together at Colonia Dublan on 20 March. Pershing then decided that the best strategy to catch Villa was to set up three parallel columns moving rapidly southward. They would

13. Arthur S. Link, *Woodrow Wilson and the Progressive Era, 1910–1917,* pp. 107–44; Robert B. Johnson, "The Punitive Expedition: A Military, Diplomatic and Political History of Pershing's Chase After Pancho Villa, 1916–1917," p. 9. See also Clarence C. Clendenen, *Blood on the Border,* pp. 213–342, for a good account of the whole Punitive Expedition; R. B. Johnson, "The Punitive Expedition," pp. 81–85.

14. R. B. Johnson, "The Punitive Expedition," pp. 96–104; 142–43.

try to locate and capture the bandit and at the same time prevent him from going over the mountains into Sonora. Two of the three columns consisted of squadrons of the Tenth. This choice indicated Pershing's high opinion of the ability of the black troopers.[15]

The two squadrons of the Tenth began their chase with a train ride. Although the train ride had been planned as a rest, it turned out to be quite the opposite. When the Mexican train arrived, the regiment discovered that the motley collection of twenty-eight box cars and flat cars had previously been used by the Mexican army which, among other things, had chopped holes in the cars. First the Blacks had to patch up the cars and then cut windows and doors to be used as entrances by the soldiers and horses. The next problem was to find places for all the men to ride. When the inside of the train was full, soldiers rode on the roof, which was hemmed in with bales of hay. When the accommodations for troops were finally ready, the engine needed so much wood that they had to tear up a corral (the United States Government later had to pay $1,900 for the damage). During the trip, the soldiers were always busy supplying the engine either with wood or with water or both. Despite the barriers placed on the roof, soldiers often fell off of it in their sleep.[16]

After leaving the train, the two squadrons began a month-long search for Villa. During that time they were provided no Government rations, nor forage, nor a cent of Government money or aid of any kind. They either improvised supplies or purchased them with the small amount of cash collected from among the officers and men. Despite the handicaps, including the indifference or hostility of the local populace, they searched constantly for Villa and his band but rarely found even traces. On 27 March Col. William C. Brown, known to his men as "Water Closet," received word that some Villa troops were occupying a ranch about eight miles from camp. He decided to attack the Mexicans at dawn. The official diarist of the Tenth reported, "Arrived as per plan and surprised the inhabitants some sixty-five or more in number and undoubtedly Villistas but proof of same lacking." Several days after this disappoint-

15. Robert S. Thomas and Inez V. Allen, *The Mexican Punitive Expedition,* 2:11; 3:1.

16. Orlando C. Troxel, "The Tenth Cavalry in Mexico," *Journal of the United States Cavalry Association,* p. 201. See also Edward L. Glass, *History of the Tenth Cavalry, 1866–1921,* p. 70.

ment the advance guard of the regiment unexpectedly encountered some of Villa's men, commanded by Beltran, on the outskirts of Aquas Calientes. There they pursued Beltran and his men for seven miles. Because night was approaching and the horses were exhausted, the Americans were forced to stop, and when the troops could resume the chase, the bandits had disappeared.[17]

On 12 April the regiment arrived at Sapien and made preparations to spend the night. About 6:30 P.M. three troopers of the Thirteenth Cavalry, the other part of the pursuit force, brought news that their regiment had been attacked at nearby Parral by the Carranza garrison and was in retreat toward Santa Cruz de Villegas. Quickly the black soldiers packed and within fifteen minutes were on their way to aid their white comrades. About fifty minutes later they arrived at Santa Cruz where they found the Thirteenth barricaded in and the rooftops manned with riflemen, ready for an attack. As soon as the Tenth arrived the Carranza forces retreated. This incident ended the pursuit of Villa, during which the regiment had marched 750 miles in 28 days.[18]

After some discussion, Pershing decided to move his troops slowly northward though always on the lookout for bands of Villistas. In May the regiments were ordered to assemble in Colonia Dublan, which remained the base of the expedition until its withdrawal from Mexico in February 1917. Reinforcements, including the Twenty-fourth Infantry, now joined the cavalry units. During these months the cavalry regiments were kept busy patrolling. On one such patrol the Tenth marched along a river, having to cross it seventy-one times in the space of a few miles. Pershing was well aware that the Mexicans disliked his presence in their country and knew that they would seize any opportunity to drive him out. For this reason he felt it necessary to send out the patrols to see what the Mexicans were doing, even though there was always the possibility of a clash between a patrol and some Carranza forces. Toward the end of June, the general learned of a concentration of Mexican forces at Villa Ahumada, which might be a threat to his line of communications back to Columbus. Pershing decided to dis-

17. Troxel, "The Tenth Cavalry," p. 199; 10th Cav War Diary, 23–24 March 1916; 28–29 March 1916; 1–3 April 1916. See also 10th Cav Org Ret, April 1916.

18. 10th Cav War Diary, 12 April 1916. See also 10th Cav Org Ret, April 1916; Troxel, "The Tenth Cavalry," p. 200

patch a patrol to find out the size of the Mexican forces in the town. Upon his request, the commander of the Tenth provided him with a trustworthy and discreet troop leader, Capt. Charles Boyd, C Troop.[19]

The patrol, which consisted of C and K troops, Tenth Cavalry, never arrived in Villa Ahumada. They clashed with some of the Mexican government's troops at Carrizal, and the skirmish almost resulted in war between the United States and Mexico. Because some historians have suggested that Pershing tried to maneuver Wilson into a full-scale war with Mexico through this incident, the specific instructions in Pershing's order to Boyd are significant. Pershing told Boyd of the large concentration of Mexican forces assembled at Villa Ahumada, and he warned him that "a clash with Mexican troops would probably bring on war and for this reason was to be avoided." With this guidance, Boyd and his patrol left the main camp of the expedition and headed toward Villa Ahumada. That evening they camped at a ranch about thirty miles from their destination. Boyd received a report that there was a force of Mexicans at Carrizal, about eight miles from his camp. Their presence blocked his road to Villa Ahumada. After consulting with the other two officers under his command, who advised caution, Boyd decided to proceed with his mission. It was to prove a fateful decision for Boyd and his men. It is possible that Boyd believed that Pershing really wanted him to force the Mexicans into a position where they would fire the first shot and cause an incident that would lead to a full-scale war. It is more than likely, however, that he felt a firm show of force would disperse the Mexicans, as it had in similar situations in the past. [20]

On the morning of 21 June 1916 the two troops left the camp site and marched toward Carrizal. Upon their arrival at a field outside of town, the troopers dismounted and rested. Captain Boyd spoke with the Mexican officers commanding the garrison in Carrizal and requested permission to pass through and move on to Villa Ahumada. The Mexicans refused. While the discus-

19. 10th Cav War Diary, 17 May 1916; R. B. Johnson, "The Punitive Expedition," p. 614; Thomas and Allen, *The Mexican Punitive Expedition*, 4:20.

20. Punitive Expedition Commander to Inspector General, *Records of the American Expeditionary Forces (World War I) 1917–1923*, NA, RG 120 (material on the Carrizal battle is contained in Boxes 70–71 of RG 120); AGO 2377632. See also Thomas and Allen, *The Mexican Punitive Expedition*, 4:22; AGO 2377632; Harold B. Wharfield, *Tenth Cavalry and Border Fights*, pp. 29, 33–34; see also R. B. Johnson, "The Punitive Expedition," p. 647n18.

sion continued between the officers, the soldiers who were waiting became more worried. On opposite edges of the field the Americans and the Mexicans began to form lines for battle. When Boyd returned, the Americans advanced across the field toward the ditch that the Mexicans were using as a defensive position. The officers of the American patrol noticed that the Mexican forces outflanked them, but there was nothing they could do because they were greatly outnumbered. The tension increased; Boyd sent the horses to the rear and apparently decided that a show of force could still succeed. As the black troopers moved across the field, some of the Mexicans began to fire. Although the firepower of the Americans initially drove some of Carranza's forces from the field, their smaller forces caused the Americans' downfall. Two of the officers, including Captain Boyd, were killed, and the ammunition supply was exhausted. In the resulting chaos, each man was on his own. Some managed to escape, twenty-four were captured, two officers and eleven enlisted men were killed, and one officer and ten enlisted men were wounded. If Pershing had wanted to provoke an armed clash, Boyd and his black soldiers had provided one. However, it is most likely that the incident was the result of a miscalculation on the part of Captain Boyd.[21]

When news of the disaster reached Pershing, he claimed that he was "surprised" and "chagrined" that Boyd had disregarded his orders. In the United States public opinion against Mexico grew, but President Wilson refused to be stampeded. He persisted in his view that no further escalation should be undertaken. For the black community, however, a declaration of war was not the central issue. They saw the dead black soldiers as heroes and deserving of "unstinted praise." A large crowd paid homage to the dead soldiers when they arrived at El Paso. The War Department arranged to have six of the dead heroes sent to Washington for burial at Arlington. Crowds lined the route from Union Station across the Memorial Bridge to the cemetery. Secretary of War Newton D. Baker and the Chief of Staff, Maj. Gen. Hugh L. Scott, were among those who attended the burial of the soldiers as a testimonial to the regard that the War Department held for them. [22]

21. AGO 2377632; R. B. Johnson, "The Punitive Expedition," pp. 614–53; Wharfield, *Tenth Cavalry and Border Fights,* p. 36. 10th Cav Org Ret, June 1916; Harold B. Wharfield, "The Affair at Carrizal: Pershing's Punitive Expedition," p. 38.

22. AGO 2377632; Thomas, *The Mexican Punitive Expedition,* 4:30; *Savannah*

In the months in Mexico after the Carrizal incident, Pershing made sure that the men were kept busy. Patrols, training problems, and small-scale tactical maneuvers kept the expedition occupied. About three weeks after the incident at Carrizal, for example, Pershing dispatched a fifteen-man patrol from G Troop, Tenth Cavalry, to scout an area northwest of the main camp at Colonia Dublan. They found no one. During the time when the troops did not have military assignments, they were busy occupying their leisure time. Since the Mexican population remained hostile, the United States Government and some private businessmen provided places for the soldiers to spend their pay. In addition they participated in athletics, such as baseball and boxing. Thanksgiving gave the soldiers an excuse for a big celebration. The cooks of D Troop, Tenth Cavalry, roasted turkey in adobe ovens built into the walls of their adobe kitchens. They also served potatoes, sage dressing, cranberry sauce, scalloped corn, three types of cake, pumpkin pie, fruit, and nuts. The men closed this marvelous celebration with cigars and coffee.[23]

The Wilson Administration first tried negotiating the matter of the Punitive Expedition with Mexico, but all attempts were fruitless. Then the possibility of a war with Germany became more acute, and Wilson decided the best policy was to bring the troops home. On 5 February 1917 the soldiers of the expedition left Mexico and were reviewed in Columbus, New Mexico. The troops then received orders to return to their preexpedition posts. The Tenth Cavalry resumed its stations guarding the border, and the Twenty-fourth Infantry now joined them.[24]

The reaction of military leaders to the Blacks' conduct during the Punitive Expedition indicated the respect they still had for black soldiers in combat. The fact that the army stationed them on the border almost guaranteed that they would take part in the expedition. However, Pershing did not have to give them a major role in his campaign. The fact that they formed two-thirds of his flying column during the pursuit demonstrated the army's confidence in them. It is fitting that this last great cavalry expedition, reminiscent of the Indian Wars in so many ways, upheld the proud tradition of the Blacks in combat that had

Tribune, 24 June 1916. See also *ANJ,* 22 July 1916, p. 1512. *The Crisis* 12:4 (August, 1916):165; 12:4 (August, 1916):194; *The Freeman,* 29 July 1916.

23. *ANJ,* 16 December 1916, p. 506.

24. 10th Cav War Diary, 5 February 1917.

been formed during the fighting on the plains in the nineteenth century. Despite the renewed evidence that these black Regulars could fight, most whites felt Blacks were cowards. White officers continued to be influenced by their predispositions about the race rather than the concrete evidence of the soldiers' performance.

IV

RACIAL ATTITUDES AND MORES

After 1890, the United States military no longer had to depend on Blacks to fulfill its need for troops, so long-submerged prejudices were allowed to surface. Even though the soldiers' conduct was proof of their combat capabilities, their status was to decline.

The policy of racial separation had been implemented in every facet of American life, and the army was no exception. Military leaders acted on the assumption that black soldiers could not be allowed to mix with whites. There was never any discussion of integration of the infantry or cavalry units. Segregation was a policy that apparently was universally accepted by whites. In some cases it resulted in confusing situations, for it was not always possible to use skin color as a criterion to distinguish the races. In one case a soldier who was in the Tenth Cavalry claimed that he had once served in the artillery, where officially no Blacks were allowed, and requested a transfer out of his black regiment. The War Department gave careful attention to the request. Either the man had "misrepresented" his color when he had served in the artillery, or, if he had legitimately served there, he had "no business in a colored regiment serving in the grade of a private." A similar case in 1912 emphasized the futility of efforts to positively define the races. The white wife of a man in the Tenth Cavalry requested that the War Department transfer her husband to a white regiment. She claimed that the soldier's parents, both white, had died when he was very young, that a black family had taken custody of the child, and consequently the soldier had grown up believing that he was a black man. The medical officer of the post examined the man in question and reported that he had the features of a white man but that his skin color could have been that of "either a very light mulatto or a dark complexioned white man." The War Department decided that because the man had served in a black regiment for a long time, the evidence would not justify "the change in the soldier's status" that had been requested.[1]

The races were not merely separated through their assignments to regiments. On occasion, the army sent a few white recruits to the posts where black soldiers were stationed. Normally the recruits would have eaten with the Regulars, but if all the Regulars happened to be black, the recruits were given separate accommodations. While the Twenty-fifth Infantry was stationed in Washington, the War Department ordered the white recruits to be quartered and messed at the post hospital. In addition, the army specifically ordered the black NCOs not to drill or give any instruction to these white recruits.[2]

The insistence on racial separation was probably carried to its most ridiculous extreme in 1916. In that year the War Department issued a pamphlet, *Experiences of a Recruit in the United States Army.* The author, a newspaper reporter, chronicled his experiences while undergoing training at the Columbus Barracks recruit depot in Ohio. The first edition of the pamphlet included a set of before-and-after pictures showing a group of rookies at the beginning of the training program and then twelve days later. The groups pictured included ten men, eight white and two black. Some officers objected to this implication that there was intermingling of the races. As a result, in the second edition the two Blacks were deleted from the picture.[3]

The army did more than just enforce segregation. It also made sure soldiers would observe the prevailing racial mores. When a white woman married a soldier of the Twenty-fifth in 1911, the army found a pretext to discharge him. They said the marriage made him "unfit for further association with other soldiers," for his wife was of "dissolute character." Another instance occurred in New Jersey in 1904 when a white soldier married a black woman. The army discharged him on the grounds that his action made his "further retention in the service prejudicial to the public interest."[4]

For a long time military leaders believed that the ability to command was largely a matter of race or family inheritance, so Blacks obviously were not suited to be officers. This view, in a slightly different form, was held also by knowledgeable Blacks.

1. LS, 10th Cav, 5 September 1902; AGO 1870439.
2. AGO 1572333. See also AGO 1543200.
3. U.S. Department of War, *Annual Report of the Secretary of War, 1916,* 1:24; AGO 2496329.
4. AGO 1848699; AGO 333328. See also *ANR,* 22 October 1904, pp 12–13.

Charles Young, the third black graduate of West Point, expressed a similar attitude. He wrote in 1912 that the black man was "by nature more dependent and has less initiative than his Anglo-Saxon comrade." However, he believed that the performance of the black officers in command of the black volunteer regiments in the Spanish-American War and the Philippine Insurrection had shown that Blacks could command other Blacks.[5]

In both of these conflicts the War Department enlisted regiments of volunteers, including six regiments of Blacks, four in the Spanish-American War and two in the Philippine Insurrection. On both occasions one of the pressing issues the War Department had to deal with was whether there should be any black officers, and if so, at what rank. Naturally Blacks wanted very much to receive commissions, and to back up their demands some said that if they could not have officers of their own color in the federal service, then they would not serve. As *The American Citizen* (Kansas City, Kansas) stated, "It is an insult to tell us that we are incapable of holding the rank of an officer— no officers, no soldier, is our motto." Despite their pleas, during the Spanish-American War the army complied with only token commissioning of Blacks in ranks no higher than lieutenant in the line companies. Whites still retained control by holding all the staff positions and the higher line commissions. In selecting the black officers the War Department decided to give preference to those men who had been noncommissioned officers in the Regular Army or who had distinguished themselves in the Cuban campaign. Many Blacks believed that this decision was an affront to the courageous Blacks who were promoted. Chaplain Theophilus G. Steward of the Twenty-fifth Infantry, a Black, said that the commissions "were too short-lived, and too circumscribed, to be much more than a lively tantalization, to be remembered with disgust by those who had worn them." When the army disbanded the volunteer regiments in 1899, these officers returned to the Regular Army as enlisted men.[6]

5. Richard C. Brown, "Social Attitudes of American Generals, 1898–1940," p. 179; *ANJ*, 11 November 1899, p. 238; William W. West, Jr., questionnaire in possession of author (see Appendix B); Robert L. Bullard, "The Negro Volunteer: Some Characteristics," p. 32; Charles Young, *Military Morale of Nations and Races*, p. 214.

6. *The American Citizen*, 17 June 1898; AGO 159424. *The Bee*, 13 August 1898; Theophilus G. Steward, *The Colored Regulars in the United States Army*, p. 251; *The Gazette*, 10 December 1898. For a more complete discussion of the black vol-

The army's opinion of the competence of these officers was rendered within the year. In 1899 the Government decided to raise more volunteer regiments to fight in the Philippines. Among the twenty-four regiments raised were two black units, the Forty-eighth and the Forty-ninth United States volunteer infantry regiments. The army announced that all line officers below the rank of major would be black. At the suggestion of President McKinley, the War Department offered Charles Young the senior captaincy in one of the regiments. Young refused, for he felt that Blacks would be upset by this appointment. They had expected him to lead the entire regiment, and, he commented, "The consideration of seven millions of a race is not to be ignored by me." At the same time the army also asked the commanders of the four black regiments to recommend enlisted men whom they felt "are best qualified for commissions as company officers." Most of the men appointed had had experience in the volunteers in the Spanish-American War and/or the Regular Army. Alfred Ray, appointed to the Forty-ninth, had been with the Tenth Cavalry for twenty-six years and had served as a first lieutenant in the Tenth United States Volunteer Infantry (one of the federally raised regiments that was used during the Spanish-American War). The army believed that soldiers who had long service in the Regular Army would be the best-trained black officers. However, control of the units was still in the hands of the whites.[7]

The members of the War Department also based policies on beliefs they had concerning the character and physical stamina of Blacks. They were convinced that they performed better in warm rather than cold climates and that they were resistant to tropical diseases. For this reason, in 1899 the Major General Commanding the Army opposed the stationing of the Twenty-fourth in Alaska. This theory also influenced the decision to assign the Twenty-fourth Infantry as nurses at Siboney during the Spanish-American War. There were ten federally raised volunteer regiments composed of men "possessing immunity

unteer units in the Spanish-American War see Marvin E. Fletcher, "The Negro Soldier and the United States Army, 1891–1917," Chap. 10.

7. Otis Report, pp. 343–44; AGO 272860; AGO 281270; AGO 238307; *ANJ*, 11 November 1899, p. 245; 4 November 1899, 219. See also *ANJ*, 14 October 1899, 145. *ANJ*, 21 October 1899, p. 169; 18 November 1899, p. 279. For a more complete discussion of the black volunteer units in the Philippine Insurrection see Fletcher, "The Negro Soldier," Chapter 11.

from diseases incident to tropical climates." Of these "immune" regiments, four were black. As late as 1915 this concept was still widely accepted in the military. An Army War College study of that year stated that black troops gave "better service in the tropics than white troops." [8]

These ideas were held even though army officers had much evidence to disprove them. The black soldiers had served long periods in the cold climates of Alaska, Montana, Wyoming, Washington, and North Dakota. Their performance there was the same as the white troops stationed in similar climes. When the soldiers of the Twenty-fourth Infantry served as nurses at the yellow fever hospital at Siboney, a geat many of them contracted the disease. As one knowledgeable officer said, "The Negro born and bred in a temperate climate is but little, if any, better suited to a prolonged stay in the tropics than a white man."[9]

Many whites believed that Blacks were generally more joyful and musical, even under stress. Whites commented that during the siege at Santiago, despite the heat and disease, the Blacks sang and told jokes. Charles J. Crane, an officer in the Twenty-fourth Infantry before the war, noted, after a long march the men would set up camp "and then . . . they would begin to sing and dance, showing a cheerful disposition, fine physical condition and satisfaction with things generally." It is hard to tell whether this image was real or whether it was a device used by Blacks to deceive whites. However, whites did accept and expect this sort of behavior. It reaffirmed their belief that Blacks needed white officers to guide them and that they were not very intelligent.[10]

The military leadership limited Blacks to service in the infantry and cavalry because many army officers felt Blacks lacked the intelligence to perform more complicated tasks. Many whites also argued that the law creating the four black regiments had specified in which type of duty Blacks could participate and that any change in this stipulation would have to originate in Congress. The old arguments of the 1870s about the inferiority of the Blacks were renewed, and it was on the basis of these misconceptions that the army was able to maintain the

8. AGO 240357; U.S., Congress, House of Representatives, *Congressional Record*, 55th Cong., 2d sess., 1897–1898, p. 4736; AGO 2290791.

9. AGO 22220160. See also *The Illinois Record*, 9 April 1898.

10. Charles J. Crane, *The Experiences of a Colonel of Infantry*, p. 115.

status quo. The War Department could use Congress as a scape-goat when its recruitment policies were questioned.[11]

Several bills brought before Congress in the years before the Spanish-American War dealt with the reorganization of the army. The authors of these measures usually wanted to reduce the manpower and thus the cost of the army. However, few detailed how the black regiments would be affected. After the gross deficiencies of the army were evidenced during the Spanish-American War, Congress went to work earnestly to correct them. In the end, Congress legislated an increase in the number of men in the army by expanding the size of the regiments and by adding five regiments of infantry and five of cavalry. No new black regiments were created. The War Department believed that the increase in the number of Blacks resulting from the enlargement of each regiment was sufficient. Other attempts in the next few years to add more black soldiers failed and for many of the same reasons.[12]

By 1915 it appeared to even the most casual observer that something had to be done to prepare our armed forces for the possibility of war. The War Department and Congress began to draw plans for the reorganization and enlargement of the army. Eventually Congress passed a bill to expand the size of the army through five annual increments to sixty-five infantry and thirty cavalry regiments. Black citizens and organizations constantly agitated for the inclusion of one or more new black units to be organized under the law. The NAACP pointed out to Secretary of War Baker that there would be little difficulty in recruiting black soldiers "because of the restricted industrial opportunity for colored people and their great pride in the four existing regiments." They also tried to use political pressure on the Wilson Administration. The black organization warned that rejection of the plea for more black soldiers "will increase the feeling of the colored people of the country that the Wilson administration has been anything but fair to them." The Secretary of War replied that he was in favor of opening up opportunities in the military to Blacks to the "largest extent possible," but he did not intend to create more black regiments. On this question, Secretary Baker hid behind the old law; he said that

11. Brown, "Social Attitudes," p. 179; *ANJ*, 29 December 1906, p. 486.

12. For an example of such a bill in the 1890s see U.S., Congress, House of Representatives, *A Bill to Reorganize and Increase the Efficiency of the Infantry Regiments, Army of the United States of America*, H.R. 7338, 53d Cong., 2d sess., 1893–1894; *ANJ*, 27 April 1901, p. 837; AGO 370613.

only Congress could designate the composition of a regiment. In response to further entreaties he replied that all units authorized under the first increase had already been formed and that consequently the Blacks would have to wait at least another year. As the years went by, the percentage of Blacks in the service steadily decreased. The army made no effort to persuade Congress to reverse the process.[13]

White racists objected to retaining any black regiments; they asked why Blacks should not be eliminated from the service. One former army officer, Capt. J. A. Judson, expressed quite clearly the ideas behind this attitude. There were enough whites in the country, he wrote in a letter to the *Army and Navy Journal*, to fill the service. There was no need for "Negroes or any other alien race." Several different legislators translated these ideas into a number of bills. One such bill called for the discharge of all Blacks from the army by the middle of 1907. Another method proposed to achieve the same goal was to repeal those sections of the Federal statutes that specifically authorized the four regiments. The proponents of a similar plan before 1890 had seen it as a method to allow Blacks to participate in all aspects of the service. A third plan was put forward in a bill introduced in the Sixty-third Congress (1913–1914), which prohibited Blacks from serving as commissioned or noncommissioned officers in the army or the navy. These bills never reached the floor for a vote. Each time the War Department informed Congress that it was opposed to the idea. Secretary Baker said that the "gallant service" of the black troops from the Revolution to Carrizal was a cogent reason for killing the bill.[14]

All of the elimination bills were proposed after the Brownsville affray (1906), and at least one was introduced in each Congress from 1906 to 1916. Two Democrats from Texas, Reps. John Nance Garner and James L. Slayden, introduced the first two bills in Congress in December 1906, the first meeting of the

13. AGO 2375469; AGO 2445888; AGO 2392349; AGO 2429203.

14. *ANJ,* 19 January 1907, p. 558; U.S., Congress, House of Representatives, *A Bill to Discontinue the Enlistment and Appointment of Negroes in the Army of the United States,* H.R. 20989, 59th Cong., 2d sess., 1906–1907; U.S., Congress, House of Representatives, *A Bill to Repeal Sections 1104 and 1108, Revised Statutes, Edition of 1878,* H.R. 20094, 59th Cong., 2d sess., 1906–1907; U.S., Congress, House of Representatives, *A Bill to Make it Unlawful to Appoint as Commissioned or Non-Commissioned Officers in the Army or Navy of the United States Any Person of the Negro Race,* H.R. 17541, 63d Cong., 2d sess., 1913–1914; AGO 2453857, 1599158.

national legislature after the Texas shooting incident. Garner, who introduced similar bills in the next three congresses, represented the district in which Brownsville was located. Slayden represented the district that included San Antonio, the nearest big city to Brownsville and the site of the two courts-martial that resulted from the incident. Later Reps. Frank Park of Georgia and Thaddeus H. Caraway of Arkansas took up the cause.

The War Department also resisted efforts to allow Blacks into the artillery. Early in 1898 Congressman George White, a black Republican from North Carolina, proposed that a provision for a black artillery regiment be included in the legislation to expand the army, which was then being discussed. He felt that it was "a sad commentary" that he had to submit a special amendment to achieve this purpose. He stated that Blacks should have been allowed to enlist in the artillery without enabling legislation. "It is reasonable to suppose that those rights would be accorded to us without any specific statute designating that such would be the case." The proposal was ignored. In 1901 the Blacks resurrected the idea, but on a larger scale. Blacks in Kansas and Illinois requested that Congress press legislation organizing two black batteries of artillery. The petitions cited the valor of the Blacks on the battlefield and their deportment in the service as reasons for the request. The Congress took no action.[15]

In 1904 some military leaders took up the project. Brig. Gen. Thomas H. Barry, commander of the Department of the Gulf, and Maj. Gen. Henry C. Corbin, commander of the Department of the East, recommended that Blacks be admitted to the artillery. Reaction was swift and predictable. A Congressman from Georgia protested the idea as a "mistake from every standpoint." The Secretary of War, on the other hand, considered the suggestion serious enough to ask the opinion of the legal branch of the army. He inquired if the army could add any black artillery units without approval from the civilian government. After much study the Judge Advocate General replied that he felt the original law of 1866 was "mandatory and restrictive." Only Congress could add or delete any black troops. Any addition by the army would be an infringement on the legislative power. The Secretary of War then let the matter drop.[16]

---

15. U.S., Congress, House of Representatives, *Congressional Record*, 55th Cong., 2d sess., 1897–1898, p. 2556; AGO 375206, 379437.
16. AGO 925354; AGO 932159; AGO 937667.

Blacks did not forget the idea. In February 1907 an old veteran of the Tenth Cavalry, Presley Holliday, wrote to Emmett J. Scott, secretary to Booker T. Washington, and suggested that with help from the President, they might be able to secure some black artillery units. Scott thought well of the idea and wrote to President Roosevelt, outlining his reasons for recommending the creation of black artillery units. Scott stated that because of the Blacks' bravery in war, their ability to shoot, their low rate of desertion, their intelligence, and the progress they had made, they had earned the right to serve in the artillery. Privately Scott told Washington that he felt the time was ripe for his proposal. One factor was "the President's present temper," that is his actions in the Brownsville incident, and his feeling about the violent anti-Roosevelt attitude of the black community. Apparently Scott believed that Roosevelt would act favorably on his request as a means of placating black voters. Initially Roosevelt made no such favorable response. He passed Scott's letter onto the War Department, which forwarded it to the Army War College for study.[17]

The report of the War College first dealt with Scott's arguments for admitting Blacks to the artillery. It stated that neither the bravery of the black troops nor their marksmanship was in question because neither contributed to making a good artilleryman. More importantly the members of the War College felt that the military aptitude of the black man "developed more slowly than in the case of the white soldier." As a result, few Blacks possessed the necessary technical knowledge for this branch. They therefore recommended that Blacks should not be admitted. If the War Department still persisted in an effort to incorporate Blacks into the artillery, however, the planners suggested how to handle this situation. They recommended that some units be integrated, with white men continuing to occupy the important positions. If the Blacks' performance proved satisfactory then the whites would be removed. If the experiment failed, then the Blacks could be easily removed.[18]

There was also a minority War College report on the question of the admission of Blacks to the artillery, which went further in its condemnation of Blacks and probably was a more accu-

17. Presley Holliday to Emmett J. Scott, 24 February 1907, Box 350, BTW, Papers; Scott to Washington, 6 March 1907, Box 359, BTW, Papers; Scott to Theodore Roosevelt, 8 March 1907, BTW, Papers.
18. AWC, file 4483, NA, RG 165.

rate expression of the way most officers felt. The intelligence of the black man, the dissenting officer wrote, was "inferior to the white race . . . . From our knowledge of the Negro, from his evident mental inferiorty, it *is* fairly to be concluded that he is *not* fitted for the modern technical artillery service." [19]

The question then passed into the hands of Secretary of War William Howard Taft. At first he was favorably inclined to grant Scott's request, but political complications soon arose. Taft sought the nomination to the presidential candidacy in 1908, and because Blacks opposed the Republican party, in general, and him, in particular, his attitude changed. "I had just about decided to give the order to organize one of the new artillery regiments with colored men when the Brownsville affair suddenly took a political turn." At this point Taft felt any action he took would appear to have been inspired by "political motives rather than [by] my own personal convictions." He decided to postpone action to see what would happen in the Brownsville investigation. The forces that Scott felt would push Roosevelt to act favorably in this question only moved Taft to do nothing. Scott had lost. The question remained dormant until the expansion of the army in 1916. Blacks again petitioned the War Department, and as before these pleas were pigionholed.[20] Not until the United States entered World War I were Blacks given positions in the artillery.

Despite the army's insistence upon racial separation and purity, there were white enlisted men among the four black regiments, the regimental chief musicians. At the same time as his appeal on the admission of Blacks to the artillery, Emmett Scott suggested to Secretary Taft that the army conform to regulations and exclude all white enlisted personnel from the four black regiments. Secretary Taft was noncommital and replied that he would study the matter. Scott would not accept this answer and continued to press the War Department for a decision. Finally they gave in and announced that in the future bands in black regiments would be led by Blacks. Implementing this decision was difficult because the regimental commanders were opposed to it and the War Department made no effort to force them to comply. Scott continued to agitate. Finally in

19. Ibid.

20. William H. Taft to Washington, 5 February 1908, Box 7, BTW, Papers; AGO 2370015. See also *The Independent,* 16 June 1898, as quoted in Jack D. Foner, *The United States Soldier Between Two Wars: Army Life and Reforms, 1865–1898,* p. 137.

November 1908 President Roosevelt wrote that he wanted "all the colored regiments supplied with colored bandmasters." Very shortly thereafter segregation was complete. Scott told the story of his victory to a group of black newspaper editors, who printed accounts that give Scott due credit. As *The Freeman* said, "Mr. Scott's brave and manly fight has opened a new and fruitful field of endeavor to the progressive Afro-American, and he cannot be praised too highly." However, the triumph was minor because only four men benefited from it, and it did not change the army's policy of racial segregation. Most importantly, it was the only demand of the Blacks to expand their role in the army that was met.[21]

Segregation presented different problems in the two branches where Blacks and whites mixed, the Signal Corps and the Hospital Corps. The members of both of these branches were small in number and highly trained. There were only a few Blacks in each of these select branches, but they presented a constant problem because their duty was not in keeping with the army's practice of segregation by units. In the early twentieth century, of about nine hundred enlisted men in the Signal Corps, four were Blacks. The chief signal officer accepted these men very reluctantly and did not want more. A black soldier from the Twenty-fifth Infantry requested a transfer into the corps, but the Signal Corps rejected the application because it was not "under conditions which would demonstrate the advisability of such action to be in the public interest." The philosophy of the Signal Corps was that Blacks would be accepted "when of exceptional ability, and when needed for the public interests." These circumstances did not occur often.[22]

There were more Blacks in the Hospital Corps. The corps also had no segregated units but assigned men to a particular post or hospital. In some instances whites and Blacks had to work together because the army had stationed them at the same hospital. In a few cases black NCOs were in a position to give orders to white privates. The army tried to avoid this situation, but not always successfully. In 1913 an individual who identified himself as "Blanco," wrote a long complaint to the *Army and*

21. Scott to Taft, 12 December 1906, Box 5, BTW, Papers; Scott to R. W. Thompson, 26 October 1908, Box 42, BTW, Papers; Elting E. Morison, ed., *The Letters of Theodore Roosevelt*, 6:1365. Scott to several newspaper editors, 19 December 1908, Box 378, BTW, Papers. Scott to Charles W. Anderson, 3 June 1907, Box 35, BTW, Papers; *The Freeman*, 2 January 1909.

22. AGO 1003923.

Navy Journal about such a situation. When detachments were mixed, the question of racial separation was posed continually. "If in the minority, the colored men will allege discrimination in the nature of the duties assigned to them; on the other hand, the white contingent will claim that the colored men are unduly favored." However, if the Blacks were in the majority, and especially if black NCOs commanded whites, then the whites were very resentful.[23] These few breeches in the barrier between races, and the problems they presented, only further convinced leaders of the army that maintaining segregation was the best policy for peace between the races in the service.

Although there were a few black officers, their service was not consistent with the army's attitude about the capabilities of Blacks. It did not place any special barriers in the way of any Black who wanted to get a commission, but neither did the military authorities encourage this ambition. In this period there were three methods of obtaining a commission. Most officers graduated from the military academy at West Point. The army filled other vacancies first with enlisted men with a minimum of two years of service or with civilian candidates. The War Department required these last two groups to pass a qualifying examination. Because of a number of factors, very few Blacks attempted to begin any of the processes, and even fewer completed them.

Between 1866 and 1936 there were only three black graduates of West Point, all of whom received commissions before 1890. Between 1870 and 1889 there were twenty-three Blacks appointed and twelve who passed the entrance examination to the academy, but only three of these graduated. After noting this record some people charged that the army limited the number of Blacks entering the military academy. The military authorities claimed that they would accept any black man who was appointed and passed the entrance examination, but most Blacks did not have the education, as some believed, or the intelligence, as most whites believed, to pass them. Even if they could overcome this hurdle, and most black applicants did not, they still had to face four years of verbal and physical hazing. Life for the black cadets was very difficult. Since there were very few, they lived a lonely existence. Henry O. Flipper, the first black graduate, wrote that he "had little or no intercourse

---

23. *ANJ*, 27 September 1913, pp. 103–4.

with" the other cadets during his four years at the academy. Some white cadets did try to break the barriers of silence, but the reaction of other cadets stopped them from renewing the attempts. As Charles Crane, a white cadet of the period, wrote, "No one openly associated with him, and anyone seen doing so would have been 'cut' by the Corps." The black cadet survived by minding his own business. Straying from this line, even the slightest, resulted in trouble, as the case of Johnson Whittaker illustrated. Whittaker entered the academy in 1877 and tried to follow Flipper's example of meeting ostracism with silence. However, early in Whittaker's career he clashed with the unwritten rules of the academy. When a white cadet struck him, Whittaker did not fight back but instead turned in the offender. By 1880 the cadet corps had put him under tremendous pressure. One morning several cadets found him in his room, bound to his bed, with blood all over him and his head partly shorn. Initially the cadets and officers accepted Whittaker's story that he had been attacked by several masked men, but they quickly came to doubt it. They felt that the assault had been feigned as a way to divert attention from his academic deficiencies. After more than a year of investigations and trials, which made national headlines, the court-martial board convicted him. Shortly thereafter the Academy dismissed him for academic deficiencies. It was clear from the manner in which the army acted and the testimony and statements of the white cadets and officers that whites felt that ostracism was a fair policy. If the black cadet could not accept it, then he could not graduate. They did not want black cadets to feel equal socially and expected them to abide by this view.[24]

There were two successful black cadets in the 1880s. The second and third black graduates of West Point, both from Ohio, graduated in the last years of the decade. John H. Alexander entered the Academy in 1883 and graduated with his class in 1887. His army career was short, for he died of natural causes in 1894. Charles Young, whose career spanned the period under study, was born near Mays Lick, Kentucky, in 1864, the

24. Thomas D. Phillips to author, 24 January 1969; AGO 2304855; Henry O. Flipper, *The Colored Cadet at West Point,* p. 125. Nathaniel F. McClure, ed., *Class of 1887, United States Military Academy, A Biographical Volume to Commemorate the 50th Anniversary of Graduation at West Point, New York, June 1937,* p. 25; Crane, *Experiences of a Colonel,* p. 55; Joseph C. King questionnaire in the possession of author; John F. Marszalek, Jr., *Court-Martial: A Black Man in America,* pp. 39, 274–80.

son of former slaves. When he was quite young, his parents moved about fifteen miles north across the Ohio River to Ripley, Ohio. In Ripley he received an education in the public schools. In his teens he went to a Jesuit academy in Cincinnati, where he studied Greek and Latin. Apparently encouraged by the success of Alexander, who was also from Ohio, Young competed for the nomination from his state and won out over twenty-eight applicants. After passing the difficult entrance examination, he entered the academy in the summer of 1884. He ran into difficulties toward the end of his last year, which some observers in the press attributed to racial prejudice, and was put back a year. He finally graduated in 1889. After his departure from West Point no other Blacks were admitted to the military academy as students until after World War I. The first black graduate after Charles Young was Benjamin O. Davis, Jr., who became a second lieutenant in 1936.[25]

In most years the graduates of West Point filled all the available slots for officers, and the enlisted men had no real opportunities. However, in 1901 and 1911 the officer corps expanded, and the army turned to enlisted candidates to fill many vacancies. In 1901 many Blacks applied, including those who had served as volunteer officers in the Spanish-American War or the recently concluded Philippine Insurrection. A number of men signed up for the qualifying examination while still in the Philippines, and the results were typical of what happened to other black officer candidates. One was disqualified for physical disabilities, and four withdrew of their own accord before the administration of the test. Among the different reasons given by these enlisted men for their withdrawal was a feeling that they were not prepared for the examination. The only successful candidates were two enlisted men who had served in the Regular Army, John E. Green and Benjamin O. Davis. Davis had been an officer in the Eighth United States Volunteer Infantry during the Spanish-American War. He then enlisted with the purpose of qualifying for a commission and was assigned to the Ninth Cavalry. At his new station, Charles Young encouraged and tutored Davis. As a result Davis scored a ninety-one on his final examination.[26]

25. *Colored American Magazine* 4:3 (January-February, 1902):249; *The Gazette*, 16 July 1898.

26. U.S., Congress, House of Representatives, *Report of the Secretary of War, 1902,* House Document 2, vol. 1, 57th Cong., 2d sess., 1902–1903, p. 289; AGO 388481; AGO 387486; *The Colored American,* 18 May 1901.

The case of Hiram Parker better illustrates the problems that many Blacks faced. In the first years of this century Sgt. Hiram Parker, Tenth Cavalry, took the preliminary examination for a commission. The examining board judged him to be mentally and morally qualified, although they noted that he was slightly deficient in his weight and chest measurements. They recommended, however, that these qualifications be waived and that he be allowed to continue. The department commander rejected this recommendation and, after reviewing the evidence, the surgeon general agreed. Blacks were upset about this decision and protested. B. K. Bruce, a black citizen, appealed to Booker T. Washington to intercede.[27] He pointed out that the "entire future of our people in the Army is at stake on this issue." Washington, in his typical fashion, refused to do anything unless President Roosevelt asked him. Bruce then wrote directly to the President. Whether this pressure had any impact is unclear, but the army did allow Parker to continue. Unfortunately he was unable to take advantage of this reprieve, for he failed the examinations. The written exam, which was the same for all applicants, included questions on English grammar, surveying, logarithms, algebra, geography, history, international law, and army regulations. The items that Parker had to answer were usually in the form of short-answer questions. Though Parker received a seventy-seven in grammar, his average was sixty-one, four points below passing. In addition, the officers who tested him recommended that he not be commissioned. [28]

The Parker case and others like it raised charges of discrimination, which the army denied. They said they placed no special obstacles in the way of a black man. They noted that there were "relatively fewer colored than white men in the army who were able to meet the educational requirements for a commission." Because of the way Blacks were treated both at West Point and in the line and the educational requirements necessary to pass the several levels of examinations, all but four Blacks were excluded from the commissioned ranks without the need of any special devices.[29]

27. This is not former Mississippi Sen. Blanche K. Bruce, who died in 1898, nor his only son, Roscoe C. Bruce.

28. *ANJ*, 18 June 1904, p. 1099. AGO 929892; Bruce to Washington, 16 June 1904; 10 July 1904, Box 2, BTW, Papers; AGO 929892, 933931, 924309.

29. AGO 1793797. See also *New York Age*, 29 June 1905. George Schuyler to author, 29 May 1967. Clarence Lininger, quesionnaire in possession of author;

The concepts that influenced much of the army's treatment of the black soldiers and officers had not really changed much from the Indian War period. They had always believed Blacks were ignorant, dependent upon white officers, better suited to hot than cold climates, and could resist tropical fevers. The only differences in the situation after 1890 were that there were more opportunities to practice these ideas, and white society in general was emphasizing separation and purity of the races.

Benjamin O. Davis, Sr., interview with Edward M. Coffman and author, 2 June 1968.

V

ON DUTY

After 1890 the racial concepts of white America began to be manifested in many aspects of military life, even the most routine. The daily activities of the black soldiers were usually no different from those of the white enlisted men, but little by little the differences began to appear. In spite of this change for the worse, Blacks continued to be attracted to the army.

There were many reasons why people of both races enlisted in the army in this period, such as financial considerations, a romantic view of the army, and a desire for travel. Blacks had additional reasons. In civilian society the black soldier, as opposed to the black civilian, was not relegated to a position of total subservience to the white man. According to George Schuyler, a former black enlisted man, black citizens were impressed by "their superb order and discipline, their haughty and immaculate noncommissioned officers, and their obvious authority." Jasper Johnson, who served in the Twenty-fourth Infantry, was motivated to join by his father, who had served during the Civil War. Some Blacks who had served in the volunteers believed that joining the Regular Army would provide them security. As Richard Johnson, a member of the Forty-eighth Volunteer Infantry, said, "Having discovered the security of the army I had shed that forlorn and homeless feeling that once possessed me." Finally, there were some areas of the army in which advancement was not hindered by the restrictions of segregation.[1]

The typical black recruit was an unskilled, barely literate southerner. This lack of education hindered his career in the service. One troop commander in the Ninth Cavalry reported

---

1. George Schuyler, *Black and Conservative: The Autobiography of George S. Schuyler,* p. 28; Jasper Johnson, questionnaire, Spanish-American War Survey, Twenty-fourth Infantry Regiment Papers, United States Army Military History Research Collection, Carlisle, Pa.; Richard Johnson, "My Life in the U.S. Army, 1899 to 1922," p. 7.

that about one-third of the men could not read and write, while others were able to do so in a purely "mechanical" way. This situation had existed since the original formation of the regiments, but the problem was compounded after 1890 as the army began to modernize and technical skills became more important. Several officers made suggestions to improve the situation. One idea was to open temporary recruiting offices at black colleges. This practice was instituted at Tuskegee Institute in 1904. Another officer suggested that recruiting parties include black enlisted men who would be better able than white officers to talk to prospective black recruits. The idea of such a mixed recruiting party was opposed by southerners because "it would be almost impossible to house and feed them." At times verbal opposition to recruiting parties erupted into physical violence. In Nashville, farmers restrained Blacks from entering the service because they needed them as farmhands.[2]

Once the man had made the decision to enlist and had gone to the recruiting officer, a physician gave him a physical examination. After successfully passing this examination, the recruiting officer administered the oath of allegiance to the soldier and accepted him into the army. Next, the soldier was sent to the recruit depot for training.

There were three recruit depots, one on David's Island in New York Harbor, another at Columbus Barracks, Ohio, and a third at Jefferson Barracks, Missouri. The depot on David's Island looked to a black recruit, George Schuyler, like a "college campus." In the middle there was a large parade ground, on one side red brick barracks for the enlisted men, and on the other the officers' quarters. When Schuyler and other recruits arrived at the depot they received a copy of the *Soldier's Handbook*, a pocket-sized, leather-bound volume that furnished them with a basic knowledge of what the army expected of them and what pitfalls to avoid. The average recruit spent about three months at the depot before being sent to a regiment, but this was not always the case with the black recruits. If remaining at the depot posed challenges to the racial lines, the black recruits were sent on to the regiments. Prior to the Spanish-American War the drill companies were sometimes mixed, but later segregation became the normal practice. In addition, at both Columbus and Jefferson Barracks, facilities were segregated. When black civilians objected, the War Department answered with

2. Sec War 1906, p. 597; AGO 473477; AGO 933620; AGO 482475; AGO 118486.

two reasons. One was that the recruits involved had not complained about this policy. They also believed that if they abolished segregation, there would be serious repercussions.[3]

After the new soldier finished his training, the War Department assigned him to a regiment, where his real army career began. In white regiments the arrival of a new recruit was not an unusual occurrence; reenlistment rates were not very high and desertion rates, not very low. The black regiments had differed in this respect since the Indian War period. In 1893 the Ninth Cavalry had more than 300 men with more than five years' service in the army, while the Twenty-fourth Infantry had more than 260 such men. In other words about half of the enlisted men of each regiment had reenlisted at least once. In addition, the black regiments had a very low rate of desertion. In 1908 less than 1 per cent of the black soldiers deserted while nearly 5 per cent of the whites did. The desertion rate in the black regiments began to rise toward the end of the period under discussion, and the number of reenlistees began to fall.[4]

Army posts of this period were all built on the same general plan. The buildings surrounded the parade ground; the soldiers barracks and the officers quarters were on opposite sides of the drill field. The enlisted men's quarters very seldom contained indoor plumbing, and the men slept in iron bunks with their equipment stored in footlockers. Yet each post had its own peculiarities. Some of the posts were in nice locations with pleasant climates, while others were not very desirable. One black soldier's description of Fort Washakie, Wyoming, encompasses all of these differences. He explained that it was located in the Rockies, 150 miles from the nearest railroad. "Here, with our trees and grass and flowers, with the cool river at our feet, we live the life of the free and healthy mountaineer." However, when winter and heavy snowfall came, the post was isolated, and the men were "lonesome during the long winter evenings."

3. Schuyler, *Black and Conservative*, p. 33; Don Rickey, Jr., *Forty Miles a Day on Beans and Hay: The Enlisted Soldier Fighting the Indian Wars*, p. 38; Alfred Reynolds, *The Life of an Enlisted Soldier in the United States Army*, p. 11. Herschel V. Cashin, *Under Fire with the Tenth United States Cavalry*, p. 59; Rickey, *Forty Miles a Day*, p. 38; AGO 1932951.

4. U.S., Congress, House of Representatives, *Report of the Inspector-General, 1893*, House Executive Document 1, pt. 2, vol. 4, 53d Cong., 2d sess., 1893–1894, p. 683; U.S. Department of War, *Annual Report of the Secretary of War, 1908*, 1:396. For another example see Sec War 1916, 1:259; James M. Bryant, Co. M, Twenty-fourth Infantry to Beverly Perea, 8 September 1914, Beverly Perea, Papers.

Sanitary conditions at these isolated posts were not always very good. At Fort Duchesne, Utah, bathing facilities varied, according to the season, from the mosquito-infested, rocky-bottomed river, to hand-filled bathtubs with their stove-heated water.[5]

Once the recruit became familiar with his fellow soldiers and his post, he began to familiarize himself with the daily routine of the army, which was generally the same for soldiers of both races. A typical day began with reveille at 5:45 A.M., followed by breakfast, then fatigue call at 7:30, recall from fatigue at 12:15 P.M., lunch, fatigue call at 1:00 and school for some of the enlisted men and NCOs at the same time, recall from fatigue at 4:30, drill from 4:45 to 5:15, guard mount at 5:30, dinner, tattoo at 9:00, followed by taps. The soldiers broke this routine on Sundays and holidays. On these occasions the unit officers suspended all duties except the necessary guard and fatigue duties.[6]

The food in the black regiments was not the same as that served in white regiments and sometimes was characteristic of the black culture. These foods were most often served on holidays but could also be found in the regular daily menu. Army regulations allowed soldiers at least twenty minutes for breakfast and lunch and thirty minutes for dinner. A typical menu submitted by an officer of a black regiment to The Adjutant General follows:

Breakfast: puffed rice, sugar and cream, stewed beef, baked potatoes, toast, tea or coffee.

Lunch: cream of potato soup, oyster crackers, beef pot pie, steamed rice, lima beans, radishes, steamed pudding, vanilla sauce, bread.

Dinner: pickled pigs' feet, chili con carne, hot biscuits, butter, syrup, and tea.[7]

The individual companies were instructed in horseback riding and marksmanship. For the cavalry, daily riding practice was a necessity regardless of the weather. During the winter at one western post, the men of the Tenth Cavalry went outdoors in buffalo overcoats and protected the animals with heavy blankets, but even this activity was discontinued when it got really cold. At posts like Fort Ethan Allen, Vermont, which had in-

---

5. Edward M. Coffman, "Army Life on the Frontier, 1865–1898," pp. 194–95; *ANJ,*27 June 1903, p. 1089; Sec War 1892, pp. 538–39.

6. *The Freeman,* 29 April 1893.

7. *Regulations for the Army of the United States, 1895,* no. 384; AGO 1299977.

door riding halls, the men were able to practice even during the coldest times of the year.[8]

Marksmanship was one of the key skills in the soldier's learning experience. The training on the rifle range began with firing at a stationary target from distances of two hundred to one thousand yards. The next phase was the skirmish run during which the men started running toward the target from five hundred yards away and did not begin shooting until they were two hundred yards away. In order to prepare properly for target practice, they made great sacrifices, for high scores eventually resulted in increased pay. Some gave up smoking and drinking and got lots of sleep. On the range the soldiers studied the wind direction and the brightness of the sun, adjusting their sights to take these factors into account. In later years practice in using Maxim silencers and telescopic sights was added. George Schuyler, who had served in the Twenty-fifth Infantry, noted that it was "uncanny to see a line of riflemen firing with silencers and not hear anything more than a hissing sound."[9]

At irregular and infrequent intervals high-ranking officers would inspect the entire garrison, and the black soldiers usually did well on these occasions. When Lt. Gen. John M. Schofield reviewed the Ninth Cavalry in 1895, the men marched by the reviewing stand in full dress then changed into fatigues and marched past with the wagon train, packmules, gun detachment, and signal detachment. Col. James Biddle put the regiment through a number of movements in the cavalry drill regulations and then formed the regiment for battle. An officer accompanying the inspecting team reported that the men were "simple perfection. We saw nothing on our trip which quite equalled the display made by Col. Biddle's regiment."[10]

The lessons learned in company and regimental drill were put to use each year during the required practice march. Here again there were no racial differences. Typical was one held by the First Battalion, Twenty-fourth Infantry, which covered 474 miles in 29 days. Training outside the post involved more than marching. Some men of the Twenty-fourth joined others in a heliograph signaling experiment in 1893. The department commander ordered them to send a signal from a point near Fort

8. Pershing, "Memoir," Chap. 6, JJP, Papers; *ANJ*, 29 June 1895, p. 723.
9. Edwin R. Van Deusen questionnaire in possession of author; Schuyler, *Black and Conservative*, p. 57.
10. *ANJ*, 29 June 1895, p. 732; 17 August 1895, p. 844.

Grant, Arizona, to Fort Bayard, New Mexico, via Table Mountain and Fort Huachuca, a distance of 406 miles. Even though the men did not expect this type of signal practice at that time of the year and many of the officers and men had never before been at the specified locations, the men did a good job. The Blacks had received the same training as the white soldiers and performed with a high degree of competence.[11]

One of the most onerous parts of military life was fatigue duty. As far as many soldiers were concerned, they were being used as free labor. In 1912 the Twenty-fourth Infantry was assigned to dismantle Camp Jossman in the Philippines. It took over a month, even though the men worked on the task most of the time they were there. The black soldiers complained that this job was an example of the way the army discriminated against them. However, the army did not assign Blacks more of this type of work than it did whites.[12]

The white officers of the black regiments had mixed feelings toward their black soldiers, and their attitudes at times affected the way in which they treated them. Rarely did the officer choose to be assigned to a black regiment. One indicator of this aversion was the type of cadet assigned to the regiments from West Point. There are three variables we will consider; geographic origins, class rank, and time.

An examination of the sectional distribution of the graduates indicates that southerners usually made up about 30 per cent of each class. About one-third of the new officers sent to the four black regiments also came from the South. These percentages did not change appreciably during the period under study. Apparently the army did not try to send a disproportionate number of southerners, even though they supposedly knew and understood the Blacks better than other white men did.[13]

The accurate indicator of the general attitude toward the black soldiers is the class rank of the graduates who commanded them. Admittedly it is an imperfect index to judge the quality of the officers, for it is a combination of both academic rank and behavior. However, the army used it as a factor in determining

11. Ibid., 1 October 1904, p. 103; Sec War 1893, pp. 673–74, 665–66.

12. For examples see LS, 25th Inf, Scrapbook, 7 November 1892. 25th Inf Org Ret, November 1894, January 1915; *ANJ*, 20 July 1912, p. 1473. AGO 1949387.

13. See Appendix C for a numerical division by assignments of the background of the new officers for each year of this period. See Appendix D for a statistical breakdown for each year.

where the graduate was assigned. First the graduates applied for a branch, such as the engineers, artillery, cavalry, or infantry, usually preferred in that order, and then the military authorities assigned them to their choice, if possible. The higher a person ranked in his class, the better his chance of getting the branch he wanted. By examining the rank-class ratio of the men assigned to the four black regiments one can get a general idea of the opinions of the graduating cadets toward black regiments, the way in which the War Department evaluated them, and whether their status changed over time. From the time the black infantry regiments were formed until 1917, the lowest-ranking officers in each graduating class were usually assigned to black soldiers. Appointments to the black cavalry regiments, however, show a different pattern. Initially they received low-ranking graduates, but by 1890 the army appointed men who ranked high in their classes. This situation continued until 1900. Then the rank-class ratio of the second lieutenants assigned to the black regiments began to fall. Between 1891 and 1900 eight appointees to the black cavalry were in the top half of their class, but after 1900 not one officer was in this group. Similarly, prior to 1900 only three out of twenty-two graduates appointed to the black cavalry regiments were in the last quarter of their class, but after that date twenty-five out of thirty-four were. Whatever the motivation for the requests by the cadets and the assignments by the War Department, one factor is clear, the quality of the officers as measured by a rank-class ratio declined after the Spanish-American War.[14]

Most of the white officers did not like serving in the black regiments. John J. Pershing, an officer in the Tenth Cavalry in the 1890s, felt that service with the black men "was not especially" to be sought after. When Andrew S. Burt was promoted to colonel and assigned to the Twenty-fifth Infantry, he did not look forward to the move. His wife wrote in her diary, "My heart was heavy, but my husband was too good a soldier to utter a word of regret." This attitude grew out of both a repugnance to serve over inferior people and a fear of the consequences such service would have on their social life with civilians. As Charles Crane wrote, "Wherever we went we officers found ourselves at a great disadvantage, socially, as compared with the officers of white troops."[15]

14. See Appendix E.
15. Pershing, "Memoir," Chap. 6, Box 376, JJP, Papers; Burt, Papers, p.

This situation was not new in 1890, but it intensified thereafter because of white society's increased hatred of Blacks. While on the frontier, contacts between black troops and white civilians were few. After 1890 these increased greatly as the army concentrated its garrisons, moved some of the black units into the East and near population centers. White officers bore the stigma of being associated with the black troops. Service in these regiments became less desirable and was avoided if possible. This attitude hurt the relationship between officer and enlisted man. One soldier claimed that the officers of his regiment, in an effort to discredit the intelligent Blacks of the unit, deliberately chose the most ignorant Blacks for duties where they would come in contact with the public. The officers at Fort Missoula, Montana, refused to allow the men of the Twenty-fourth to hold a reception and ball in honor of Emmett Hawkins, who had recently won first prize in a rifle tournament. The soldiers felt that this restriction was a result of the officers' enmity toward them.[16]

Another facet of on-duty life was the relationship between the few black officers and the white officers. Though these encounters occurred infrequently, they did upset the whites. The commander of the Ninth Cavalry protested when he heard that Charles Young, then recently graduated from West Point, was to be assigned to his regiment. The white said that they already had the other black officer, John Alexander, and the addition of Young might cause "officers not to apply for assignment to the regiment." The War Department replied that the regimental commander's request regarding Young's transfer could not be complied with because it would complicate an already-difficult situation. Young was one of the new graduates who could not immediately be assigned to a regiment. In that position "he was liable . . . to have a vacancy fall to him in a *white* regiment." In order to avoid such a possibility, the War Department transferred him to the Twenty-fifth Infantry, with the understanding that when a vacancy occurred in a black cavalry regiment he would be returned to that branch. The vacancy in the Ninth was the first one. The incident demonstrated that the War Department was determined to keep the black officers in black regiments. It also made clear that whites did not want a

262; Charles J. Crane, *The Experiences of a Colonel of Infantry,* p. 255.

16. R. W. Thompson to Washington, 25 December 1908, Box 42, BTW, Papers; *The Gazette,* 14 November 1903. See also *The Freeman,* 4 March 1893.

84

black officer. The black soldiers sensed this animosity toward the black officer, and their relations with their white officers worsened.[17]

There was more to the army than drill, fatigue duty, and enmity between officer and men. Among the different assignments that the black soldier received were to participate in parades, give band concerts, and display his military prowess in competition with other soldiers.

After 1898 the army began annual summer maneuvers involving Regular Army and National Guard regiments. The War Department and the new General Staff wanted to give the men and their leaders a chance to experience the problems of large-unit tactics. The army included the black units in the activities whenever they were stationed in the area of the maneuver. Among those in which the black troops participated were the ones at American Lakes, Washington; Atascadero, California; Pole Mountain, Wyoming; and Pine Camp, New York. In 1913 several regiments of cavalry, including the Tenth, went to Winchester, Virginia, to try out some new techniques of cavalry drill in another type of maneuver. The Tenth Cavalry marched from Fort Ethan Allen to Winchester, a distance of 706 miles, in little more than a month. When the regiment arrived, they paraded through the southern town. Appropriately, the regimental band played "Dixie." Following the maneuvers the cavalry units marched to Washington, D.C., and put on a display of horsemanship for President Wilson. The black citizens of Washington then feted the black cavalrymen. Maj. Gen. Leonard Wood addressed the group and said that the Tenth Cavalry had a splendid record and a great responsibility, as a representative of the black race, to keep up that good record. After an evening of speeches and congratulations, the regiment boarded trains and headed back to Vermont and the daily drudgery.[18]

For some men this monotony was interrupted by competition in individual military skill contests. Among the different events included were broadsword, horse training, machine-gun competition, tent pegging, and bayonet races. In the Department of Colorado in 1896 two black and six white regiments held an interregimental competition. The Ninth Cavalry won first prize. A blacksmith of that regiment won the most points by

17. AGO 192–1890.
18. *ANJ*, 2 August 1913, p. 1501; 11 October 1913, p. 179.

taking first place in three different events and coming in second in two others.[19]

The expert marksmen of the black regiments also competed in rifle contests. At a rifle match at Fort Sheridan, Illinois, in 1904, Quartermaster Sergeant Proctor, E Company, Twenty-fourth Infantry, took first place; enlisted men of the black regiments took second and third. The winners of such competitions advanced to the armywide tournament. The purpose of this level of competition, which was begun after the Spanish-American War, was to choose an army infantry and cavalry team to enter into the national rifle matches. Usually these all-army teams consisted entirely of officers, but there were a few enlisted men able to qualify, and the black soldiers were not excluded. In 1906 the infantry team included Q.M. Sgt. William Tate, L Company, Twenty-fifth Infantry, and Sgt. Oscar Fox, M Company, of the same regiment. One of the members of the cavalry team of the same year was Sgt. Robert Johnson, K Troop, Tenth Cavalry. In the 1903 national competition Q.M. Sgt. Emmett Hawkins, Twenty-fourth Infantry, recorded the highest total at 1,000 yards, 43 out of a possible 50.[20]

Blacks performed equally well in riding competitions. At a horse show near Washington, D.C., in 1913, a corporal of C Troop, Tenth Cavalry, won the Secretary of War Cup, awarded for first place in the soldiers' jumping class. The trophy was presented to the soldier by the Secretary of War, Lindley M. Garrison. In all these competitions, color proved no barrier. Unlike civilian society, Blacks were able to compete against whites.[21]

Soldiers could also participate in the regimental bands. The quality of these organizations depended upon the members whom they were able to recruit and the competence of the chief musicians. The black band leaders compared favorably with their white counterparts. The chief musician of the Ninth Cavalry, Wade H. Hammond, a Black, in 1912 received permission from the War Department to attend a course at the Royal Musical School for Bandmasters, near London, England. Frank H. Damrosch, a German-American conductor and educator,

19. Mary Curtis, *The Black Soldier: or, The Colored Boys of the United States Army,* p. 30. *ANJ,* 17 October 1896, p. 113. See also: *The Burlington Free Press,* 2 January 1913. AGO 2285947; *ANJ,* 31 October 1896, p. 139.

20. *ANJ,* 6 August 1904, pp. 1278–79; 25 August 1906, p. 1450; 3 October 1903, p. 105.

21. *The Burlington Free Press,* 3 May 1913.

offered five scholarships for the instruction of bandmasters and set up a series of rigid examinations to select the winners. One of the winners of a course at Damrosch's Institute of Musical Art in New York City, which later became part of the Juilliard School of Music, was Chief Musician Alfred J. Thomas of the Tenth Cavalry. He attended the military bandmasters' course for two years on a full scholarship and received his diploma in June 1914.[22]

On the post, on escort duty, in concerts, and at dances, the regimental bands were constantly busy. At the post the band turned out daily to play during guard mount and also gave concerts several times a week. Included in the concert programs of the Twenty-fifth Infantry band were the following numbers: Suppe, *Pique Dame Overture;* Lehar, selections from *The Merry Widow;* Verdi, duet from *I Due Foscari;* Sousa, "Jack Tar March"; and Weber, selections from *Der Freischutz.* Similarly the Twenty-fourth Infantry band had a repertoire of about one thousand numbers and a music library valued at more than $6,000. On different occasions the regimental bands accepted invitations from civilians to perform. In most black communities there was a celebration of Emancipation Day, 1 January. The black regimental bands usually took part in the events of nearby cities. In addition, each regimental band doubled as an orchestra and was available for hire. The fees were added to the regimental fund and used for special occasions like dances and holiday dinners.[23]

Compensation came in other than monetary forms in some instances. John Philip Sousa invited the band of the Twenty-fourth Infantry to be his guests at a concert to be given by his band to honor the gallantry of the whole regiment in the recently concluded conflict in Cuba. In 1914 the Douglas, Arizona, Chamber of Commerce minted one thousand copper commemorative medals in honor of the Ninth Cavalry's band. The inscription read, "Ninth U.S.A.—A Live Band From A Live Regiment." In early 1915 the mayor of the town presented a diamond-studded gold medal to the leader of the Ninth Cavalry band. It had been purchased with funds raised among the

22. *The Chicago Defender,* 18 May 1912; *The Crisis* 5:2 (December, 1912):63. *The Chicago Defender,* 19 October 1912; Judson Ehrbar, Registrar, Juilliard School of Music, to author, 16 January 1969.

23. *ANJ,* 27 February 1909, p. 716; 30 August 1902, p. 1325; *Broad-ax,* 25 September 1897. *ANJ,* 7 July 1906, p. 1265; LS, 25th Inf, Co. C, 11 September 1903.

townspeople in recognition of the fine music that the band had provided the town for the preceeding two years. Army officials also recognized the quality of these musical groups. The managers of the 1904 St. Louis World's Fair requested the army's best bands to perform at the fair. The band of the Twenty-fourth Infantry was one of the few chosen. The army was willing to judge these black soldiers on their miter and accord them the honors due their performance. It was also an area in which, according to the racial stereotype, Blacks had a great deal of ability.[24]

The black regiments, like all those in the army, had ceremonial duties, including acting as escorts and marching in parades. Two troops of the Ninth Cavalry escorted President Roosevelt when he visited San Francisco in 1903. The occasion was, according to a newspaper account, "the first instance in the West where negro soldiers have held the position of honor in a public procession." The same regiment also participated in the 1905 presidential inaugural parade. The unit received a warm round of applause from President Roosevelt and the many citizens who had gathered to see the parade. One observer described them as "one of the best drilled and most soldierly organizations in the parade." After the parade the black cavalrymen were the guests at a reception at a Washington church. There were more than two thousand people present at the event, which lasted until midnight. Appropriately black soldiers took part in a celebration of the fiftieth anniversary of John Brown's battle at Osawatomie, Kansas. For the black community the appearance of black soldiers in these events was a source of pride. It encouraged them to feel that Blacks could achieve recognition despite a generally indifferent or hostile white population.[25]

Competing in military skills, drill, and training was preparation for active duty. In this period of peace such duty was quite varied and often hazardous. During the 1890s, an era of industrial violence, the army was occasionally called up to preserve law and order, which really meant that the men acted as strikebreakers. The black soldiers had their share of this duty.

During a strike by the miners' union at Coeur d' Alene, Idaho, in 1892, strikers blew up some of the mines. The army

24. *ANJ*, 18 March 1899, p. 684; 22 August 1914, p. 1648; *The Crisis* 9:5 (March, 1915):218; AGO 512625.

25. *The New York Times,* 13 May 1903; *ANJ*, 11 March 1905, p. 745; 18 March 1905, p. 777; 1 September 1906, p. 7. See also *The Chicago Tribune,* 18 October 1892, 22 October 1892. Benjamin C. Truman, *History of the World's Fair,* p. 93.

ordered the regiments of the Fourteenth and Twenty-fifth Infantry, stationed nearby, into the area to quell the disturbances.
A rumor was circulated that the black troops were coming and
this upset the miners. They felt that to have scabs protected by
black soldiers was "an aggravation of injury by insult." Once
the soldiers arrived at the scene of the strike, the miners dis-
persed. After two weeks military authorities on the scene decided that order had been restored and ordered the troops to be
sent home. Civil and military leaders in the region commended
the soldiers, both black and white, for their good conduct while
on this difficult duty.[26]

Black troops also served at the Pullman strike two years later.
When Eugene V. Debs and the American Railway Union went
out on strike against the Pullman Company, and eventually all
of the nation's railroads, the Government decided that it had to
step in. President Grover Cleveland directed army officers to use
force to remove obstructions to the mail and protect the railroads. Detachments of the black units rode in the trains or
guarded tunnels, bridges, and switch yards from any attempts
to destroy them. The strikers in Missoula, Montana, admitted
that if the Government had to use troops, there could have been
none better than those of the Twenty-fifth Infantry who were
stationed in that town. The commander of the Department of
the Dakota expressed his "high appreciation" to the battalion
of the Twenty-fifth stationed at Fort Custer for the way in which
they carried out their duty.[27]

In many parts of the western United States at this time, the
army was often the only large organized group that could enforce the law, so civilian authorities often called upon it to
perform a great variety of duties. Again the War Department
dispatched black soldiers in the same way as white troops. The
army stationed detachments of the black regiments, as well as
of the white units, at different times in the national parks in
California—Yosemite, Sequoia, and King's Canyon—to pre-

26. Sec War 1892, p. 107; Mary H. Foote, "Coeur D'Alene," p. 108; Sec War
1892, pp. 108, 112.
27. Letter, 8 July 1894, Records of U.S. Army Continental Commands,
1821–1920, Department of the Platte, Letters Sent, 1891–1898, NA, RG 393;
John H. Nankivell, *History of the Twenty-fifth Regiment of United States Infantry,
1869–1926*, p. 54. See also *Inter-Ocean* (Chicago, n.d.), as quoted in *The Enterprise,*
18 January 1896; letter, 5 September 1894, Records of U.S. Army Continental
Commands, 1821–1920, Department of the Dakota, Letters Sent, 1891–1898,
NA, RG 393.

vent and extinguish forest fires and to protect game. Although the Indians no longer engaged in direct confrontations with the army, the military still had to patrol the reservations and quell small disturbances. Part of the Tenth Cavalry, including Lt. John J. Pershing, spent June and July 1896 rounding up some 525 Cree Indians who had come from Canada and were stealing cattle and horses. The soldiers covered more than one thousand miles, over some of the most rugged terrain in the country along the Continental Divide, and finally escorted several bands back across the border into Canada. The last group, when it was finally gathered together, included 190 men, women, and children. The journey was long and arduous. It was difficult to keep all of the Indians together, but after much travail they finally reached the border. At first the Canadian authorities refused to allow the disease-ridden Indians to re-enter the country, but after higher authorities were contacted by telegraph the question was settled.[28]

When called upon, the army enforced law and order among civilians. At the request of the governor of Texas and the mayor of Laredo, a troop of the Tenth Cavalry went into that city to disperse a mob. The troops had only to use rifle butts to quiet the town, and "were warmly complimented for their discretion." Black troops were also used in Spokane, Washington, to stop mob violence. The city council commended the men for their action. The army did not hesitate to use black troops to put down civil disturbances even in white communities in the South.[29]

On the other hand, there were discrepancies between the types of duties assigned to black and white officers. Many whites felt that a black officer posed a threat to them. They feared the possibility of a black officer commanding his white subordinates or other white soldiers. Before World War I only Charles Young posed this threat. In one instance a white officer objected to the possibility of serving under Young and asked that Young be transferred to another battalion of the Tenth Cavalry. The chief of staff replied that the white officer would have "to take the

28. *ANJ*, 13 May 1899, p. 874. Muster Rolls, Troop C, Ninth Cavalry, June–August 1904, Records of The Adjutant General's Office, Muster Rolls, Ninth Cavalry, 1891–1912, NA, RG 94. For another example see *ANJ*, 6 October 1900, p. 128; 10th Cav Org Ret, June–August 1896, Pershing, "Memoir," Chap. 6, pp. 7–10, Box 377, JJP, Papers. Donald Smythe, "John Pershing at Fort Assiniboine," p. 21. *Freeman*, 15 April 1899.

29. AGO 215358; *New York Age*, 27 January 1910.

same chance as other officers in the 10th Cavalry." A more sensitive aspect of black-white relations concerned the social amenities. Both groups attempted to avoid as many uncomfortable situations as possible, without forcing any confrontation over social equality. The solution to these problems was to keep black officers away from their regiments on different special assignments as long as possible. The passage of a law to cut down on the length of time that an officer could serve away from his regiment posed a threat to this policy. Army officers considered lobbying for amendment to the law to exempt black officers or to retire them, especially Charles Young, but in the end the authorities accepted the new rules.[30]

One of the normal assignments for a black officer was as Professor of Military Science and Tactics at Wilberforce University, a small black school near Xenia, Ohio. Alexander, Young, Davis, and Green all served tours of duty at the school. At times they complained that the school officials did not really support their administration of discipline, but the officers managed to train the students in some basic rudiments of the military arts. Young also taught French, German, and mathematics and coached the school's glee club and drama group. While at Wilberforce he greatly impressed the president of nearby Antioch College. As a result, he was asked to set up a course in military training there. More than sixty white students attended the classes that Young taught.[31]

Another assignment that the black officers received was as military attaché to United States embassies in the two black republics of the time, Haiti and Liberia. The only instance in this period when the United States had a military attaché on the island of Santo Domingo came during a time of unrest in 1904–1907. Haiti was financially unstable, and the United States Government feared that some foreign nations might attempt to use force to collect their debts. It was at this time that the War Department decided to send Young to the island. Some members of the military and of the civilian government believed he would be better received because he was black. The *Army & Navy Journal* commented, he would probably "command the immediate confidence and good will" of the citizens. One of the

30. AGO 2354040; *New York Tribune*, n.d., as quoted in *ANJ*, 25 July 1914, p. 1501.
31. *The Washington Post*, 26 May 1929, Magazine Section, pp. 11, 14; *The Burlington Free Press*, 8 April 1912.

jobs assigned to Young as an attaché was to obtain information about the military forces and the terrain. Information about the terrain was especially important in case troops would have to be sent there to protect United States interests. One section of the country needed to be mapped, and Young made great efforts to do this. He first offered money for the information. When this approach was unsuccessful, he did the work himself. He disguised himself and "at the risk of his life" worked night and day in the unmapped area. He completed an excellent map and a detailed monograph on the conditions of the country. W. F. Powell, the United States ambassador to Haiti, said that Young worked "even at times against the advice of his physician." He also compiled a "Handbook of Creole as Spoken in Hayti" and sent it to the War Department. All of this work was of great benefit a few years later when the United States did occupy the country. However, his achievements were hardly noticed by the black press.[32]

Three of the black officers served tours of duty in similar capacities in Liberia. At this time Liberia was weak and at the mercy of its stronger neighbors, colonies of Great Britain and France. Since Liberia could not resist, the two powers were able to take over several pieces of her border territories. In 1909 the situation became critical. The Liberian Government fired the commander of the Liberian Defense Force, a British citizen, and he took most of the corps of officers with him. The Liberian Government turned to the United States for aid. In March 1909 Congress created a three-member commission to study the situation and see what the United States could do "which would constitute the most effective measures of relief." The group, headed by Emmett J. Scott, sailed for Liberia and investigated the country's problems. The next year they submitted their report to Congress. One of the Scott Commission's recommendations was that the United States help Liberia "in organizing and drilling an adequate constabulary or frontier police force." They recommended that three black officers or NCOs from the American army could achieve this goal. Such service "would be

---

32. Ludwell L. Montague, *Haiti and the United States: 1714–1938*, pp. 182, 187; *ANJ*, 7 May 1904, 939; "Extracts-Colonel Young's Record," mimeographed sheets in possession of author; W.F. Powell to Elihu Root, 20 October 1905, Dispatches from United States Minister to Haiti, 1862–1906, General Records of the Department of State, NA, RG 59. See also Powell to John Hay, 1 February 1905, 5 April 1905, in the dispatches; Charles Young, "Handbook of Creole as Spoken in Hayti."

peculiarly attractive to such men and offer them, . . . opportunities for more rapid advancement in their profession than could be hoped for at home." The United States Government made no decision on this proposal at the time the commission submitted it.[33]

Further study seemed necessary, and Benjamin O. Davis was designated as military attaché to do it. Davis had just completed four years of college duty at Wilberforce and wanted to return to his regiment. He accepted the offer, however, because he felt, "If I can be of service to the United States in this capacity, I am willing to undertake the work." Upon acceptance of his assignment, he received a confidential memo from the General Staff outlining his duties. They included investigating of the Liberian military establishment and its organization, strength, staff, mobilization system, and transportation network. He was to submit reports at least once a month with a summary "of important military events." His instructions allowed him to visit parts of the country, but he had to keep in mind "a strict regard for economy."[34]

Upon his arrival in Monrovia, the capital of Liberia, he rented a house and began his investigations. His work was soon interrupted when he contracted blackwater fever, a common complaint of new arrivals to Liberia, and he was confined to his bed for two weeks, during which time he lost twenty-eight pounds. Even when he was able to get around again, he was not fully recovered. For the next six months he had to take a daily dose of five grains of quinine. As a result of his illness, his initial hope of taking part in the reorganization of the Liberian Frontier Force had to be shelved, and he was recalled.[35]

When Davis returned to the United States in 1911, he discussed the situation in Liberia with officials on the General Staff and offered them his recommendations. He felt that a force of about fifteen hundred men would be "sufficient for all purposes. . . . For most efficient service there should be at least four trained officers preferably from the [American] regular army." This recommendation was based upon his evaluation of the training and qualifications of the Liberian officer corps. He

33. Robert E. Anderson, *Liberia: America's African Friend,* p. 88. *New York Age,* 9 December 1909; U.S., Congress, Senate, *Affairs in Liberia,* Senate Document 457, 61st Cong., 2d sess., 1909–10, pp. 2, 11, 17–19, 34–35.

34. AGO 1590249; AWC File 6926–2; Matthew Hanna, Second Section, General Staff, to Benjamin O. Davis, Sr., 13 December 1909, BOD, Papers.

35. Davis to Matthew Hanna, 21 December 1911, BOD, Papers.

pointed out that there might be difficulties in getting the Liberian Government to go along with these major changes, however, and warned that unless the Liberian Government agreed in advance and in writing to abide by the decisions of the American advisors, trouble would ensue, and the effort would be "a waste of time and energy." [36] In general his recommendations were an elaboration of the points made by the Scott Commission.

The Liberian Government continued to request help. In April 1911, Liberian Secretary of State F. E. R. Johnson stated that his government wanted the officers, as recommended in the Scott report, and asked for Davis as the senior officer. United States Secretary of State Philander Knox put him off with the comment that the request would receive "due consideration at the proper time." By November, as plans for a $1.7 million loan from American bankers to Liberia neared completion, the United States State Department began to move. Secretary Knox asked the War Department for an officer to carry out the reorganization of the Liberian Defense Force. [37]

The War Department complied with the request of the State Department and named Charles Young, senior black officer, to carry out the recommendations of the Scott Commission and Benjamin Davis. Booker T. Washington had strongly urged Young to help Liberia. Because of this pressure and his own sense of duty for "our race in particular," Young was convinced to accept the position. He received permission to organize the new Liberian army and to nominate some American Blacks to high positions in it. However, his nominees were not current members of the Regular Army as Davis had suggested, but men with previous experience in either the volunteers or the Regular Army. Young's status, as he saw it, was "that of helper and advisor. I have done everything short of taking actual command of troops in aiding this reorganization." The other American Blacks became the actual, operational leaders of the Liberian Defense Force. As Davis had predicted, Young's efforts at reform were not greatly appreciated by some Liberians. The officials that had been displaced because of his activities, including the Secretary of War, resigned rather than work with the American attaché. [38]

36. Ibid.
37. U.S.–Liberia Records, 882.20/-; 882.00/443.
38. AWC File 6926–3; U.S.-Liberia Records, 882.20/5; 882.20/13.

In addition to purely advisory work, Young on occasion also had to command troops in the field. Capt. Arthur A. Browne, one of the Americans Young had brought with him to Liberia became trapped, deep in the jungle, by rebellious Liberians. The Liberian Secretary of War asked Young to lead a rescue force. All the other officers, according to the Liberian, were already in the field. The rescue attempt took more than a month to execute. In his report on the expedition Young noted that on Christmas Day, "We found ourselves lost in the jungles of Liberia, surrounded by man-eating Manos, with about four clips of ammunition to the soldiers." During one skirmish, Young was wounded in the right arm but continued to lead the rescue mission. They finally reached Browne and his men, and the combined force was able to fight its way back to the coast. Despite the risk, Young considered it an "arduous but pleasant task" because through it he was helping Liberia, a country he considered "a heritage for the blacks of the U.S. and for their children's children for all time."[39]

Young was very successful at his job during the four years that he was in Liberia. When he left, he received commendations from his host and from the United States ambassador. The latter wrote, "The actual result of work so well performed through your boundless energy and personal application leaves behind you a testimonial of your true work." In addition, the Blacks in the United States felt that his work was very worthwhile. In 1916, the year he left Liberia, he received the Spingarn Medal of the NAACP. This medal was given each year to the American black man who made the greatest contribution in the preceeding year "in any field of honorable or elevated human endeavor."[40]

After Young left Liberia, he was replaced by John Green, who remained there through 1917. Green continued to supervise the Liberian Defense Force and help the Liberian Government settle its many border disputes with its British and French colonial neighbors. In December 1916 Green received permission to go to the French West African border and survey it with Liberian assistance.[41]

Black officers were also involved in the training of black

---

39. U.S.–Liberia Records, 882.30/14, Enclosure A; 882.00/451; and AGO 2596616; U.S.–Liberia Records, 882.20/37.

40. AGO 2370224; *New York Age*, 24 February 1916.

41. AGO 2501593.

National Guard units. Army officers were often detached during the summer months to assist at state National Guard training camps. The black officers received such assignments but only with black troops in those few areas that still had them. Benjamin Davis was assigned to the First Separate Battalion, District of Columbia National Guard, a black unit. In 1908 they took part in joint maneuvers between the District of Columbia National Guard and the Coast Artillery. When no black officers were available for this duty, the army sent black NCOs. In one instance a sergeant of the Twenty-fourth Infantry was assigned to this same District of Columbia battalion.[42]

Evaluating the military career of the black soldier and officer who served in this period is not difficult. Generally the army used them as it did white soldiers. Only in the case of the black officers were the differences very apparent. The Blacks continued to perform well in those tasks given them by the military authorities. The variety of these assignments helped keep up the reenlistment rate for most of this period.

42. *ANJ*, 13 June 1908, p. 1126; AGO 1688892.

VI

OFF DUTY

When not on duty the black soldier and officer had a wide range of opportunities for recreation and education. In some areas, such as sports, Blacks took advantage of the opportunities to participate in activities from which they were excluded in civilian society. Yet even in these situations racism began to intrude.

The basic social unit was the company, but often this group was augmented by the families of the enlisted men. In 1892 the number of married men in the black regiments ranged from fifteen in the Ninth Cavalry to sixty-four in the Twenty-fourth Infantry, and the number of children per regiment varied from fourteen to forty-eight. These figures were similar to those of the white regiments. According to army practice, when an enlisted man wanted to marry, he had to receive the permission of his commander. If he ignored this rule, he would not be allowed to reenlist when his term expired. One officer of a black regiment made it a practice to check into the character of the prospective bride and then require the soldier to agree to allot half his pay to his wife because otherwise some soldiers neglected to send their wives any of their pay.[1]

The black soldiers, like many white officers and enlisted men, often married the relatives of other soldiers. In a ceremony at Fort Harrison, Montana, Sgt. Eugene Farris, Twenty-fourth Infantry, married Miss Nannie T. Coles, the sister of the battalion sergeant major. Of course, soldiers also chose brides from the civilian population, and one unusual wedding of this nature was conducted via telephone wires. Samuel Wheeler, a private in H Troop, Ninth Cavalry, while stationed at Fort Wingate, New Mexico, married Lizzie Hummons, a girl then in Winchester,

---

1. U.S., Congress, House of Representatives, *Report of the Inspector-General, 1892,* House Executive Document 1, pt. 2, vol. 4, 52d Cong., 2d sess., 1892–1893, pp. 426–43; Guy V. Henry, Jr., to author, 21 August 1966; as an example see AGO 364578.

Kentucky. The post chaplain was present with the soldier and the Reverend S. P. Young of Lexington officiated at the bride's end. While in the Philippines, some of the soldiers married native girls. At one such wedding in 1900 Pvt. Willie Redding, K Company, Twenty-fifth Infantry, married Señorita Senung Marcalina. The mayor of the town, the bride's father, performed the ceremony in a flower decked house, using rites that were a combination of the American and Filipino religious cultures. When the troops were ready to return from their tour of duty in the Philippines, however, some soldiers did not want to take their native brides back home with them. The War Department authorized the regimental officers to require the men to keep their wives or face the possibility of a discharge without honor. In one instance in 1902, five men of the Twenty-fifth complied with the order, while another forty decided to leave the service.[2]

Life was hard for the men and their families, but most soldiers' wives were aware of the problems and, as one black soldier's wife said, accepted army life "improving it as circumstances and conditions" made it possible. At most posts housing was either insufficient or nonexistent, so the men created substitutes with the materials on hand. At Fort Ontario, New York, several old buildings were converted to housing for the enlisted men's families, even though they were grossly inadequate. Because of poor facilities at Fort Robinson, Nebraska, two children died when a fire started in a barracks in which seven families were housed. Though the soldiers tried to get through the flames and evacuate everyone, a sergeant's two children perished. Despite these inconveniences, the soldiers and their families usually tried to stay together, even in the harsh climate of the Philippines. While families were not permitted to live with the soldiers during the Insurrection, afterwards the army allowed the wives to join their husbands. However, they had to agree to stay in the Philippine Islands for the entire two-year tour of duty.[3]

The community of enlisted men and their families on each post was of necessity tightly knit, especially in the black regiments. Usually these small groups were isolated from any black

2. *ANJ,* 14 January 1905, p. 510; 30 December 1899, p. 417; *The Richmond Planet,* 16 June 1900; AGO 440772; *ANJ,* 23 August 1902, p. 1286.

3. *The Enterprise,* 4 April 1896; *ANJ,* 4 April 1908, p. 836; 2 April 1898, p. 582. See also AGO 1205636; AGO 368444.

civilians. Self-help became the key. The men of the Tenth Cavalry looked after the widow of one of their first sergeants, and as one soldier said, "That woman ain't going to want for bread while the 10th Cav has a ration left."[4]

These family groups celebrated special events and holidays with parties and dances. On Washington's Birthday, Troop I, Ninth Cavalry, held a dance for the men and officers. At the dance the band sat beneath a hugh Japanese parasol that was draped with ribbons and crepe paper. The menu at a Thanksgiving dinner given by H Troop, Tenth Cavalry, featured turkey and cranberry sauce. The meal also included roast pork, possum, mashed potatoes, sugar corn, canned peaches, and was concluded with cake, tea, and coffee. The regiment celebrated the same holiday in Vermont in 1911 with a different twist. They had a "Wild West" show in the riding hall. There were bucking broncos, trained horses, and bareback riders. As a grand finale, the soldiers re-created an attack on a stage coach and a settler's cabin by a group of "Indians." These attackers were put to flight by a band of cowboys and soldiers. The program, directed by First Sergeant Alexander, D Troop, and managed by Chaplain Louis Carter, both black, was described as a "spendid success" by the enthusiastic spectators.[5]

At Christmas most posts decorated a tree, distributed gifts to the children of the officers and enlisted men, and had an elaborate meal. It was the usual practice for each company to invite its officers and their families to share this festive dinner with them. At one such meal A Troop, Tenth Cavalry, had as its centerpiece a large cake designed to represent the battleship *Oregon*. "The cake was the admiration of all in the post, as it was a work of art." When black regiments invited officers to these social functions, they followed different procedures than the white regiments. In the white regiments the officers and their wives would make only a token appearance and then depart. The black regiments had a more complicated system, and the enlisted men expected the officers and their wives to stay the entire evening. According to Grace B. Paulding, wife of a commander of the Twenty-fourth Infantry, the dances of the black enlisted men were more elaborate than those conduct-

---

4. *ANJ*, 7 December 1892, p. 236. See also *The Freeman*, 22 February 1896. *ANJ*, 12 June 1915, p. 1298.

5. *ANJ*, 5 March 1910, p. 779. See also *ANJ*, 6 March 1909, p. 771; *The Richmond Planet*, 3 December 1898; *ANJ*, 9 December 1911, p. 454. See also *ANJ*, 14 December 1895, p. 263; 5 December 1903, p. 353; 3 December 1904, p. 348.

ed by the officers. The colonel and his wife had the first dance, then she danced once with the regiment's ranking enlisted man. After that they sat on the sidelines while the Blacks danced. Only much later did the officers retire as the soldiers continued the festivities late into the night.[6]

Other social activities of the garrison included plays, movies, and music. The men of B Troop, Tenth Cavalry, put on a production of the "Court Scene" from Shakespeare's *Merchant of Venice*. Many members of the garrison community attended and enjoyed the entertainment. At some army posts live entertainment was supplemented with movies. The chaplain at one post in the Philippines bought an electric light plant and used it to power a movie projector. The equipment was paid for by charging admission to the shows. However, the Blacks were not always pleased with what they saw on the screen. At least three times in six months in 1915 black soldiers stationed in Hawaii prevented antiblack movies from being shown, once by pelting the theater with rocks.[7]

Some members of the black regiments formed volunteer musical groups of various kinds. A minstrel troupe composed of members of the Twenty-fourth Infantry band gave performances at a theater in Manila in 1899 and earned about $500 a day. However, the NCOs of the regiment objected to this type of entertainment, for they felt that performing as minstrels was degrading to Blacks. Aside from these types of shows, the men channeled their musical abilities into many different activities. A Troop, Ninth Cavalry, formed a volunteer band of twenty pieces, a vocal quartet, and a group of mandolins. Not only did they entertain their peers but also the Blacks often used their skills to help others. The Tenth Cavalry Mandolin Club donated the money it raised in a concert in September 1909 to a public library in Vermont.[8]

6. For examples see *The Burlington Free Press,* 24 December 1910. *The Freeman,* 18 January 1896; *Colored American Magazine* 8:2 (February 1905):96; Grace B. Paulding, "Memoirs" (typescript), Paulding, Papers, pp. 127–28.

7. *ANR,* 4 March 1911, p. 30; AGO 1892411, March 1912. See also *ANJ,* 7 February 1903, p. 545; 3 June 1911, p. 1216; 10 October 1914, p. 187; *New York Age,* 12 August 1915.

8. *ANJ,* 2 December 1899, p. 323. See also *ANJ,* 21 October 1899, p. 176. *ANJ,* 4 November 1899, p. 226; 18 January 1902, p. 487; 4 March 1905, p. 727; Francis H. Farnum questionnaire in possession of author. For other statements on the racial situation in the army *see New York Age,* 8 June 1905. *The Chicago Defender,* 18 December 1915. For opposing views to these see *New York Age,* 20 July 1905. *ANJ,* 25 April 1903, p. 832; 21 November 1903, p. 290; 12 January

One place where the men could spend their off-duty time on the post was the recreation or amusement room. Because many of the posts at which the army stationed the black regiments were isolated, this room was quite important to the soldiers. At Fort Huachuca, when the Blacks were at the post, there were three rooms set up for the soldiers' leisure. There was a billiard room, a room that contained card tables, dominoes, checkers and chess games, and a reading room with newspapers and magazines. It was common for a post to subscribe to periodicals, but each unit decided how much money would be spent. One company of the Twenty-fourth Infantry subscribed to such papers as the *Army and Navy Journal, Leslie's Weekly, Sporting Life, Puck,* and a black newspaper, the *New York Age.* Money for these items came from the special funds collected by the companies or regiments. Money-raising projects included band concerts, sales at the PX, and contributions by the soldiers.[9]

The off-duty time of the soldier also provided opportunities to engage in still another activity, athletics. The regiments staged competitions in baseball, basketball, and track-and-field events among the different companies, and then they chose the best men in each regiment to compete against other military and civilian teams. This activity provided one of the very few chances for the races to compete equally.[10]

Baseball was the most popular and successful sporting activity of the black regiments. One chaplain reported, "The men seem to have their minds so employed now with baseball . . . that they do not get drunk." The record of the team of the Twenty-fifth Infantry is indicative of the success of Blacks at this sport. In 1903 the regiment traveled to Fort Riley for maneuvers, and in every town where they camped, the local ball club challenged the Blacks to a game, and the soldiers always won. At the maneuvers there was a baseball tournament among the many army and National Guard regiments. Competition eventually narrowed down to the two unbeaten teams, both black. In the final game the Twenty-fifth Infantry scored the winning run in the bottom of the eleventh inning. The amusement hall of the

---

1907, p. 537; *The Burlington Free Press,* 10 September 1909.

9. *The Freeman,* 3 June 1893; *The Recorder,* 20 October 1900; LS, 24th Inf, letter sent, 1 November 1903; LS, 9th Cav, letter sent 8 September 1905.

10. For more information on this topic see Marvin E. Fletcher, "The Black Soldier Athlete in the United States Army, 1890–1916," *Canadian Journal of History of Sport and Physical Education* 3:2 (December 1972): 16–26.

regiment "was covered with banners won by the companies, battalions and the regiment in athletic contests." It was even suggested that this team, when stationed in Hawaii, tour the Pacific Coast playing civilian teams. However, the army rejected this proposal, claiming that there was "no special end of military athletic training served thereby." The regiment's supporters were greatly disappointed.[11]

The army regiments also played civilian teams, usually on weekends, and allowed civilian spectators on the post. When these games were held on Sundays some civilians protested for religious reasons. A minister in Vermont wrote the War Department that they furnished an "attraction for the young people to an environment which is not the best for them." The commander of the Tenth Cavalry, the regiment involved in this particular complaint, replied that no one was compelled to come to the game. The army responded to the pressure, however, by banning their games with civilians on Sundays. Although the commanding officer of the Tenth remarked that there was more vice just outside the post in "disreputable dives" than took place on the post in the form of Sunday baseball games, his protests did not change the new army policy.[12]

While baseball was the most popular sport among black soldiers, there was a growing interest in basketball. At posts like Fort Ethan Allen, which had properly equipped gymnasiums, the sport was very popular. During the winter the soldiers played almost every night. The regiment decided that the winner of the 1911 Tenth Cavalry company tournament would go to New York to play the New York All-stars, a black team. The members of the Tenth's team were bigger than the All-stars, but the latter were faster and won 30 to 14. The *New York Age* gave the following description of the game:

The boys in blue proved as tricky as the horses they ride, and whenever an All-Star player attempted to tackle a cavalryman by jumping on his back he was usually given a quick excursion through the air. Medical aid and sticking plaster were called into use several times, and one soldier had a sweet short dream in the second half, but no one was seriously injured.[13]

11. AGO 53910, October 1901; Richard Johnson, "My Life in the U.S. Army, 1899 to 1922," p. 75; *ANJ*, 12 September 1914, p. 57; 16 December 1916, p. 496; AGO 2494843.

12. AGO 1816297, 1826704; AGO 1933173.

13. *ANJ*, 21 January 1911, p. 611; *New York Age*, 30 March 1911.

During the summer months the black regiments channeled their athletic talents into track-and-field events, as well as baseball. There were intra- and inter-regimental events. In one intraregimental competition in the Twenty-fifth Infantry the winning time in the one-hundred-yard dash was 11.2 seconds. Several years later Private Gilbert of the same regiment equaled the world amateur record by running the distance in 9.6 seconds. Such athletic feats did not go unnoticed by whites. Many civilians were disconcerted when in 1908 members of the black regiments won the track-and-field championships of the departments of Luzon, Visayas, and Mindanao. One white correspondent for the *Army and Navy Journal* commented on this situation. "Surely this is a matter for some thought on the part of those who are responsible to the nation for the maintenance of its prestige and for its defense." The authorities made no reply to the complaint.[14]

Another sport in which the black soldier displayed interest was boxing. During an athletic meet in Manila there was a match between two enlisted men of different races, Sternberg of the Thirtieth Infantry and Murray of the Ninth Cavalry. While a disturbance drew the referee's attention from the ring, the black soldier got in a low blow. Despite this violation of the rules and the protests of the crowd, the referee awarded the black cavalryman the decision. Black soldiers were also fans of black professional fighters. The movies of the lightweight fight between Joe Gans and Battling Nelson attracted a large audience when shown to members of the Tenth Cavalry. They were even more enthusiastic about the fight of 1910 between Jack Johnson and Jim Jeffries. Jeffries, "the white hope," had come out of retirement to challenge the black heavyweight champion. Johnson KOed him in the fifteenth round. Some of the men at Fort Lawton, Washington, had rented a telegraph line to give them information about the fight, and they greeted Johnson's victory with wild cheers.[15]

While interracial boxing was permitted, swimming competi-

14. *ANJ*, 25 July 1903, p. 1185. See also *ANJ*, 19 March 1910, p. 859. *Colored American Magazine* 8:1 (January, 1905):25. *The Enterprise*, 11 July 1896; *ANJ*, 18 March 1916, p. 945. See also AGO 53445; *The Freeman*, 1 May 1909; *ANJ*, 8 February 1908, p. 595. For other examples see *ANJ*, 10 March 1906, p. 784; 28 March 1908, p. 797; 11 July 1908, p. 1243; 11 September 1915, p. 59.

15. *ANJ*, 6 February 1909, p. 632; *The Burlington Free Press*, 16 September 1909; *The Seattle Post Intelligencer*, 5 July 1910. William P. Evans questionnaire in possession of author. See also *ANJ*, 16 July 1910, p. 1385.

tions were segregated. This typical attitude of the period was evident at the pool at Camp Stotsensburg, Philippine Islands. Regulations allowed the white soldiers pool privileges three days a week and the Blacks three other days.[16]

Education and religion were other facets of the off-duty life of the black soldiers. Each post provided a range of educational opportunities for the enlisted men, from general classes often conducted by the chaplain to instruction in special skills by soldiers appointed to the job. The opportunities for such education and the need to have it both increased after 1890. Training in reading and writing was available. The number of interested soldiers varied from post to post, from a few to more than one hundred students. On some posts there were facilities for students who wanted to progress beyond the elementary level. At Fort Douglas, Utah, Chaplain Allen Allensworth included training in trades, such as printing, baking, and telegraphing, in his curriculum. He had the post printer, baker, and telegrapher teach these courses. Sgt. Horace Bivens of the Tenth Cavalry sought further training than that provided at his post. In 1897 he applied for and was granted a four-month furlough to go to Hampton Institute, Virginia, to continue his education. He also received permission to apply for a longer leave if necessary. However, the army did not allow all soldiers these opportunities. After acquiring a knowledge of colloquial Spanish while in the Philippines, a few of the black soldiers sought further training in the language. This idea was rejected by the authorities. They presumed that any conversation a soldier might have with the natives could be carried on in colloquial Spanish. Probably more important in their decision was the belief that the "education of the colored soldier . . . is not of such a nature that he is able to receive much benefit from the scientific study of a language."[17]

Education continued outside of the formal structure of the classroom. On most posts there was a library with a small selection of books, magazines, and newspapers. Among the most popular works in the Tenth Cavalry's library were histories of the black soldier. At times a literary society was formed to

16. *ANJ*, 7 June 1913, p. 1257.

17. George Schuyler, *Black and Conservative: The Autobiography of George S. Schuyler*, p. 45; *ANJ*, 22 July 1905, p. 1281; LS, 24th Inf, 1 December 1892. *ANJ*, 6 February 1897, p. 409; 16 April 1904, p. 865; Charles Alexander, *Battles and Victories of Allen Allensworth*, p. 278; *The Freeman*, 25 February 1899. See also *The Freeman*, 24 December 1892; LS, 25th Inf, 24 April 1903. See also AGO 472548.

discuss the books or debate items of current interest. The 3M Literary Club at Fort Ethan Allen held well-attended weekly discussion groups. At one such session they debated the subject, "Resolved, That Women are of Greater Value than Money." The negative side won the argument.[18]

While the chaplain was in charge of education on the post, his main duty was to look after the spiritual welfare of his men. The chaplain of a black regiment, usually a Black himself, was a commissioned officer and, like the white chaplains, received $1,000 a year, a free house, and could retire at age sixty-four with three-fourths pay. There were always many applicants for these positions in the four black regiments. The chaplain's main duty was to conduct services. On some occasions he had a full house for his services, but at other times he had to try strenuously to fill his chapel. He had to compete with the attraction of sports, such as baseball. One chaplain tried to counteract these influences by promoting his cause in a pamphlet with this message: "I need the help of every man. You have always had my best wishes and prayers. May I have, *once in a week*, your presence in church."[19]

In addition to his religious functions, the chaplain provided a variety of other services for the men. One of the functions of the chaplain in the Ninth Cavalry was to deliver a lecture to the men of each squadron on the cause and effects of venereal disease. In some cases he acted the role of public defender. Chaplain Allen Allensworth, Twenty-fourth Infantry, defended one of the enlisted men before a court-martial. The black soldier was accused of burglary. He had been caught by the guard coming out of an officer's house. Though the soldier said he was guilty, Allensworth did not believe him. Upon close questioning the soldier admitted that he had been in the house but not to rob it. He had been visiting the maid. Upon leaving he had tripped on the stairs, the maid had screamed, and the officer's wife had called the guard. In order to protect the girl, the soldier had lied about committing burglary. Allensworth convinced the court that this was the real story, and the soldier was acquitted. The regimental chaplains also supervised the Sunday school, to which the officers sometimes sent their children, arranged lec-

18. AGO 1549808. See also *The Colored American*, 8 April 1899; *The Burlington Free Press*, 24 February 1911. See also *ANR*, 9 January 1892, p. 22.

19. *The Enterprise*, 27 February 1897; AGO 1350445; AGO 1346–1892; AGO 1966–1893.

tures for the men, and assisted in conducting the educational program.[20]

Blacks also conducted a number of other types of activities. Matthew Henson, the Black who had accompanied Robert Peary on his trek to the North Pole, gave a lecture entitled "The North Pole" to the men of the Twenty-fifth Infantry stationed at Fort George Wright, Washington. Another special event was the fiftieth-anniversary celebration of the two black cavalry regiments. The Ninth held theirs in the Philippines at Camp Stotsensburg and included a parade with historical floats. Among them was one entitled "Ascending San Juan Hill— Capturing Block House—Planting Colors." Mexico was the site of the Tenth's celebration. Lt. Col. Charles Young, who was in charge of the preparations, wrote a poetic description of the regiment's history. The men then re-created scenes of historical moment, and a herald read the appropriate verses. After the various tableaux had been presented there was a call to the colors, and a "great burst of cheering ending with singing of 'Glory, Hallelujah'."[21]

Hunting was one of the most common forms of recreation for many of the officers and men stationed in the West. At one post a few enlisted men of the Ninth Cavalry organized a hunting expedition and invited several officers to go along. The resulting party included two officers, four men from the Eighth Infantry (a white unit), and the black soldiers. On the trip they got thirteen black-tailed deer, six antelope, and large quantities of small game.[22]

Black officers were more restricted in their off-duty activities than white officers. White officers disliked the possibilities of having to eat with, live near, or be commanded by a black officer, and Blacks had either to accept this general antipathy or leave the army. The black officers survived by keeping correct official relations but drawing tacit social barriers. Apparently the officers of both races built them up. William W. Hay, a fellow officer of Charles Young, wrote that he "associated very little with the other officers." In another instance Young met the social requirements of the post by inviting the other officers to

20. Alexander, *Battles and Victories,* pp. 306–9; for examples see AGO 10315, 23255, 1210098, 1616574, 1892411. *The Freeman,* 2 June 1893. *ANR,* 9 January 1892, p. 22. *ANJ,* 22 October 1904, p. 177; 13 March 1909, p. 797.

21. AGO 1620008; AGO 2129809; *ANJ,* 12 August 1916, p. 1611.

22. Frank Armstrong, "Memoir" (typescript in possession of writer's family). See also Richard O'Connor, *Black Jack Pershing,* p. 104.

functions at his house that were cancelled at the last moment because he was " 'unavoidably' called away." The black chaplains were in much the same position. The invitation of Chaplain Carter to the annual New Year's reception given by the commanding officer of the Twenty-fourth Infantry posed a problem. His solution to this compulsory social function was to arrive before the other officers, then fade into the background and quietly depart as the other officers arrived. He had fulfilled his social obligation but not really broken the color line. Some whites appreciated the situation and admired how the black officers carried off "the difficulties associated with their social equality."[23]

When the black officers did not respect the racial lines, the situation became difficult. While stationed with the Twenty-fifth Infantry at Schofield Barracks, Hawaii, Lt. John E. Green was asked to vacate his quarters for a white junior lieutenant and his wife. According to strict military etiquette he did not have to do so, but many whites assumed he would. He stood on his rank and refused to vacate his quarters. While the officers were probably upset and considered him uppity, the black enlisted men of his regiment were very proud of the stand he had taken.[24]

One other form of relaxation, which at times caused a great deal of trouble, was gambling. Within each regiment there was usually a hard core of gamblers who appeared after payday to draw in unsuspecting recruits. The old pros quickly parted the unsophisticated gambler from his money. On some posts the gamblers went so far as to set up shacks, which for several days after payday were the scenes of all-night gambling sessions. As could be expected, these games occasionally led to violence. At one game at Fort Niobrara, Nebraska, one soldier shot another because they both tried to borrow money to get into a crap game.[25]

One of the brightest aspects of the life of the black soldier and officer in this period were the times of rest and relaxation. The army opened many areas to Blacks from which they were usually restricted in civilian life. An old pattern of treating Blacks

23. Charles Young questionnaire in possession of author; John C. Pegram questionnaire in possession of author; William W. Hay, interview with Earl Stover, 17 February 1967. See Alexander, *Battles and Victories*, pp. 316, 321; William W. West, Jr., questionnaire in possession of author; Paulding, Papers, p. 129; Orlando C. Troxel questionnaire in possession of author.

24. Schuyler, *Black and Conservative*, pp. 58–59.

25. Ibid., pp. 40, 63; AGO 454487.

equally only superficially was continued in this way. In off-duty activities, this attitude was beneficial to them, but their welfare was almost always disregarded if these policies of the military were challenged by the white civilian population.

VII

THE BLACK SOLDIER AND SOCIETY

Soldiers in the black regiments became increasingly hostile toward discrimination after 1890. They were discontent over the Government's refusal to protect the Blacks' civil rights, the general hatred among whites of Blacks, the growing number of incidents of violence against Blacks, and the stationing of Blacks in the South.

Conflict usually began when the Government made the decision to move a black unit into a community. White civilians objected to having Blacks near them. Before 1898 the army, to avoid these protests, tried to station Blacks in the more isolated and less desirable posts. At times there were exceptions to this policy. In 1895 the army decided to move the Twenty-fourth Infantry from Arizona and New Mexico, where they had been stationed for a number of years, to a "northern station," Fort Douglas, located near Salt Lake City, Utah. Chaplain Allensworth claimed that he had made great efforts toward this end. He had begun by asking a recently discharged black soldier to write a letter to the *New York Age* explaining that one reason he had decided not to reenlist was the regiment's poor stations. After it was published, Allensworth had the article sent to a black representative, John Mercer Langston of Virginia. Langston in turn took the complaint to the commanding general, Nelson A. Miles, to introduce the issue of assigning black regiments at better stations. The commanding general agreed that something should be done, and as a result sent the Twenty-fourth to the post in Utah.[1]

Stationing the black soldiers became a more complex problem after 1898. The War Department had to decide whether to send Blacks to the United States' new island possession in the Pacific, the Philippines, when in 1905, through the rotation

---

1. *New York Evening Post,* 4 June 1898, as quoted in Jack D. Foner, *The United States Soldier Between Two Wars: Army Life and Reforms, 1865–1898,* p. 133; AGO 15000; Charles Alexander, *Battles and Victories of Allen Allensworth,* pp. 288–91.

system, the black regiments of the infantry were scheduled for return there. Some officers feared that because segregation was not practiced in the Philippines as in the United States, the black soldiers would be very dissatisfied when they returned to America. Even rumors of their conduct during their previous tour in the islands entered into the discussion. A well-known and widely respected army officer, Matthew Steele, who was an instructor at the Army staff school at Fort Leavenworth and author of the widely read *American Campaigns*, stated that the army recalled the black soldiers in 1902 upon the demand of the civil governor because they had aroused fear in the civilian population. Though not stated, it was implicit that he was referring to sexual relations between the black soldiers and civilians. However, there was contrary evidence. Colonel Burt of the Twenty-fifth Infantry said, in opposition to the general opinion, that there was not a single place in the islands "whose inhabitants have not been sincerely sorry when we have been ordered to leave their towns." The commander of the Department of Mindanao, Brig. Gen. George W. Davis, commented in 1902 that the black soldiers and the natives got along well without any signs of "racial antipathy."[2]

The army weighed the contrary evidence on the conduct of the black soldiers in their previous tour in the Philippines and then, in 1905, decided to make a test using the Twenty-fourth Infantry. They did not want to subject the Christian Filipinos to the experiment first, so they decided to send the regiment to Mindanao, which was mainly inhabited by Moros, a tribe of Muslims. The War Department believed that the Moro tribesmen could defend their women against the expected sexual activities of the Blacks. Before the soldiers reached their destination, however, the army reversed its decision and assigned the soldiers to the Visayas, another island group. The reason given was that they feared the probable conflicts between the Moros and the black soldiers.[3]

The following year, however, when the regiments overseas again had to be replaced, the War Department had to face the question again. They did not want to send more black troops to the Philippines, because in their study of the Blacks' first tour

2. Matthew F. Steele, "The 'Color Line' in the Army," p. 1288; *ANJ*, 4 October 1902, p. 106; George W. Davis to Maj. Gen. Adna R. Chaffee, 17 April 1902, Elihu Root, Papers.

3. AGO 1077761. See also AGO 1200795. *ANJ*, 28 October 1905, p. 232; AGO 1128850.

of duty there, the soldiers had reportedly come into "too close contact" with the natives, and this had been the cause of much of the trouble. The War Department was at a loss to find an alternative station for the Blacks. In Alaska, they claimed, the white signal corpsmen did not want the necessary close living conditions. The planners eliminated as possible stations Cuba or many parts of the United States because they feared civilian protests. Consequently their only solution was to send the other three regiments to the Philippines. Sen. Benjamin R. Tillman of South Carolina objected to this decision because he felt the black soldiers would attack the native women. He believed the army should keep the soldiers at home, where, if they committed outrages, "We can shoot them, as we ought to do, and not inflict them, with their brutalities, upon a helpless people." The War Department informed the regimental officers that they had to pay special attention to the relations between the men and the natives.[4]

Whenever the War Department considered assigning the black soldiers to a domestic station, they had to face great pressures exerted by the military and civilian American public. The officers of the black regiments often requested better stations for their men. Capt. William B. Cochran, Twenty-fourth Infantry, suggested that the army discriminated by stationing black soldiers only west of the Mississippi River. The army responded by sending the Twenty-fourth Infantry to upstate New York and the Tenth Cavalry to Fort Ethan Allen, near Burlington, Vermont. At the same time civilians tried to influence the army to keep Blacks out of their areas. The army displeased one group by pleasing another. It was a very difficult situation, but most often the army was more responsive to civilian pressures than to military requests.[5]

Civilians advanced a number of reasons to buttress their arguments against having black soldiers in their vicinity. "Some people" in Salt Lake City feared that many local Blacks would follow their soldier friends and be the cause of much friction. If, on the other hand, there were few black women in the area, then the black soldiers would turn to white women, and rape and prostitution might plague their towns. Whites also feared that the black soldiers would not only reject the practice of separation but would use force to change it. Throughout the country

---

4. AGO 1192804; *The New York Times*, 7 January 1907.
5. *ANJ*, 24 November 1906, p. 334; 25 August 1906, p. 1454.

there were many areas in which, according to local custom, bars were off limits to Blacks. When soldiers broke these customs the bartenders raised the prices of drinks or smashed the glasses that the soldiers used. In one case in Watertown, New York, the management raised the price of a glass of beer to twenty-five cents and a drink of whiskey to fifty cents. The soldiers were aware of the implications of these actions and merely avoided these bars. The army made no real effort to prevent these acts of discrimination except to refrain from stationing black troops in the South.[6]

Neither did the military try to defend the soldiers' civil rights. In one case two black soldiers were detailed from Oklahoma to a government hospital in New Mexico, and the Government requested they ride in Pullman berths. When the soldiers arrived in Texas the conductor removed them from the Pullman car, in accordance with a Texas law which forbade Blacks in such railroad cars. The army investigated the facts and then asked the Department of Justice for an opinion on the case. Even though there seemed to be a violation of the spirit if not the letter of the Fourteenth Amendment, the Justice Department reported that the soldiers' only remedy was to take action themselves. Since the soldiers obviously did not have the funds to undertake such a case, the army's inaction indicated that they intended to accept discrimination.[7] Another incident occurred when Charles Young went to Leavenworth, Kansas, to take an examination for promotion. He tried to find a place to stay in the hotels in town but was refused. He had to go to Kansas City to find a hotel room, and the authorities did not protest. The army did not always back up black soldiers when they were carrying out controversial assignments. In one instance, a sergeant of the Ninth Cavalry was detailed to pick up a white deserter in a town in Okalhoma. In reaction a riot almost started in the town. The War Department took note of this reaction and stated that it did not consider it advisable to use black soldiers for this type of duty "particularly at this time."[8]

6. For examples see *Helena Independent* (Montana), 27 August 1904, as quoted in *ANJ*, 3 September 1904, p. 8. *Pacific Commericial Advertiser*, n.d., as quoted in *ANJ*, 16 March 1912, p. 880. AGO 1973086; *ANJ*, 3 October 1896, p. 71. See also *Herald* (Neibart, Montana), 14 September 1895, as quoted in *ANJ*, 28 September 1895, p. 53; *The Seattle Post Intelligencer*, 6 October 1909; *ANR*, 21 September 1907, p. 13; AGO 1368775.

7. AGO 941110, 989512; *ANJ*, 19 September 1896, p. 40; *The New York Times*, 14 September 1896.

8. AGO 1224153.

In many cases the black soldiers were able to live amicably within the confines of the established racial patterns. There were some instances of violence, however, as one group objected to the conduct of the other. While most of these incidents took place in the South, there were also occurrences in the North and West. The army assumed that any accusation against a black soldier was true without considering the validity of the evidence. Though there were no real violations of the letter of army regulations in dealing with black troops, there was a distinct attitude against believing what black soldiers said and toward making them prove their innocence.

The praise given Blacks for good conduct was often tainted. The Ninth Cavalry won the plaudits of the Douglas, Arizona, Chamber of Commerce. They said that by their actions the black cavalrymen had "dissipated the racial prejudice and have won the tolerance of the people of this community." The chamber had sponsored the distribution of commemorative medals to the band as a token of this feeling. Yet, as one soldier said, the citizens liked them because they were "good little fellows," in other words they accepted segregation. There were also instances of good black–white relations in the South. When the Tenth Cavalry arrived in Winchester for the 1913 cavalry maneuvers the local authorities expected trouble. There was not any because the conduct of the troops was quiet and orderly. Even more unexpected was the request made by the citizens of Laredo, Texas. They asked the War Department to permit the Tenth to remain there because they felt that no other group of troops would be as acceptable as the black soldiers. It is likely that when whites tolerated the black troops, it was because they behaved in a servile manner. As long as they said and did nothing to break the racial patterns already established, they were accepted.[9]

The relationships were usually much more unhappy, however. In 1899 part of a train carrying the Tenth Cavalry was fired upon near Meridian, Mississippi, and near Houston, Texas. The officer in charge of the train asked the War Department for help so his troops could pass through a region they were supposed to protect "without danger from hidden assassins." The request was ignored. The police in Macon, Georgia, initiated another incident when they arrested several soldiers from the Seventh United States Volunteer Infantry, a black volunteer

9. AGO 2252389; *New York Age,* 4 March 1915; *ANJ,* 2 August 1913, p. 1489; AGO 230808.

unit from the Spanish-American War, who were in the custody of the Provost Guard. The soldiers then received reinforcements from the regiment, turned on the police, knocked down several white bystanders, took away a policeman's gun, and beat him on the head with it. The police were able to rally their forces and arrest these men on charges of disorderly conduct and avoiding arrest. They were tried swiftly, and the prosecutor insulted them with such names as "yellow man" or "black s__ b____."[10]

Such incidents were not limited to the South. One of the most famous took place in Suggs, Wyoming, in the 1890s. In 1892 there were a series of battles between the large and small cattle ranchers and part of the Ninth Cavalry were among those soldiers sent in to quell the disturbance. Camp Bettens, established on the Powder River, about five miles from Suggs, was the site of the Ninth's camp. It was a region with few black civilians and a transient white population. The whites disliked the presence of the black soldiers and made no secret about it. Whenever the Blacks went into town the townspeople verbally harassed the soldiers wherever they went. Some of them followed the soldiers from store to store insulting them at every stop. Several local businesses refused to serve them. The situation was ripe for an incident; the Blacks were ready to fight back. One night Pvt. Abraham Champ, G Troop, visited a white prostitute whom he and other Blacks had visited earlier when she lived near their post in Nebraska. In Suggs, however, her white customers would not permit her to accept Blacks, and she refused Champ. He and another soldier then headed for the local saloon. As usual the white patrons insulted the Blacks, but this time the black soldiers drew their pistols, as did many of the white patrons of the bar. The bartender convinced them to leave town before any violence began. Someone shot at them while they were riding back to camp. Several nights later a group of about twenty soldiers rode into town, determined to teach the townspeople a lesson. They fired a volley into the air and then began to shoot at the buildings. Some of the whites shot back, and Pvt. Willis Johnson, I Troop, was killed in the exchange. Though the local papers tried to stir up more trouble with sensational headlines, the officers of the unit were able to restrain their men and this was the end of the action. The army

10. AGO 184450; *The Gazette*, 18 March 1899. See also *The Richmond Planet*, 3 December 1898. AGO 207070.

buried the records of the affray and made no effort to protect the soldiers' rights. They did not urge the civilian authorities to find the soldier's killer or to stop the harassment that initiated the incident. Such repeated examples more firmly convinced the soldiers that they would have to defend their own rights.[11]

Although Blacks were considered inferior in all parts of the country, intolerance was greater in the South. In 1899 the army mustered out the volunteer regiments and sent them home. One train carrying a load of the recently discharged Tenth United States Volunteer Infantry, another black unit from the Spanish-American War, was scheduled to pass through Nashville, Tennessee. The citizens of the town accepted without question reports about the "turbulent misconduct" of some other black soldiers after they were discharged and were determined to take care of "the rioters before they had time to break out." When the train approached, the city police, together with a large number of white civilians, detached the locomotive and stationed men at the car windows. With the exits blocked, other whites, armed with revolvers and clubs, "entered the cars and beat the men, most of whom were asleep, over the heads and bodies, and robbed some of them of money and tickets." As the Blacks had come to expect, the authorities turned a deaf ear to their pleas for help.[12]

One of the unique factors that shaped the course of black civil-military relations was the continued pride of the black soldier in his uniform, position, and tradition. The men of the Tenth Cavalry were proud to be the first black regiment to make the trip home from the Philippine Islands via the Suez Canal. On the voyage the soldiers were on their best behavior. One white said that the members of a black infantry regiment that he had observed acted at all times as though each believed that any bad action of his would be an injustice to his uniform and the flag. They behaved as if the privileges of citizenship might come to them as a result of the performance of their duties.[13]

---

11. Robert A. Murray, "The United States Army in the Aftermath of the Johnson County Invasion," p. 72; Letter sent, 4 June 1892, Records of United States Army Continental Commands, 1821–1920, Letters Sent, Department of the Platte, 1891–1898, NA, RG 393; Summary Discharge, p. 382. AGO 29763–1892; Frank N. Schubert, "The Suggs Affray: The Black Cavalry in the Johnson County War," pp. 57–68.

12. AGO 209169.

13. *ANJ*, 21 August 1909, p. 144; *Tribune* (Salt Lake City), 24 October 1897,

At the same time the Blacks were quite aware of their position in society and how it was changing. This was one of the themes of an address given by Charles Young at a Stanford University meeting in 1903. Young told the assembled students that the system of race relations espoused by Booker T. Washington had not worked in the past and would not work in the future. "When the black man has learned the industrial trades and seeks work he runs into the unions, where he is told that no negroes need apply." The black officer felt that following Washington's policy led to submission by the black man and by following it he could gain nothing. Young's goal was for Blacks to be allowed to use their abilities without interference from society. "All the Negro asks is a white man's chance, will you give it?" The answer was usually no, both from white society and from the army.[14]

In this situation the black soldiers took action. Signs such as "No Negroes served here," or "This place for blacks" raised their hackles. The Jim Crow streetcars, which the men of the Ninth Cavalry encountered in San Antonio, Texas, in 1911, greatly upset them. They proceeded to attack the cars and start a small riot. In several other cases they even used the weapons at their command to protest discrimination. In Florida during the Spanish-American War a black soldier ordered a drink of soda water at a local restaurant. The waiter refused to serve him and the Black greatly resented this action. A scuffle ensued, and a bystander was shot. In another case a barber would not serve a black soldier, "Whereupon the soldier stepped outside and firing his pistol through the window killed the barber." On a higher level the Blacks ignored the civilian authorities when they felt that they were being harassed. The police in Tampa, Florida, arrested a member of the Ninth Cavalry for carrying a concealed weapon. His black comrades felt that he would be convicted on this trumped-up charge solely because of his race, and they stormed the jail and freed him. Though a large group of police and civilians tried to stop the raid, they decided not to dispute this group of well-armed soldiers. The assertiveness of the black soldiers and the dismay that it caused were well stated by the *Tampa Morning Herald* in 1898: "The men insist upon being treated as white men are treated and the citizens

as quoted in *ANJ*, 6 November 1897, p. 173.
14. *The Daily Palo Alto*, 9 December 1903.

will not make any distinction between the colored troops and the colored civilians."[15]

The Blacks found it difficult to avoid the pressures placed upon them by white civilians and officers. Almost any event was a possible source of trouble. There were very few black girls near Fort Ethan Allen, and the black soldiers of the Tenth Cavalry associated with some white girls who lived in the surrounding area. Several officers greatly disapproved of this practice and put the soldiers in the guard house.[16]

The daily press, in its reporting of racial incidents and its handling of the conduct of the black soldiers, also stirred up trouble. The press in Seattle, Washington, to cite but one example, played up any incident involving black soldiers. They were not so much interested in what really happened but only in a black man's involvement. One contemporary writer, Asa Mercer, blamed the trouble at Suggs, Wyoming, on the "viciousness" of the black soldiers. Even though the black private had been murdered, he called the retaliation of the soldiers "unprovoked."[17]

Another source of racial friction was money. The people who owned real estate near Fort Lawton, Washington, believed that their property values were declining because the fort was manned by black troops. When the army stationed the Twenty-fifth Infantry at Fort Logan, near Denver, Colorado, many of the saloonkeepers refused to serve the black soldiers. Since the owners of the saloons did less business when they excluded the soldiers' trade, they asked the War Department to remove the black regiment and replace it with a white one. When the black soldiers refused to patronize white money lenders, there were complaints. On the other hand, when the men were delinquent or refused to pay their bills, the whites also complained. All of this hostility drove one black editor to ask if there were no place

15. *The Gazette*, 8 April 1899; *The Crisis* 2:1 (May, 1911):35–36. *Savannah Tribune*, 4 February 1899; John Bigelow, Jr., *Reminiscences of the Santiage Campaign*, p. 36. John B. Atkins, *The War in Cuba: The Experiences of an Englishman with the United States Army*, p. 22; John J. Pershing, "Memoir," Chap. 7, Box 380, JJP, Papers. See also Bigelow, *Reminiscences*, p. 24; *Tampa Morning Herald*, 5 May 1898, as quoted in Willard B. Gatewood, Jr., "Negro Troops in Florida, 1898," pp. 3, 13.

16. AGO 1612264.

17. *ANJ*, 25 June 1910, p. 1284; Asa Mercer, *The Banditti of the Plains: or, The Cattlemen's Invasion of Wyoming in 1892*, p. 82.

in this country that was safe from the "severity of the powerful white man." To many black soldiers and officers there seemed to be none.[18]

This possible pattern of action and reaction involving the black soldier and his civilian neighbors was always considered before the army decided to station black troops in an area. Once the local citizens heard of the decision, they protested, but after a while frequently came to tolerate the troops. In those few places where the people treated the black soldiers as human beings, relations were usually harmonious. In the many other localities where the racial patterns insisted that blacks be subservient to whites or where the civilian authorities went out of their way to see that the black soldiers were made to feel unwelcome, trouble often resulted. They wanted to be given "a white man's chance." The reaction of the army, as well as that of the civilian society as a whole, was to quickly put down any such action, often before anyone produced evidence of the Blacks' guilt. There was no attempt to view the situation from the blacks position or to demand equitable treatment. Relations grew worse as contact became more frequent and white racism intensified and spread after 1890. Blacks became firmly convinced that they were the only ones who were interested in protecting their rights. They showed on numerous occasions, such as at Suggs, that they would be willing to use force or the threat of force to prove to whites that disregard of their rights would no longer be tolerated. As white racial discrimination increased, so did black militancy. Unlike the black civilian population, however, the black soldiers were in a position to do something about the situation. Many of these conditions are evident in the incidents that led up to and followed the Brownsville raid of 1906.

18. AGO 1828510; AGO 200551; LS, 9th Cav, Order Book, H Troop, 4 November 1902, 20 March 1903, 22 October 1903. See also AGO 1700024; *The Rising Sun,* 8 November 1906.

VIII

THE BROWNSVILLE RAID
THE VERDICT

In August 1906 a shooting incident occurred in a small town in Texas, which quickly led to the discharge without honor of 167 black infantrymen. The events leading up to and proceeding the incident followed a pattern similar to all other towns in which soldiers were discriminated against. To many black soldiers and civilians the reaction to these events of white leaders, such as President Roosevelt and Secretary Taft, demonstrated that the underlying prejudice against Blacks had existed for a long time and was now merely coming to the surface.

The events that led up to the incident began in May 1906. In that month the War Department ordered two battalions of the Twenty-fifth Infantry, then stationed at Fort Niobrara, to Forts McIntosh and Brown in Texas. A Company, First Battalion, then on temporary duty at Fort Washakie, Wyoming, was to go to Texas as soon as it completed its assignment. A few weeks later the War Department modified its original orders. First the units were to participate in the maneuvers of the Regular Army and Texas National Guard units to be held at Camp Mabry, Texas, and then they were to go to their permanent stations. The officers of the Twenty-fifth Infantry protested this new order. They feared a repetition of a series of incidents that had occurred three years earlier when the black soldiers had come into conflict with some Texas national guardsmen at the maneuvers at Fort Riley in 1903. The chaplain of the regiment, Theophilus G. Steward, was also concerned about "the present state of feeling among the younger element." He too advised against going to the maneuvers. "Texas, I fear, means a quasi battleground for the Twenty-fifth Infantry." As a result of these protests the regimental commander requested that the regiment be sent directly to its new station, and the War Department complied.[1]

1. Court of Inquiry, pp. 1671–72; 1665–68; 1390; Macklin Court-martial, p.

Brownsville was a small town with a population of about seven thousand, 80 per cent of which were Mexican, and only ten families of which were black. The citizens were not eager to receive the black troops. In early June one of the residents wrote a letter of protest to United States Sen. Charles A. Culberson of Texas, who in turn discussed the matter with Secretary Taft. Taft replied that the conduct of the black troops had usually been good and that many communities had changed their minds about the troops once they had arrived, but the Texans were not reassured. They vowed that if there was any trouble from the Blacks, they would be ready to retaliate in kind.[2]

B, C, and D companies arrived at the end of July 1906. They quickly encountered Jim Crow in most parts of the town, including the saloons. Taking advantage of the situation, two black soldiers, Pvts. William Allison and John Holloman, set up a bar of their own near the post. Although it quickly captured a major share of the liquor trade of the soldiers, racial friction was not eliminated. During the first two weeks of the soldiers' stay, there were several incidents that, though seemingly unimportant at the time, assumed a greater significance after the raid on 13 August. One of the first involved Pvts. James W. Newton and Frank J. Lipscomb. The two privates were out for a Sunday stroll when they encountered a party of ladies and a male escort on a narrow sidewalk. The two privates attempted to pass the women by walking on the inner part of the walk. The male escort, Fred Tate, a local customs official, struck Newton on the head with a revolver and knocked him into the street. The other black soldier, Lipscomb, quickly fled from the scene. As soon as Private Newton regained consciousness, he heard Tate say, "I'll learn you to get off the side-walk when there is a party of ladies on the walk." Newton reported this incident to his commander, Capt. Edgar A. Macklin, and seemed satisfied with Macklin's promise that he would investigate the matter.[3]

The second incident occurred the following Sunday, the day after the soldiers were paid. That evening several soldiers, including Pvt. Oscar W. Reid of C Company, were on their way

---

239. (Parts of Chaps. 8 and 9 were based upon James A. Tinsley, "The Brownsville Affray.")

2. Summary Discharge, p. 301; Court of Inquiry, pp. 2121–22. For other such sentiments see Court of Inquiry, pp. 2116–19, 2122–24. Summary Discharge, p. 180.

3. Court of Inquiry, pp. 61; 69.

back from a visit to Matamoros, Mexico, right across the Rio Grande from Brownsville. Private Reid who was somewhat drunk, quarreled about his fare with the man who was running the ferry. When the boat reached the American side of the river, A. Y. Baker, a customs official, joined the discussion. He urged the soldier to pay his fare, but when Reid did not, Baker pushed him into the river. Baker later reported that as Reid got up and walked off, he had said, "We will see about this tomorrow." [4]

The third incident took place that same Sunday afternoon. A man, later identified as a member of the garrison, attacked Mrs. Lon Evans. When she screamed, her assailant fled. The local paper, the *Brownsville Daily Herald,* printed the story the following day with a very suggestive headline: "Infamous Outrage—Negro Soldier Invaded Private Premises Last Night and Attempted to Seize a White Lady." Knowing that in Atlanta a similar incident and newspaper article had recently stirred up a lynch mob, the mayor of Brownsville, Frederick J. Combe, and Mr. Lon Evans visited the battalion commander, Maj. Charles W. Penrose. They asked Major Penrose to take appropriate precautions. The mayor thought it would be easier to control the soldiers than the civilians. In line with this thinking, Major Penrose issued an order confining all the soldiers to the post after 8 P.M. that evening and revoking all passes. Since a number of men had left by the time the order was issued, the officer of the day, Captain Macklin, sent out several patrols to see that the black soldiers were back on post in time. By 10 P.M. all but about three members of the Twenty-fifth Infantry were inside Fort Brown. The officers assumed that their precautions had eliminated the possibility of racial violence arising from the Evans incident.[5]

Around midnight a group of about ten to twenty men gathered at the entrance to Cowen's Alley, a narrow passage just across the road from the post wall and B Company's barracks. After a brief pause, the men entered the alley and began firing into the buildings along the way. One of the first houses attacked was that of Mr. Louis Cowen. They narrowly missed Mrs. Cowen and her five children. The riflemen continued up the alley, apparently firing at the lights that appeared in their line of sight. Near the intersection of the alley and Thirteenth Street, about a block from the garrison road, the raiders severely

4. Ibid., p. 40.
5. Court of Inquiry, pp. 1668–69; Summary Discharge, p. 33.

wounded the lieutenant of the Brownsville police. The party of men then divided in half. One group continued up the alley about half a block and, firing into a saloon, killed a bartender, Frank Natus. The other group went up Thirteenth Street to the next major cross street and fired a volley into the house of Fred E. Starck, who lived next door to Mr. Tate. After this ten-minute shooting episode, the raiders disappeared.[6]

The frightened townspeople emerged from their houses to survey the damage and see if anyone had been killed. They all quickly jumped to the conclusion that the firing had been done by the black soldiers and considered attacking the fort. Mayor Combe, who was well acquainted with the amount of munitions at the fort and the training of the soldiers, realized that such an attack would be suicidal and dissuaded the people from attacking the post. At that point a patrol under the command of Capt. Samuel P. Lyon, commander of D Company, arrived on the scene. Mayor Combe now learned that the people in the post believed that the raiders had been civilians who had been firing at the fort. Major Penrose had sent the patrol out to find Captain Macklin, who was missing from the post and whom Major Penrose feared had been hurt in the shooting. Lyon escorted the mayor back to the fort, where the two leaders had a brief discussion. Penrose still believed that civilians had been firing at the post. During the shooting, he had the company commanders take roll, and all of his men were reported as "present or accounted for." However, in order to mollify Combe, he ordered another roll call, a thorough inspection of all the rifles at sunrise, and a careful check of the garrison. While the soldiers secured the fort for the night, Mayor Combe went back to the town and began his own investigation. He retraced the route of the raiders and found seven cartridge cases, one cartridge, and one empty rifle clip, into which the cases fitted perfectly. He identified them as ammunition that was used in the army's new Springfield rifle, Model 1903, and this evidence further convinced him that the soldiers were guilty.[7]

The next day Mayor Combe initiated the first of a series of inquiries into what happened. He helped create a committee of prominent local citizens to carry out an investigation to determine who had done the shooting. The committee called

6. Court of Inquiry, pp. 2159, 2199–2208; 2212–14, 2219–27, 2237–42.
7. Senate Hearings, pp. 2380–2451; Summary Discharge, pp. 30–31, 63; Senate Hearings, pp. 2388–89.

twenty-two witnesses, eight of whom claimed they had seen black soldiers shooting. The testimony was not taken under oath and was proved unreliable. Charles C. Madison, one of the witnesses, identified the soldiers as the raiders by their voices alone. "I was raised among them [Blacks] and know their voices pretty well." The information gathered by the committee was limited to evidence against the soldiers, for they had their minds made up before they began the investigation.

Q. We are inquiring into the matter of last night with a view to ascertaining who the guilty parties are. We know they were Negro soldiers.

On 15 August, two days after the shooting, the committee reached its conclusion: The soldiers had raided Brownsville.[8]

The army now began its own investigations. The first was conducted by Major Penrose. Early on the morning of 14 August Captain Macklin examined the garrison road near Barracks D and B, where he found several cartridge cases and a few clips of government ammunition concentrated in a small space, about ten to fifteen inches in diameter. He did not find a single bullet hole in the walls of the barracks. All the ammunition was accounted for and all the rifles were clean. At this juncture, Mayor Combe arrived and presented the evidence he had gathered the previous evening. This put a new light on what Major Penrose already had found and brought him to the conclusion that his men had carefully planned and executed the raid. This conclusion was also reached by the second army investigator, Maj. Augustus P. Blocksom, assistant to the Inspector General, Southwestern Division, who was sent by President Roosevelt. Blocksom arrived on 18 August, and within two days he had submitted a report. The raid, he said, was provoked by the civilians' slights to the soldiers because of their race and was carried out by nine to fifteen soldiers. He had made no attempt to see if there was evidence for any other explanation of the event. As a result of his findings, he recommended the removal of the troops, "the sooner the better." The President agreed to order the troops out of the town and into a post "where there are white troops." The War Department selected Fort Reno, Oklahoma.[9]

8. Senate Hearings, pp. 2393–94; Summary Discharge, pp. 82, 84; 446.
9. Summary Discharge, pp. 31, 34, 38.

Major Penrose faced a problem before he could leave for Oklahoma. He had to decide what to do with twelve of his men charged by the state of Texas with murder and/or conspiracy to murder. He did not want to turn the men over to the civil authorities, for he feared local lynch law. He telegraphed for instructions. After studying this question, Roosevelt ordered Penrose to leave the prisoners under the control of the military authorities at Fort Sam Houston in San Antonio pending a final decision by the Cameron County Grand Jury. When the grand jury was unable to find sufficient facts to indict those soldiers who were charged or any of the men, the state dropped the case. Instead of freeing the black soldiers, however, the army continued to hold them.[10] This disregard of the principles of justice typified the actions of the Government in the whole incident.

While the soldiers moved to Fort Reno, Major Blocksom continued his investigation of the incident. In his final report he noted that black soldiers and civilians were "much more aggressive" in their attitudes "on the social equality question" than they used to be. He reiterated his conclusion that the soldiers had raided the town. As causes of the riot he credited the reports about the attitude of the Texas militia, the opposition of the residents of Brownsville to the black troops, the Tate-Newton affair, the Reid shoving, and the Evans attack. His conclusions were mainly drawn from the eyewitness accounts, while the bullets, cartridge cases, and clips found in the town merely corroborated this source. Blocksom believed that undoubtedly many of the soldiers knew who had done the shooting but refused to tell. He suggested that if they did not disclose which of them had done the shooting, all "should be made to suffer." Major Penrose, however, was not satisfied with Blocksom's efforts and intensified his attempts to find the guilty parties. As the battalion commander reported a month later, in late September, Penrose felt that extra work and confinement to the post would encourage the soldiers to confess. When this method did not work, he recommended two new plans. His favored plan was to hire three black detectives to pose as soldiers and then put all the black soldiers back on the preconfinement routine. He believed that if they felt they were no longer suspect the Blacks would begin talking about the shooting. The alternative proposal was to announce to the three companies that if no one

10. Ibid., pp. 46–51; 107; 66.

confessed his guilt, he would arbitrarily discharge 20 per cent of the companies each month, until only the final 20 per cent remained. The department commander, Gen. William McCaskey, felt that both of these plans were rather drastic, especially the latter, and recommended that neither be accepted.[11]

President Roosevelt made the next move. He studied the sworn statements collected by Col. Leonard A. Lovering, acting Inspector General, Southwestern Division. Colonel Lovering had questioned many of the men about what troubles they had encountered in Brownsville prior to 13 August, what they had been doing during the shooting, whether they knew of any men who had been absent around the time of the shooting, or whether they heard any talk that might implicate any of the soldiers. The men had all denied having raided the town. Roosevelt weighed these assertions, along with the contrary reports of Majors Penrose and Blocksom, and then made his decision. He ordered Gen. Ernest A. Garlington, the Inspector General, to find the men in the regiment who had committed the shooting. Following the line suggested by Major Blocksom and also partially by Major Penrose, Roosevelt authorized General Garlington to deliver an ultimatum to the men: If the guilty parties were not revealed within a certain time then the entire three companies would be discharged without honor from the service and barred from reenlistment or from appointment in the civil service.[12]

General Garlington began his mission in San Antonio where he interviewed each of the twelve prisoners separately. As soon as he began to discuss the incidents at Brownsville, "The countenance of the individual . . . assumed a wooden, stolid look." They all denied any knowledge of the affray or of anyone involved in it. General Garlington interpreted their reactions as evidence to reinforce his preconceived idea that some soldiers were guilty. Even though he presented his ultimatum, the threat was unsuccessful in producing any admissions of guilt or new evidence. Garlington interpreted this reaction not as an expression of innocence but as evidence of a conspiracy of silence. He then went on to Fort Reno where his efforts had the same results. In this report of 22 October General Garlington recom-

11. Ibid., pp. 65; 61–64; 105. See also AGO 1166395; Summary Discharge, p. 107.

12. Summary Discharge, pp. 110–11, 116. The complete report including 143 statements is found on pp. 110–77; 109.

mended to President Roosevelt that all the soldiers in B, C, and D companies, Twenty-fifth Infantry, be discharged without honor. He said that they all stood together "in a determination to resist the detection of the guilty; therefore they should stand together when the penalty falls." He felt that they were guilty men engaged in a conspiracy of silence, even though he could "find no evidence of such [an] understanding." President Roosevelt accepted the findings of his Inspector General, and on 9 November, the day after the congressional elections, the order was made public. The black soldiers did not resist being discharged, though many of them cried as they turned in their rifles and left the service. A total of 167 enlisted men were discharged. More than half of them had spent five or more years in the service, and 10 of them had spent fifteen or more years in the army.[13]

To people in different parts of the country, the decision appeared to be influenced by racial prejudice. Though Secretary Taft denied this implication in the War Department's annual report, the fact that soldiers were black and had allegedly raided a white community invited this accusation. The immediate reaction of many black civilians to the dismissal of the three companies was outrage. To them it was worse than the lynchings and the miscarriages of civilian justice that were common in this period. Participation in the army was one of the few ways in which Blacks could show that they were citizens. The discharge of the soldiers was bad enough, but because Theodore Roosevelt implemented the order, it seemed a betrayal. The Blacks had supposedly saved his life in Cuba, and he was purported to be a friend of the race.[14]

They vented their frustration and anger upon the Republican party and especially upon Booker T. Washington. He did not publicize any of his efforts to mitigate the effect of the discharge order or to get it reversed. Although these attempts were completely unsuccessful, he somewhat successfully tried to tone down the black press's attack on the Roosevelt Administration. In the long run, however, he failed. Though Blacks were able to forgive the Republicans and continued to vote for their candidates, they never forgot that Washington did not come to the defense of the soldiers but instead defended the President.

13. Ibid., p. 179; pp. 180–82. The complete report is found in Summary Discharge, pp. 178–83; 183, 185–86; *ANJ,* 17 November 1906, p. 314.

14. Sec War 1906, p. 34.

Washington's role in the Brownsville incident was one of the contributing factors to his loss in power. At the same time the President, Secretary of War, and the War Department were inundated with letters, post cards, telegrams, petitions, resolutions, and newspaper articles denouncing the action of the President. The administration could not ignore the uproar. In late November President Roosevelt wrote to Silas McBee, a close friend and editor of the *Churchman*, that it had been shown "conclusively that some of these troops made a midnight . . . assault" upon Brownsville, and all of them "instantly banded together to shield the criminals." He was under pressure, he wrote, from "sentimentalists" and northern politicians who wanted to keep the black vote, but in this case he would not "for one moment consider the political effect." He felt that he could use this case to teach Blacks that they should not "band together to shelter their own criminals."[15]

Pressure mounted for a reopening of the case. The Constitutional League of the United States, usually called the Constitution League, made the first efforts. This racially mixed organization was founded in 1904 and was largely financed by John H. Milholland, a prosperous white manufacturer and progressive Republican politician. This group wanted to defend the rights of helpless Blacks through the courts and the law, a strategy that was later adopted by the NAACP. In those states where Blacks were disfranchised, the Constitution League wanted to enforce the second section of the Fourteenth Amendment, which would have proportionally reduced that state's representation in Congress. When the controversy over Brownsville began, Milholland was working to end disfranchisement on the grounds that the Republican party could not afford to lose black votes. The League quickly added defense of the Brownsville soldiers to its tasks. Mrs. Mary Church Terrell, a prominent black leader and a member of the league, talked with Secretary Taft about the discharge order. Milholland, the president of the organization, arranged to send an investigator, Gilchrist Stewart, to obtain information from the soldiers. In his initial report, made in late November, Stewart presented different findings than Major Blocksom. He believed that if any

15. Ann J. Lane, "The Brownsville Affray," p. 155; AGO 1201054; AGO 1185681. For other protest letters also see AGO 1188426, 1190580, 1182886, 1182834, 1183637, 1183977, 1181130, 1181630; Theodore Roosevelt to Mr. Silas Lynch, 27 November 1906, as quoted in Tinsley, "The Brownsville Affray," pp. 59–60.

soldier had participated in the shooting, he would have been too far from the post to have made it back for roll call. He also noted that the patrol headed by Captain Lyon, and dispatched after the affray, found men in town "in khaki uniforms and regulation hats" who were armed with rifles. It was later discovered that these men were policemen. Stewart also dealt with the physical evidence used to prove the soldiers had done the shooting—the cartridges, cases, and clips found in the town. He stated that Government ammunition could have been used in the rifles owned by the townspeople, that the clips and cartridge cases could have been found on the target range at the post, and that the soldiers of the Twenty-sixth Infantry had given away Springfield rifle ammunition to the townspeople in the months before they left. He felt that the evidence of the cartridge cases could as easily be used to prove that some citizens in Brownsville had done the shooting. As for the previous investigations of Major Blocksom and General Garlington, Stewart felt that both men had been biased against the soldiers and did not allow the men to give any testimony not directly supporting their prejudices. This report and a final summary report issued later convinced the Constitution League to call for a congressional investigation to check on the facts and then to propose and pass remedial legislation. As was to be expected, the military authorities denied the validity of Stewart's reports. Secretary Taft stated that the idea that the citizens had framed the soldiers was "so grotesque in its improbability and absurdity as hardly to call for discussion or comment." Major Blocksom commented that little new evidence had been brought out in Stewart's reports. Congress did not cease its demands for an investigation.[16]

By late November 1906 many of the basic points in the case had been established. The army regarded the Blacks as guilty, their punishment as lenient, and looked down upon those that questioned their ideas and conclusions. The opposition felt the Blacks had not been proven guilty and that their punishment consequently was unjustified. These two opinions led to several years had delivered its verdict.

---

16. Ann J. Lane, *The Brownsville Affair: National Crisis and Black Reaction*, pp. 26–27; Roi Ottley, ed., *Sketch and History of the Constitution League of the United States; Summary Discharge*, pp. 196–200; 205–22; 15; 236–37.

IX

THE BROWNSVILLE RAID
THE HEARINGS

After the black soldiers were discharged by President Roosevelt, they began to try to defend themselves. However, never in the hearings that ensued during the next four years were the soldiers given the benefit of even marginally acceptable judicial procedures. The Administration continued to believe the soldiers were guilty and demanded that they prove their innocence, but they were never told exactly what measures they should take.

The leader of the attack on the Roosevelt Administration, which began with the opening of Congress in December 1906, was Sen. Joseph B. Foraker, a Republican from Ohio. When he had first read about the President's decision in November 1906 he felt that it was rather drastic but probably based upon evidence that had not yet been made public. However, when he saw Roosevelt's evidence, he felt that it was "flimsy, unreliable and insufficient and untruthful." Foraker then decided that he must urge an investigation. Some people suspected Foraker's motives, and believed he was more interested in obtaining support for the presidential nomination than in seeing justice done. Foraker's resolution for an investigation provoked a strongly worded message from the President, which defended his course of action. In the message Roosevelt called the raid a "horrible atrocity" without any excuse or justification, and claimed that it was "unparalled for infamy" in the annals of the army. He repeated that "there can be no doubt whatever" that many of the noncommissioned officers were privy to the attack either before or after it occurred. If the black soldiers decided to stand by "criminals of their own race" they had to beware of "the most dreadful day of reckoning."[1]

Senator Foraker continued to press for the Military Affairs

1. Joseph B. Foraker, *Notes of a Busy Life,* 2:234; *New York Times,* 5, December 1906, 26 December 1906; Summary Discharge, pp. 2–9.

Committee to conduct an investigation. This idea, now in the form of a motion, was hotly debated in January and February 1907, for the prestige of the Administration was being questioned. Sen. Henry Cabot Lodge, a friend of Roosevelt's, offered an amendment to the motion, which said that Roosevelt was within his powers in the actions he took. Those who opposed the Lodge amendment, including Foraker, in effect opposed the President. Roosevelt then tried to heal some of the divisions in the party. He revoked the provision in his order that had barred the soldiers from entering the civil service and even admitted that he should not have made the decision at all. He also sent to the Senate the results of the second investigation into the shooting incident by the War Department. The President had sent Major Blocksom and Milton D. Purdy, the assistant to the Attorney General, to Brownsville in December 1906 to make a thorough investigation. In his summary the President said that the evidence again showed "beyond any possibility of honest question" that some soldiers had done the shooting and that most of the soldiers at the post had knowledge of the incident. At the end of the message, in an apparent attempt to draw support from Senator Foraker, he extended an offer that if any of the soldiers individually showed to his satisfaction "that he is clear of guilt, or of shielding the guilty," he would readmit the man to the army.[2]

In the report that accompanied the presidential message the two investigators detailed the procedures they had followed. They had gone to Brownsville, gathered together the eyewitnesses, and questioned them under oath. An example of the quality of the evidence is the testimony of James P. McDonnel. He said that when he heard the firing he went down near the post and "instantly" recognized the men as being soldiers. He made this statement, even though he admitted they were half a block away from him and there was no light. A guest at the Miller Hotel, Hale Odin, testified that he was able to identify the uniforms and skin color of the men from the light of the flashes from their rifles. The two investigators also found new evidence to support their conclusions, the bullet holes in the houses. A bullet had grazed the lintel of Ygnacio Garza's porch, and by sighting along the groove Blocksom and Purdy were able to determine that the shots were fired from B Company's bar-

2. U.S., Congress, Senate, *Congressional Record,* 59th Cong., 2d sess., 1906–1907, pp. 552; 684–85; 687–88; *New York Times,* 5 January 1907; Summary Discharge, p. 2; i–vi.

racks. The investigation also explored another facet of the evidence, the bullets, cartridges, cases, and clips found in the town. Capt. Hanson E. Ely, Twenty-sixth Infantry, testified that these pieces had convinced him that the black soldiers had committed the shooting. Some bullets had been extracted from the buildings and had the marks of four lands, or grooves, on them. These marks could only have been made by an army weapon, such as the Springfield rifle, that was issued to the troops only in April and May 1906. The clips and cases found in the streets were also clearly identified as ammunition issued by the army for the Springfield rifle. Since the rifle and the shells were the newest military equipment, they were available only to the black troops, not to the citizens.[3] It was clear that the investigators sought only evidence to support Roosevelt's actions.

President Roosevelt also tried to deal with another issue against his discharge of the soldiers, the claim that his action had no precedent. Roosevelt asked the War Department to back him, but although it conducted "a protracted search" of the military records, it failed to find a precedent. Roosevelt then ignored this charge.[4]

The Purdy-Blocksom report and the accompanying message succeeded in robbing Senator Foraker of much of his support. A compromise version of the resolution that was accepted by the Ohio senator and his friends was passed. It read: *"Resolved,* That without questioning the legality or justice of any act of the President . . ."* a committee investigation of the Brownsville raid would be conducted. The modified Foraker resolution was accepted by a vote of 46 to 19. The investigation that the Senator had long been promoting was now to begin.[5]

Amidst the discussion of the Brownsville raid and the discharge of the black soldiers, questions were raised as to why the regimental officers were not also punished. Originally the War Department had planned no action. As far as they were concerned the officers at Fort Brown "did everything that could be expected of them to detect the guilty soldiers." However, as the debate intensified, this conclusion came under scrutiny. The Army General Staff began an inquiry into whether the officers at the post had really been performing their duty and had done

3. Summary Discharge, pp. 30–32, 77; 43; 163–69. See also Summary Discharge, pp. 170, 175, 192, 195.

4. Summary Discharge, p. 311.

5. U.S.,Congress, Senate, *Congressional Record,* 59th Cong., 2d sess., 1906–1907, pp. 1434, 1512.

everything to find the guilty parties. There was also some question about where Captain Macklin had been during the shooting, since all efforts to find him had failed. After some deliberation the War Department decided that both Major Penrose and Captain Macklin, the officer of the day on 13 August, should be court-martialed. In essence the Major was being tried for not taking the proper precautions to prevent the raid by the Blacks and not being diligent enough to detect the guilty soldiers after the shooting had occurred.[6]

The month-long court-martial proceedings took place at Fort Sam Houston in February and March 1907, the same time as the Senate hearings began. In order to win his case, Capt. Charles Hay, Judge Advocate, felt he had to prove the soldiers' guilt. The defense, headed by Lt. Col. Edwin F. Glenn, tried to establish that there was reasonable doubt that the soldiers had done the shooting and that given the situation prior to midnight 13 August 1906, Major Penrose had taken adequate precautions to prevent any incident. As a result, for the first and only time the witnesses to the shooting were subjected to a rigorous cross-examination in a courtroom.

The first group of witnesses were townspeople who testified as to what they saw the night of the raid. Colonel Glenn was quite thorough in his cross-examination, and the flimsiness of most of their testimonies became apparent. George W. Rendall, who lived across the road from the post, testified that he saw the soldiers firing from inside the walls of the fort. Under cross-examination it became apparent that Rendall, who was seventy-two years old and blind in one eye, made this identification on a dark night, about one hundred feet from the raiders. He also admitted that he had discussed the events quite often with his friends. As a result of these talks, he had changed some of the facts he had given in earlier testimony. The prosecution next placed on the stand the various investigators, such as Major Blocksom, in an attempt to prove that Major Penrose should have known that a riot was imminent. The defense cross-examined Major Blocksom on his idea that the raid was premeditated. The major stated, "All of them [the soldiers] couldn't have

6. *ANJ,* 17 November 1906, p. 315; Summary Discharge, pp. 294–95; File 20754, Records of the Office of the Judge Advocate General, Document File, 1894–1912, NA, RG 153; U.S., Congress, Senate, *Proceedings of a General Court-Martial Convened at Headquaters, Department of Texas, San Antonio, Tex., February 4, 1907 in the Case of Maj. Charles W. Penrose, Twenty-fifth United States Infantry,* Senate Document 402, pt. 2, 60th Cong., 1st sess., 1907–1908, p. 4.

had a spontaneous resolution to do this at one time." The eyewitness accounts of the townspeople and the investigators from
the War Department furnished the major part of the case presented by Captain Hay.[7]

The defense questioned a number of black soldiers, who testified about conditions in Brownsville and the events that occurred at the time of the raid. In cross-examining, the prosecution tried to emphasize discrepancies between the accounts
the soldiers had previously given to other interrogators like
Colonel Lovering or the Senate Military Affairs Committee and
the ones they were giving in the courtroom. Corp. Samuel
Wheeler had testified before the Senate committee that he had
heard horses riding away from the post at the time the first shots
were fired. Because he had never mentioned the occurence before, Captain Hay was suspicious and questioned him closely on
the point. The soldier retorted: "That's the first time I had an
opportunity to tell anybody. I have been cut off when trying to
tell other people about that."[8]

The next phase of the defense began with the testimony of 1st
Lt. Henry A. Wiegenstein, Twenty-fifth Infantry. He testified
about a series of night experiments he had conducted to determine what one could see in a situation similar to that which
existed in the streets of Brownsville on the night of the raid. He
had stationed ten men in an arroyo, or deep gulley, and then
placed several officers up on the bank, at about the same height
and distance that many of the citizens were from the raiders
they identified as black soldiers. The soldiers in the experiment,
both black and white, were dressed in the uniform that was
worn by the black soldiers stationed at Fort Brown. They tried
to approximate as closely as possible the lighting conditions of
that dark, moonless night of the raid. The soldiers fired their
Springfield rifles, and the officers tried to identify the skin color
of the men. All they could see was the flash of the rifle. Another
experiment began with a series of walls and boxes, which sim-
ulated the construction of the buildings in Brownsville. The
experimenters then fired bullets through them from various
distances. The experiments proved that the bullets did not con-
sistently follow the same type of path, so one could not really
tell where they were fired from. "The effect, generally, was that

7. U.S., Congress, Senate, *Proceedings of a General Court-Martial,* pp. 9–25, 613.
8. For an example see the testimony of Battalion Sergeant Major Spottswood
W. Taliaferro in Ibid., pp. 760–96.

the bullet was deflected from its original course and in no two instances the same." The defense claimed that the Purdy-Blocksom evidence obtained by sighting along the grooves in Garza's house was meaningless.[9]

The last major witness for the defense was Major Penrose. On the stand he stated that at first he had been convinced that civilians were shooting at the post, but the lack of any bullet holes in the barracks, along with the cases and cartridges found by Captain Macklin and Mayor Combe, convinced him that some black soldiers were guilty. He believed it was a planned raid because all the rifles were clean the next morning, and "the ammunition was carefully and accurately accounted for." Major Penrose attempted to exonerate himself but maintained that the Blacks were guilty. The prosecutor sensed he had not made his case and therefore, in his final argument, cautioned the court that an unqualified verdict of not guilty would be a proclamation not only of Penrose's innocence but also of the Twenty-fifth Infantry's. The court found Penrose not guilty but the black soldiers guilty. They did not blame Penrose for his failure to prevent the raid, but they still felt that the men of the Twenty-fifth had committed the shooting.[10] This verdict is what one would expect from a tribunal composed of army officers. If they had ruled differently, they would have had to face the wrath of Roosevelt. Although the defense had cast a reasonable doubt on the idea that the black soldiers were guilty, in this court that was not sufficient.

The charges brought against Captain Macklin avoided the issue of the guilt of the soldiers. The major charges at this court-martial concerned why he had not appeared when the shooting started and why, when he had been found asleep, the soldiers could not awaken him. During the proceedings, it became evident that he was a very sound sleeper and that most of the men sent to arouse him apparently went to the quarters of another officer. As a result, the court found him not guilty and made no mention of the conduct of the black soldiers in its findings.[11]

After the court-martial, attention shifted to the chamber of the Senate hearings. The hearings of the Senate Military Com-

9. Ibid., p. 874. His whole testimony is found in the proceedings on pp. 870–77; 989–94; 995–1011.

10. Ibid., pp. 1149–51; 1167; 1222–24; 1227–36; 1238–39; 1242–47; 1248.

11. AGO 1191361. Macklin Court-martial, p. 4. See also pp. 6–7; 247.

mittee were conducted sporadically from February 1907 to February 1908. Over fifty of the discharged soldiers testified before the committee. A great variety of topics was raised in the course of the proceedings. The senators closely questioned the soldiers about their feelings toward the residents of Brownsville before 13 August, the events that occurred during and shortly after the raid, and their belief in the innocence of the regiment. The soldiers all denied knowledge of any conspiracy or of having any real provocation to raid the town.[12]

Other questions were designed to provide evidence for Senator Foraker's new theory on the origins and perpetrators of the riot. The basic premise was that some whites in Brownsville wanted to get rid of the black soldiers, so they staged a raid, while dressed in army uniforms. The pseudo-black raiders left old army cartridge cases on the ground to implicate the soldiers. The senators closely questioned a number of enlisted men of the Twenty-sixth Infantry, the regiment that had preceeded the Twenty-fifth in Brownsville, about the reaction in the town to the news that the Twenty-fifth would be arriving, whether army ammunition was available to the citizens, and whether the white soldiers had discarded part of their uniforms before they left town.[13]

Senator Foraker used the thirty-three cartridge cases found in the town to further develop his theory. The cases had been sent to the Springfield Arsenal, where the army ordnance experts compared the marks on the cartridge cases with those made by all of the rifles available to the men of the Twenty-fifth Infantry. The report showed that all of the cases had been fired from only four different rifles. These particular rifles belonged to men in B Company. Three of the Blacks who owned the rifles denied having been involved in the shooting. The owner of the fourth rifle, Sgt. William Blaney, was on leave when the firing occurred. Lt. George Lawrason of the Twenty-fifth also testified that on the night of the shooting he had checked B Company's storeroom. In order to get to the arms chest that contained Sergeant Blaney's rifle and several other arms in storage, he had to remove bunks and other heavy items. In addition, all of the stored rifles were coated with cosmoline oil, which made it

12. Senate Hearings, pp. 25–53; *Springfield Republican,* n.d., as quoted in *ANJ,* 23 February 1907, p. 696.

13. For an example see the testimony of 1st Sgt. Nelson Huron, Twenty-sixth Infantry, Senate Hearings, pp. 1111–48.

almost impossible to fire them. The lieutenant also testified about a large case of undecapped cartridge cases that the company had taken with them from Fort Niobrara and then left on the porch of the barracks at Fort Brown. Within a few days of the regiment's arrival, a guard had to be stationed at the barracks to stop the citizens from taking things. Lawrason also testified that cases ejected from the Springfield rifles usually were distributed in an area of about eight to ten feet from the rifle.[14] This testimony helped add evidence for Senator Foraker's theory. Some citizens, according to the Ohio senator, had taken cartridge cases from the box and live ammunition and uniforms from the discards of the Twenty-sixth Infantry. These unknown civilians, dressed as soldiers, had then raided the town and dropped the cases obtained from the Twenty-fifth Infantry. This theory was to form part of Senator Foraker's plea for readmission of the black soldiers into the army.

Foraker's supporters also wanted to disprove General Garlington's belief that there was a conspiracy of silence. Harry S. Grier, a second lieutenant of the Twenty-fifth Infantry, raised several points which he felt made the idea invalid. Despite the widely held opinion, black soldiers in his experience were not more secretive than white soldiers. He cited several examples including the fact that Corporal Madison had reported the incident concerning Reid to him. He doubted any conspiracy because the soldiers had remained silent even after being confined to the post and threatened by General Garlington. However, an even sterner and previously unreported test occurred during the confinement at Fort Reno. Five black soldiers had been captured after leaving Fort Reno. They were given the choice of eighteen months in the stockade and a dishonorable discharge, or, if they could tell the commander all they knew about the events at Brownsville, their sentences would not be so severe. The men insisted that they knew nothing and went to prison.[15]

The statements of the regimental officers concerning the guilt of their men varied during the hearings. In September and October 1906 Captains Macklin and Lyon, as well as Major Penrose, all testified that they were quite certain that some men in their battalion had committed the crime. However, the evidence presented before the Penrose court-martial and the Sen-

---

14. Ibid., pp. 1309; 1440–41; 1582; 1599–1607.
15. Ibid., pp. 1740–41.

ate Military Affairs Committee began to change their minds. As Captain Macklin said, the longer the investigations were continued "the more I feel satisfied that the men did not do the shooting." [16]

Foraker also made the point that the officers' judgment of the black soldiers was affected by their conceptions about race. General Garlington admitted that he would not believe the word of a black man when he was testifying about a crime. Garlington claimed that the basis of his statements about the secretiveness of the Blacks came from "a lifetime of my experience with them." His position indicated that his whole effort at San Antonio and Fort Reno had been a sham. Apparently he would not have believed what the black soldiers said even if they testified they were guilty.[17]

In February 1908 the Military Affairs Committee finished taking evidence. It was able to agree on very little except "That the testimony fails to identify the particular soldier or soldiers who participated in the shooting affray at Brownsville, Texas, on the night of August 13–14, 1906." The committee also could not agree to approve any one report nor send out one bill that would satisfy all parties. The majority (four Republicans and the five Democrats on the committee) stated that the shooting was done by some soldiers of the Twenty-fifth, while the minority (the other four Republicans including Senator Foraker) noted that they could find no motive for the raid and no real evidence that any of the soldiers had done the shooting. In addition, Senators Foraker and Morgan G. Bulkeley of Connecticut submitted a seventy-four-page analysis of the evidence that they used to support their theory of the events. They proposed a bill to help out the soldiers, S. 5729, which provided that an affirmation of innocence by the soldiers would make them eligible for reenlistment. The President, in an effort to counter Senator Foraker, proposed a bill, S. 6206, which would have allowed him to reinstate any man "who in his judgment" was not involved in the shooting in Brownsville or in the conspiracy of silence. Roosevelt thought the other bill was simply "a proposal to condone murder and perjury in the past and put a premium upon perjury in the future." He wrote to several people, including Sen. Francis Warren of Wyoming, that if the bill should be enacted "no reappointment would be made under it by me." Senator Foraker tried to bring his bill up for a vote

16. Ibid., pp. 1788, 1843, 1944.
17. Ibid., pp. 2720–47.

before Congress adjourned for the 1908 political conventions and the presidential campaign. Since the party leaders did not want to deal with this controversial issue, they opposed the action. The Republican leaders persuaded Senator Foraker to postpone a vote; they even promised to help him in his reelection campaign. Given the pressure and the inducement, it was not too surprising that the Senator finally agreed to postpone consideration of his bill until December 1908.[18]

While Congress debated, the Administration did not cease its efforts to find further evidence to support its actions. The Secretary of War had received a letter in April 1908 from William B. Baldwin, a private detective, and Herbert J. Browne, a Washington journalist, offering their services in locating the fourteen men from B Company who they believed had stormed Brownsville. However, they neglected to tell Secretary Taft that they had previously worked for Senator Foraker and had been fired by him because they were incompetent. Ever anxious to improve its case, the Government signed a contract with Browne and Baldwin to ferret out the guilty parties. The investigators sent out many agents to track down the soldiers. In July they reported that they had sufficient evidence to "indict, convict and hang" four soldiers, including Boyd Conyers and John Holloman. Based upon a confession obtained from Conyers, Browne felt he was able to reconstruct the whole raid. He deduced that the soldiers had expected the citizens of Brownsville to be hostile, that preparations for the shooting had been made before the men even left Fort Niobrara, Nebraska, and that cartridges had been put aside for that purpose. Once the soldiers had encountered the expected hostility, they were ready for action. Several of them met at Allison's saloon, and, led by John Holloman, they planned a midnight attack on the town. The sergeant on duty at B Company's barracks opened the rifle racks for the men, and the raiders then went out into the streets firing at the citizens. Once the raid was over, the used cartridges were replaced from a stockpile John Holloman had built up. The President sent this report to Congress in December 1908 and said that it clearly established "the fact that the colored

---

18. Ibid., pp. 3410–11; U.S., Congress, Senate, *The Brownsville Affray,* Senate Document 389, 60th Cong., 1st sess., 1907–1908, pp. 24–105; 22; U.S., Congress, Senate, *Congressional Record,* 60th Cong., 1st sess., 1907–1908, p. 3557; Elting E. Morison, ed., *The Letters of Theodore Roosevelt,* 6:967; AGO 1763692; *The New York Times,* 14 May 1908; U.S., Congress, Senate, *Congressional Record,* 60th Cong., 1st sess., 1907–1908, pp. 4710–20, 4962–69; *The New York Times,* 14 May 1908.

soldiers did the shooting." This was a fact which, according to previous messages, had conclusively been proven twice before. The President recommended again that only those men whom the Secretary of War "finds to have been innocent and whom he finds to have done all in his power to help bring to justice the guilty," be allowed back into the service.[19]

Senator Foraker responded quickly. He produced a series of letters and sworn statements, which brought into question the validity of the confession of Boyd Conyers. In one instance Browne had claimed that Conyers had confessed in the presence of the county sheriff. The sheriff swore that Conyers had not made any confession at all. The Ohio senator called the whole procedure "atrocious, revolting, shocking to every sense of fairness, justice, and even common decency."[20]

Undaunted, the detectives continued their investigation and found what they believed was further evidence to support their version of the Brownsville raid. Browne went to St. Louis and John Holloman consented to be interviewed in the presence of a white lawyer. According to Browne this interview convinced the lawyer that Holloman had participated in the raid and was responsible for it. In his report on this interview the detective suggested that a possible motive for the raid was money. Holloman had had a good business at Fort Niobrara lending money to the men, and he earned $250 to $300 a week in loans at 25 per cent interest per month. After the move to Texas he had a smaller group to work on and did not get along as well with the local merchants as he had in Nebraska. In addition, Holloman had learned that his saloon was to be closed down. According to Browne, Holloman then decided that he could improve his economic position if the battalions were reunited at another post. He goaded the men, building up their hostility toward the townspeople. "Out of this material of drunken and inflamed soldiery there was no difficulty on John Holloman's part in organizing his raiders." The Secretary of War sent this report to the President with the comment that while it had "some interesting features," further evidence was not needed to convince Congress that the Administration had acted correctly.

19. AGO 1763692; U.S., Congress, Senate, *Employment of Herbert J. Browne and W. G. Baldwin by the War Department at Brownsville*, Senate Document 626, 60th Cong., 2d sess., 1908–1909, pp. 2, 4; AGO 1763692; Special Message, pp. 9–11; 3; 4.

20. U.S., Congress, Senate, *Congressional Record*, 60th Cong., 2d sess., 1908–1909, pp. 191–94, 800–803. For Browne's reply see AGO 1763692.

The Administration was sure it was going to win the battle with Senator Foraker. The President agreed, though he noted that Browne's report again proved the black soldiers had done the shooting. The report was never sent to Congress and remained in the files of the War Department.[21]

As the Secretary of War had noted, by late January 1909 the debate in the Senate was coming to a close, helped along by a compromise proposed by Sen. Nelson W. Aldrich of Rhode Island. President Roosevelt took a hand in drafting the Aldrich compromise. He wrote to the Rhode Island senator that the board of inquiry created by the bill should only make the soldiers eligible for reenstatement. The President made it quite clear that he wanted the executive branch to have the right to make the final decision on the readmission of the soldiers to the service. This revised version of the Foraker bill gave the Secretary of War the power to appoint a five-man court of inquiry made up of retired army officers. It was up to them to decide which men were eligible for reenlistment. The bill was passed 56 to 26 on a fairly straight party-line vote. The bill then went to the House of Representatives where it also was passed by the Republican majority. Although Senator Foraker was not completely satisfied with the new law, which Roosevelt signed on his last day in office, he realized that since he was leaving the Senate, he must accept compromise or lose the fight altogether. He feared, correctly as it turned out, that the law could be construed by a hostile court of inquiry to mean that all the soldiers were guilty and that the burden of proof rested on their shoulders.[22]

The last stage of the Brownsville affray began in the first days of the Taft Administration. After some discussion, five retired officers were chosen to sit on the Court of Inquiry: Lt. Gen. Samuel B. M. Young, Maj. Gen. Joseph P. Sanger, Brig. Gens. John W. Wilson, Theodore Schwann, and Butler D. Pierce. Capt. Charles R. Howland, Twenty-first Infantry, was chosen as recorder for the court. His function was to investigate the affray and to present the evidence. Drafting the instructions for the court posed a problem for the War Department. In the

---

21. Special Message, p. 24; AGO 1763692.

22. Theodore Roosevelt to Nelson Aldrich, in Morison, *The Letters of Theodore Roosevelt*, 6:1482, 1486, 1501; U.S., Congress, Senate, *Congressional Record*, 60th Cong., 2d sess., 1908–1909, pp. 1579, 2948. *The New York Times*, 24 February 1909; U.S., Congress, House of Representatives, *Congressional Record*, 60th Cong., 2d sess., 1908–1909, pp. 3399–3400; Foraker, *Notes*, 2: 313–14.

original version there was a stipulation for the court to investigate whether the President had been correct in his actions. However, the new Secretary of War objected to this provision. He felt that it was "embarrasing" and an "annoying and unwarranted criticism" of the President and might lead to a controversy that would be played up in the press. As a result the lines were removed and the court confined to the question of the readmission of the soldiers. The court was instructed that its conclusions "should be affirmative and positive in character and based upon such preponderance of testimony as will support its specific findings." [23] The final provision stated that the soldiers had to prove their innocence, the actions of the Administration were not to be questioned, and no other theories concerning who committed the shooting were to be examined.

The court first met on 4 May 1909. The recorder announced that he was arranging all of the previously gathered evidence in groups so that the members of the court would be able to compare what each witness said at different times about the raid. Consideration of this material began on 17 May and continued until 15 November. In all, the court studied the statements of 325 witnesses. At that point in the proceedings, the court admitted counsel for the soldiers—Brig. Gen. Aaron S. Daggett, a retired army officer who had served with the Twenty-fifth Infantry from 1895 to 1899, and Napoleon B. Marshall, a black lawyer and member of the Constitution League. The court then went to Brownsville, viewed the scene of the shooting, and began to gather new information. In October 1909 B Company's barracks had burned. During the fire there were explosions, which sounded to the onlookers as if ammunition were going off. Since the barracks had not been used since the Twenty-fifth had left it, the recorder suggested that the explosions might have been from ammunition the soldiers had hidden away. A witness testified that he saw Captain Macklin picking up cartridge cases all along the garrison road the morning after the shooting. The final major new witness was James K. Powers, caretaker of the national cemetery at Fort Brown. He testified that on the morning after the shooting a soldier approached him as he was leaving the post to go shopping. At the end of a brief

---

23. AGO 1501287; Court of Inquiry, pp. 1643–44. Brig. Gen. Aaron S. Daggett, chief defense counsel, felt the officers selected for the court were hostile from the beginning. A. S. Daggett to Joseph B. Foraker, 16 November 1909, Foraker, Papers, as quoted in John D. Weaver, *The Brownsville Raid,* p. 225.

conversation the black soldier said, "I want you to understand that I am not one of those men who went out and did the shooting." Capt. Howland then informed the court that they had finished their investigation in Brownsville, though he admitted that there were more possible witnesses. However he felt that "it would merely be corroboration and would multiply the record." Neither the recorder nor General Daggett made any effort to see if any evidence could be found to exonerate the soldiers. The court then returned to Washington.[24]

In the next phase of the hearing, the court questioned many of the soldiers as to what they were doing on the night of 13 August 1906 and, if they had testified previously, tried to clear up some discrepancies in their different testimonies. Not all of the soldiers were allowed to appear before the court, including some who asked to do so. One of the soldiers who did testify was John Holloman, the ringleader, according to Browne. He said that if given the choice he would have done all in his power to prevent the raid because he felt that such an affray would have ruined his business. The court also considered the validity of Boyd Conyers's confession. They heard testimony from him, the sheriff, the detectives, and other parties in an effort to determine which group was telling the truth.[25]

One of the goals of the recorder, who was supposedly impartial but quite obviously against the black soldiers, was to cast doubt on the evidence which Senator Foraker had used to prove the soldiers' innocence. He began by examining the property book of B Company, which contained rifle numbers along with the names of the soldiers who supposedly had possession of them. As a result of his efforts, it became apparent that no one could determine "when a particular rifle was issued to a particular soldier." Captain Howland then presented evidence to invalidate the ammunition counts that had been taken after the raid. He put into the record the official ammunition returns of Lieutenant Lawrason in June and September 1906. In September the company had reported 1,260 fewer rounds than it had in June. There should have been the same amount, for no ammunition was dispensed. The missing rounds could not be accounted for. Similar discrepancies had occurred in the other companies' ammunition accounts. When Captain Macklin was asked if he had any way of accurately determining how much

24. Court of Inquiry, pp. 2–18; 23; 53–55; 68; 83.
25. Ibid., pp. 361–82; 147–239.

ammunition he had on hand before 13 August, he replied, "I don't see of any way." The recorder next considered the question of Sergeant Blaney's rifle. He got Lieutenant Lawrason to admit that he did not know which rifles were in the storeroom and that he had made no check of the numbers on the rifle barrels. With the confused company property book, no one was really sure where Sergeant Blaney's rifle was, and it could have been used in the shooting, cleaned, and then later returned to the box. Senator Foraker's theory had been fairly thoroughly destroyed.[26]

After this presentation the court quickly concluded its business. A series of final arguments was presented by both sides. General Daggett stated that there had never been any evidence of the soldiers' guilt in their testimonies, despite the long ordeal they had been through, and that the citizens had given contradictory testimony on different occasions. He felt that the citizens were the ones responsible for the raid, mainly in an effort to get rid of the soldiers. In conclusion he said:

Punish the guilty, if there are any; restore the innocent to all their rights. If no guilty can be found, be governed by the rule of law that a man is innocent till proved guilty. Better that 100 guilty escape than one innocent man be punished is the adage.

Marshall, one of the attorneys representing the Blacks, declined to submit an argument because he felt the whole proceeding was contrary to the legal concept that all men are innocent until proven guilty. He concluded his brief presentation by saying that he felt confident that truth would triumph in the end. The recorder then delivered his final argument. One of Captain Howland's contentions was that there

is a conspiracy . . . as broad as the garrison, not only by the men, but assisted intentionally or unintentionally by some of the commissioned officers of the post, and such assistance . . . is the principal reason why the facts have never come to light.

Captain Howland stated that while individuals had rights, it was more important to enforce discipline and punish collective guilt. "Until they come forward and turn in the guilty there is no way . . . of making a classification. I accordingly submit that

26. Ibid., pp. 1164, 1345–51, 1407–44, 1460; 1452–54.

the companies . . . should be held responsible . . . for their acts."[27]

After a week of deliberation, the court announced its decision. They held that the men of the Twenty-fifth Infantry were guilty of raiding Brownsville. They also blamed the unit's officers for not preventing the affray and for not detecting the guilty soldiers. Based upon these findings, they decided to readmit fourteen men. Of these, thirteen had been in the barracks when the shooting had occurred, and one had been in the guardhouse. No reasons were ever given why these particular men were readmitted while the others were not; there are no records of the court's deliberations that could explain this decision.[28]

Within a year of the Court of Inquiry's decision all fourteen men were back in the service. These men received back pay from the time of their discharge to their reenlistment. The other 153 men were, by the court's silence, convicted. The entire sequence of events was officially forgotten for the next sixty years.[29]

Then in March 1971 Rep. Augusts F. Hawkins, a black Democrat from Los Angeles, California, introduced a bill to declare all of the discharges honorable. He claimed that he was motivated to take this action by reading John Weaver's recently published study of the affray. The House Military Affairs Committee buried the proposal, but the Pentagon showed some interest and asked Hawkins for the information he had collected. In September 1972 Secretary of the Army Robert F. Kroehlke announced that he had ordered the records of the 153 men changed to honorable discharge. He also said that they were not to be awarded any back pay or allowances. It is probable that the military authorities believed that there were no survivors to be affected by this action. Representative Hawkins wanted more than the mere change of an old record. He conducted a nationwide search, aided by radio, television, and magazines, and found two survivors. Dorsie W. Willis, 87, then living in Minneapolis, announced that he had been vindicated. "None said anything because we had nothing to say. It was a frame-up straight through. They checked our rifles and they hadn't been fired." Shortly afterwards he was presented with a new discharge certificate and an American flag. Several months later

---

27. Ibid., pp. 1674–82, 1684–85; 1467–1623.
28. Ibid., p. 1635.
29. AGO 2404991.

a second black soldier, Edward Warfield, 82, one of the fourteen soldiers who had been allowed to reenlist, received his honorable discharge papers in the office of Representative Hawkins. Warfield commented that he felt "grateful" for the action. Yet for these men, and the many others who had died in the intervening years, such rewards could not heal the psychological and financial wounds inflicted by Roosevelt's actions.[30]

Representative Hawkins did not ignore this problem. He began a campaign to get the Government to pay compensation. In early 1973 he introduced a bill (HR 4382) for this purpose. He proposed two sets of payments. One would involve a sum of $40,000 for each survivor or his widow as compensation for the "pain, suffering, humiliation, and other damage" caused by the Government. In addition those survivors who had not been exonerated would receive either the value of the pension they had lost or payment of $20,000, whichever was greater. The Veterans' Administration and the Office of Management and Budget both indicated that they objected to the large payments proposed. Donald E. Johnson, administrator of Veterans' Affairs, stated that Hawkins's bill would set two bad precedents. The Veterans' Administration did not want to make peacetime service, in this case serving in the army in 1906, equal in pension status to wartime service. In addition the agency opposed the bill because it would have made grandchildren eligible to receive pensions.[31]

By the time a subcommittee of the House Committee of Veterans' Affairs, to which the Hawkins bill had been sent, held hearings on the question, the Nixon Administration had taken a more positive stance. Secretary of the Army Howard H. Callaway sent a letter to the subcommittee stating that he was opposed to a pension, but agreeing that some compensation to the survivors or the widows "is a fair objective through legislation." At those hearings Dorsie Willis testified about the way in which the actions of the Roosevelt Administration had ruined his life. He still proclaimed his innocence. "It was unjust. I was kicked

30. *The New York Times,* 3 October 1972; *San Francisco Examiner,* 12 February 1973, 19 April 1973.

31. U.S., Congress, House of Representatives, *A Bill to confer pensionable status on veterans involved in the Brownsville, Texas, incident of August 13, 1906, and to require the Administrator of Veterans' Affairs to make certain compensatory payments to such veterans and their heirs,* H.R. 4382, 93d Cong., 1st sess., 1973; *The New York Times,* 6 June 1973; U.S., Congress, House of Representatives, *Congressional Record,* 93d Cong., 1st sess., 14 November 1973, H.R. 9980.

out of the Army without a trial and my citizenship taken away from me." Another witness was Sen. Hubert Humphrey, Democrat from Minnesota. He testified that such payments would amount to about $13 million, but he believed it was worth the cost.[32]

Humphrey took a greater interest in the case of his poor black constituent than just to testify for him. On that same day he introduced another compensation bill (S. 1999) into the Senate. The monetary benefits in Humphrey's bill were similar to the Hawkins proposal, but the compensation payments for the non-exonerated survivor were to be much higher, $100,000. Senator Humphrey stated, in presenting his bill, "we in government have a duty to demonstrate that we can admit an error and can correct a terrible wrong." He wanted the men and their families to be provided "reasonable compensation for the economic deprivation and personal suffering" they had had to endure because of Theodore Roosevelt's actions. A subcommittee of the Senate Committee on Veterans' Affairs held hearing on the bill several days later. Both subcommittees reported favorably on the idea.[33]

These two bills never reached the floor of Congress in their original form. Instead the Senate Committee on Veterans' Affairs added a different version of the pension proposal onto a veterans compensation bill (H.R. 9474). The amendment, in line with the suggestions of the Nixon Administration, provided for a $25,000 pension to the living, nonexonerated soldiers, and a $10,000 payment to the unmarried widows of these men. In its comments on the bill, the Senate committee estimated that ten widows would be eligible to receive the money. Senate floor action took place on 2 August 1973. There was little debate on this bill, and it easily passed the Senate. The pension bill then returned to the House. The inequity of pensioning only one of the two Brownsville survivors was resolved naturally before the bill reached the floor of the House again. On 18 September

---

32. *The Washington Post,* 14 June 1973; U.S., Congress, House of Representatives, "Pending Non-Service-Connected Pension Legislature," *Hearings Before the Subcommittee on Compensation and Pensions of the Committee on Veterans' Affairs,* 93d Cong., 1st sess., 1973, p. 1233; *The New York Times,* 15 June 1973.

33. U.S., Congress, Senate, *A Bill to Confer Pensionable status on veterans involved in the Brownsville, Texas, incident of August 13, 1906, and to require the Administrator of Veterans' Affairs to make certain compensatory payments to such veterans and their heirs,* S. 1999, 93d Cong., 1st sess., 1973; U.S., Congress, Senate, *Congressional Record,* 93d Cong., 1st sess., 14 June 1973, S. 11129–30.

1973, Edward Warfield died. Dorsie Willis was now the only survivor.[34]

On 14 November 1973 the House took up the pension bill and its Brownsville compensation payments. Rep. William B. Dorn, a Democrat from South Carolina and the chairman of the House Committee on Veterans' Affairs, spoke out in favor of the passage of the compensation provision. He agreed with Senator Humphrey's indictment of Roosevelt's actions, calling them "wrongful and illegal." The payments were to be "long overdue" compensation for the discharges. There was no debate on the question and the House passed the bill by voice vote. The bill then returned to the Senate for concurrence with other amendments. The Senate passed the bill again on 16 November and sent it on to the President. On 6 December 1973 President Nixon signed the bill. Shortly thereafter the Government ended the Brownsville affair by awarding a $25,000 pension to Dorsie Willis.[35]

The recent turn of events really did not settle several major questions raised by the whole incident, however. It was never determined absolutely whether the black soldiers were guilty of shooting up the town and whether racism affected the way in which the Administration and the nation reacted to the incident. Despite the great quantity of evidence that was presented over the years, it is still difficult to arrive at any definite conclusion as to the guilt or innocence of the soldiers. A brief look at some of the major pieces of evidence seems to be in order.

One of the major points brought out in defense of the soldiers was the location of Sgt. William Blaney's rifle. The firing pin markings on several of the cartridge cases found in the town indicated that they were fired from the weapon supposedly assigned to Sergeant Blaney. However, the defenders of the soldiers said that Blaney's rifle could not have been fired because it was coated with oil and locked in the arms chest in B Company's barracks. This cast doubt on the assertion that the cases found in the street were fired on the night of the raid. Evidence presented before the Court of Inquiry seemed to inval-

34. U.S., Congress, House of Representatives, *An Act to amend title 38 of the United States Code to increase the monthly rates of disability and death pensions, and dependence and indemnity compensation, and for other purposes,* H.R. 9474, 93d Cong., 1st sess., 1973; U.S., Congress, Senate, *Congressional Record,* 93d Cong., 1st sess., 2 August 1973, S. 15530.

35. U.S., Congress, House of Representatives, *Congressional Record,* 93d Cong., 1st sess., 14 November 1973, H.R. 9980.

idate the contention that Sergeant Blaney's rifle was really in the arms chest. Lieutenant Lawrason did not inspect the numbers on the rifles in the chest when he opened it on the morning of 14 August. Even if he had, the company property book was so confused that the Lieutenant could not have been able to tell which rifle really belonged to a particular man. Sergeant Blaney's rifle could in fact have been fired during the raid.

Another argument used in defense of the soldiers was the fact that despite threats, promises, and other measures, no information or confession was obtained. It seemed unlikely that all of the soldiers would have accepted their punishment if they did in fact know who was responsible for the raid. On the other hand, if there was a conspiracy of silence, it was quite successful. If a few of the soldiers had raided the town, probably most of them would have known who was responsible within several days. Considering the pressure they were under, their silence contradicts the theory about a conspiracy and supports their innocence.

The roll calls taken during the firing that night were also offered as evidence by Senator Foraker that the soldiers were not guilty. Defenders of the soldiers said that no soldier could have participated in the affray and returned to his company undetected and in time to answer the roll call that was supposedly taken during the firing. However, the night was dark, there were few lights on the post, and the officers were in a hurry to repel what they thought was an attack. Consequently a number of soldiers could have been missing and still listed as present, either because someone answered present when their name was called, because the count was so hurried that they were overlooked, or because the roll call was taken after the firing was over. The roll calls provide no conclusive evidence for either side.

Similarly inconclusive was the check of the ammunition made the next morning by the company officers. At the Court of Inquiry Captain Howland demonstrated quite clearly that none of the officers really knew how much ammunition their companies had before the firing started. Any count taken after the firing was therefore meaningless.

The soldiers' rifles were the subject of much discussion. The inspection on the morning of 14 August produced only clean rifles. If the rifles had been fired the previous night, the men would not have had an opportunity to clean them well enough to pass inspection, or so claimed Senator Foraker. On the other hand, there was testimony that the soldiers could have cleaned the rifles quite easily. They could have used the materials in the butts of the rifles or, with the cooperation of the noncommissioned officers, obtained the cleaning rods that were locked in the rifle racks. A demonstration was conducted to show that a rifle can be cleaned well enough to pass immediate inspection but still be quite dirty. Thus the cleanliness of the rifles on the morning after the shooting is not a conclusive argument for the innocence of the soldiers.

The bullets that were found in the town had four lands on them, which meant that they could only have been fired from the Springfield or Krag rifles. While the former was available only to the soldiers, the latter was available to civilians. Thus, the bullets by themselves did not prove the guilt or innocence of any particular party.

Most of the visual evidence was worthless. However, there were still a few credable eyewitnesses. Among them was the servant of the Cowen's who was only ten feet from the alley when the raiders went by. These few reliable witnesses all identified the soldiers as the guilty parties.

The cartridge cases, especially the ones Captain Macklin found clustered within a small radius, were used to prove that the black soldiers did not do the firing and also that the citizens had framed them. During the proceedings of the Court of Inquiry some of the officers doubted Macklin's claim that he had found all the cases in a clump. However, even if we accept his story it is rather hard to accept Senator Foraker's explanation for their being there. He deduced that the cartridge cases found in the street were taken from the box on the back porch of B Company's barracks. The chances of picking out thirty-three cases out of over fifteen hundred and finding ones fired from only four rifles are rather remote. This piece of evidence does not support the idea of the soldiers' innocence, and even less does it prove that they were being framed. However, about two hundred shots were supposedly fired during the raid, and the remaining cartridge cases were never found. Evidence from these missing cases might have proven Senator Foraker's contention or reinforced the conclusion of the army.

The idea that there was a conspiracy to force the army to remove the black garrison is hard to accept. Probably the most important point against it is that some of the bullets were aimed at people, and one person was killed. If some of the townspeople had wanted to create a fake raid, they could have as easily damaged the reputation of the black soldiers but with much less risk if they had fired in the air or at the tops of buildings. Another flaw in this argument is the eyewitnesses who saw the soldiers in the streets.

There is still a division of opinion on the guilt of the black soldiers. John Weaver has recently stated that the Blacks were framed. When he was interviewed at the time the army was reviewing its decision in 1972, Weaver stated: "I found there wasn't a shred of evidence implicating them in the riot at all. It apparently was some local vigilante types who were sore at the black troops being stationed there and the effect on local businesses like saloons." Ann J. Lane, in her recent study, does not really take a stand on this question, but presents arguments for both views. On the other hand, James A. Tinsley, in an older study, leaned toward the conclusion that the black soldiers were guilty, and I agree with him because of the strength of the evidence, such as the eyewitnesses, the missing ammunition, the thirty-three shells. However, there is no evidence to indicate the guilt of any specific individual and still a reasonable doubt as to the guilt of all of the soldiers. If normal judicial procedures had been applied, the black soldiers probably would have been acquitted.[36]

The situation, however, was not normal, and this is the real key to understanding the Brownsville raid. Army leaders and the President assumed from the beginning that the soldiers had committed the crime, probably because they believed that the black soldiers were becoming defiant of authority and the old racial lines. They believed that Blacks were by nature secretive and would shield members of their own race. President Roosevelt therefore acted quickly, refused to go through the normal procedures of military justice, and ignored the soldiers' protestations of innocence. Despite his denials, it is questionable if Roosevelt would have reacted in the same way if it had been a white unit which had committed the shooting at a black community, or even at a white town. Historians have suggested that Roosevelt's reaction may have been a compensation to anti-integrationists in politics for the earlier invitation of Booker T. Washington to have dinner at the White House or for the appointment of Dr. William D. Crum to a position in the port

---

36. *The New York Times,* 3 October 1972; Ann J. Lane, *The Brownsville Affair: National Crisis and Black Reaction,* pp. 166–67; James A. Tinsley, "The Brownsville Affray," p. 131; Lawarence C. Cook, "The Brownsville Affray of 1906," p. 103.

of Charleston. Another possibility is that Roosevelt felt that the Blacks, who were inferior to Anglo-Saxons, had to be taught that they should be responsible individuals. Roosevelt believed he was being fair, for he had protected the black population when they stayed within the laws and punished them when they broke the laws, as at Brownsville.[37]

In addition, the black soldiers never had a chance to defend themselves. They were always required to prove their innocence, instead of their prosecutors having to disprove it. Apparently it was up to them, if they were innocent, to find the guilty parties. However, neither the President nor the War Department gave them any assistance and the resources of other groups, the Senate or the Constitution League, were not adequate to the job. Evidence that might implicate others was ignored.

The positions of most civilians on Roosevelt's punishments were determined by their views of racial problems rather than evidence. Most Blacks supported the soldiers; most whites, the Administration. Southerners were quick to see in this action a swing by the Administration to their position on the race question. The fact that Roosevelt publicly announced his decision the day after the Congressional elections indicates that he was aware of the affect that this move would have on the black population.

The action of the Nixon Administration in 1972 just raises new questions. This action implies that some civilians were guilty of the shooting. However, the Administration made no mention of this when it announced its decision. In addition, the timing of this action, several weeks before the 1972 presidential election, makes the motives behind the decision suspect.

The awarding of the compensatory pensions to Dorsie Willis and the surviving widows is based upon a continued belief in the soldiers innocence. It is now a generally accepted view that the soldiers were unjustly treated in 1906 and had to suffer for many years from the stigma attached to their discharges. Yet the few payments do nothing for the men of the battalion who have long

37. *The New York Times,* 8 November 1906; Willard B. Gatewood, Jr., *Theodore Roosevelt and the Art of Controversy: Episodes of the White House Years,* pp. 127; 38, 39. Booker T. Washington had dinner with Theodore Roosevelt at the White House in 1901. In reaction many southern whites who saw racial lines being breeched protested, especially since Mrs. Roosevelt was at the dinner. Dr. Crum's appointment in 1903 as collector of the port of Charleston also angered southern whites; Tinsley, "The Brownsville Affray," p. 133.

since died. Still left unanswered is the guilt or innocence of the soldiers. It is an issue which has been avoided by most supporters of the action giving new discharge papers and of the legislation that granted the soldiers pensions. Someone obviously did the shooting. If the black soldiers of the Twenty-fifth Infantry did not, then the guilty parties have remained free and untouched even after the changing of the records of the soldiers. Now is the time to face up to this issue also. I feel that changing the discharge records of the soldiers and awarding a few of the Blacks pensions has only dealt with the residue of the racism of Theodore Roosevelt and the white society of his time.

If some of the black soldiers actually did raid Brownsville, their guilt would tie in with similar incidents that occurred during this period. The black soldiers would no longer accept harrassment, segregation, and discrimination. Brownsville was in many respects like a frontier community. It had a small native black population and a large transient population. Because the town was in the South, racism was more intense and the town was a perfect breeding place for violence. Some of the black soldiers, as they had in Suggs in 1892 and in Florida in 1898, would not accept the status quo. They used the tools they had to take the actions the military authorities refused to take. They moved, through the use of force, to protect their rights.

The treatment of the black soldiers by the military authorities, the rationale behind their presumption of guilt, the resistance to admitting they might have made a mistake, and their answer to the protests against their decision, all demonstrate the new dimension of the army's treatment of the black soldiers. The Brownsville raid and the actions of the military before and after it point out quite clearly the negative aspects of the position of the black man in the service.

X

CONCLUSIONS

After the raid at Brownsville, the racial prejudice that had handicapped black civilians now reached the military. As the United States approached World War I, an era for the black soldiers drew to a close. Though some aspects of their lives in the army remained as they had been before 1890, they were increasingly affected by racism.

There were a number of factors responsible for this change. Whites throughout America felt ever more strongly that Blacks were inferior biologically and mentally. As a result there was no hesitation in segregating and discriminating against these second-class people. This general attitude affected the army in two different ways. Army officers generally accepted these concepts, and they allowed their decisions to be shaped by them. At the same time, increased contact with civilians who held these beliefs helped encourage army officers in their discriminatory actions against Blacks.

Also related to this upsurge in racism was the acquisition of colonies in the Pacific and the Caribbean. The army was enlarged to protect these colonial possessions. In turn, the black soldiers and officers were in closer contact with the hostile white population, so the white officers' latent prejudices came to the surface, and the percentage of Blacks in the service diminished. As racism became a more significant factor in the lives of Blacks in general after 1890, it also affected the army. However, there were still some areas in which circumstances remained as they had been before.

The experiences of the Indian War period had convinced the authorities that Blacks performed well in combat situations. Their good conduct continued after 1890, and the army acted accordingly. When mobilization for the Spanish-American War first began, the Twenty-fifth Infantry was the first regiment to be sent to the South, and all four of the black regiments played a prominent role in the expedition to Cuba. They took an active part in the fighting and acquitted themselves creditably at Las Guásimas, El Caney, San Juan Heights, during and after the siege. The use of a detachment of the Tenth Cavalry on an independent mission in Cuba further points out the high esteem that was held for their fighting abilities. In the Philippine Insurrection the Blacks continued to meet the army's high expectations in a variety of different situations, ranging from large-scale actions to guerrilla warfare. Batchelor's march deserves to be ranked with the Blacks' greatest accomplishments in the Indian Wars. Despite the attempts by the insurgents to persuade the black soldiers to defect by picturing the conflict as a race war, the black soldiers remained loyal. Another indication of the esteem in which the army held black Regulars was their use in the Mexican Punitive Expedition of 1916–1917. Gen. John Pershing designated the Tenth Cavalry to be the major part of his flying column in pursuit of Pancho Villa. Again the Blacks did not disappoint their superiors, but they were always led by white officers because the army continued to hold the premise that they were not capable of command.

In peacetime the on-duty life of the black soldier was very similar to that of the white soldier. The army generally employed Blacks as they did whites, no matter what the task. They were used to break strikes, keep the peace, escort Indians, and do fatigue work and a variety of other duties. Blacks competed with whites both in individual and regimental military competitions. The black regimental bands were directed by both white and black bandmasters, and as their talents developed, they were honored many times. The recognition of the Twenty-fourth Infantry band as one of the best in the country at the 1904 St. Louis World's Fair and the prize awarded to Bandmaster Alfred Thomas, Tenth Cavalry, are but a few. There are several possible explanations why this aspect of army life remained the same.

Until 1898 the small number of troops meant the army was restricted in the types of duty to which they could be assigned. After that date the army could be more selective but continued to use Blacks because it felt they could do these jobs well. The Blacks also had comparatively high reenlistment rates, so noncommissioned officers and privates were well trained. Consequently the small number of black soldiers in the service was highly skilled and could easily meet the demands of the army. Despite their competent performance of military duties, racial mores did not change; they were given a relatively fair chance in the military only because there was no purpose served in practicing discrimination in this aspect of life.

After 1890 the off-duty life of the soldier became more attractive in some respects. Blacks could compete against whites in athletics, something they could not do in civilian society. The Blacks frequently defeated the white teams, which helped to relieve the racial tension. Consequently, the soldiers were very interested in interregimental competition. Baseball was the most popular sport, but they also participated in basketball, boxing, and track and field. The record of the baseball team of the Twenty-fifth Infantry clearly demonstrated to whites that Blacks could excel in athletic competition if given the chance. Other leisure activities, such as education, recreation, religion, gambling, and social functions, while available also to black civilians, added variety to the life of Blacks in the service and were an inducement for enlistment. They also helped keep the reenlistment rates high during most of this period. Very seldom did these activities threaten the racial system so there was no need to change what had existed before.

Unfortunately for Blacks in the army, racism affected most other aspects of their service careers. The assignments of the black soldiers were increasingly restricted because of the racial bias of the army; the old stereotypes were applied more often, racial separation was more strictly enforced, and the army was more callous in its treatment of Blacks. Even in the areas where Blacks were allowed to progress, there were touches of the increased racism. Charges of cowardice tarnished the efforts of the black soldiers in the Spanish-American War. Theodore Roosevelt had claimed that he had to use a revolver to prevent Blacks from fleeing the front lines on the San Juan Heights. After Blacks won several track meets, a white officer wrote to the major service newspaper that he feared white supremacy was threatened. These incidents were minor, however, compared to intrusions of racial prejudice into other aspects of the service.

Racial concepts became much more important in governing the decisions of the War Department. They acted under the assumption that Blacks did not have the innate intelligence to assume new responsibilities. Although the rest of the army expanded, because this concept was applied, a smaller proportion of black soldiers was recruited. The idea was implemented after 1890 as the army put more emphasis on education and the knowledge of technical skills. Some officers even believed that the Blacks' educational deficiencies could not be remedied because they lacked the ability to absorb much knowledge.

This concept was linked closely with another—that Blacks performed well only under the command of white officers. As a result there was no support given to Blacks seeking commissions during the national emergencies in 1898 and 1899 or during peacetime. As the case of Hiram Parker demonstrated, it was quite difficult for Blacks to overcome all of the normal obstacles without any assistance. The army made no effort to give this help. White officers were also averse to serving with or under black officers. Since there was only one high-ranking black officer in this period, Charles Young, the fear was more of the future than of the present. As a result of this aversion, the army frequently isolated black officers from service with whites and assigned them to duties that were racially acceptable. They were selected as military attachés only to countries with black populations or assigned as instructors only to schools for Blacks. At the same time, service with black troops became less desirable for white officers. Indicative of this is the fact that the quality of West Point graduates who received their first assignment to a black regiment, as measured by their class standing, declined after 1900. Although opposition to the expansion of the black segment of the army was voiced vehemently only after 1890, it was merely the expression of old ideas that assumed new urgency.

Whites also accepted the idea that Blacks had a strong sexual drive. This belief played a role in the decisions concerning where they should be stationed. There was a fear that they would attack the native women in the Philippines. Again, the idea was old and certainly held before 1890, but it did not influence decisionmaking until conditions changed after that date.

Colonialism, and the racial concepts encouraged by it, also became more important after 1890. While many people had long believed that Blacks were better suited to warm than cold climates, the new colonial possessions obtained in 1898 and 1899 allowed them to put these ideas into practice. The reluctance to send Blacks to Alaska, the long assignments in Arizona and New Mexico, and the 1915 Army War College study are a few instances that attest that this concept was regarded as valid and was applied. The concept of racial superiority over and responsibility for Blacks that had long existed in the South was promoted throughout the country as the United States took on colonial interests. The army became quite concerned about keeping the races separate, all the way from recruiting stations to facilities of posts and even to the marriage of the soldiers. The most significant example of this drive for separation was the removal of the integrated picture in the 1916 recruiting pamphlet. What was new after 1890 was the pressure for separation and the opportunities to carry out the new policy.

Even the benefits of off-duty life for the black enlisted men were tainted by racism. No effort was made by the army to prevent segregation in those areas where the soldiers went during their leisure hours. When whites attacked or harassed the soldiers while they were off duty, as in Suggs, Wyoming, in 1892, the army took no action. While the officers made great efforts to restrain the black soldiers after one of their comrades was shot, they did little to urge the civilian authorities to apprehend his killers.

Black officers had always had to deal with awkward social situations. Whites did not want to associate with them socially, and the black officers found ways to avoid confrontations. Chaplain Louis Carter, a black, arrived early at social functions and left early, fulfilling the obligations yet not intruding. However, this position also meant that Blacks had little social life. Black officers could not really associate with enlisted men, and there were very few occasions when there was more than one black officer at a post. As a result, black officers were comfortable when assigned to detached service, especially to Wilberforce University, and did not protest too much at those assignments that deliberately took them away from their regiment and the mainstream of army life. The knowledge of this social isolation most likely helped to dissuade many Blacks who were prospective officers from even attempting the qualifying examinations. This effect just reinforced the whites' efforts at ostracism.

The area of civil-military relations was the one most affected by the upsurge in racism. The 1906 Brownsville affray is one of a number of conflicts, and the way in which the army rode roughshod over the rights of the Blacks is symptomatic of this new era. Stationing black soldiers now involved anticipating a great deal of civilian hostility. They could no longer be kept isolated on the frontier. The waverings over stationing Blacks in the Philippines and the arguments over whether to inflict them upon the Christians or the Muslims are typical of this new concern. Pressure on the War Department increased. White citizens who lived near prospective stations for black soldiers expressed fears that they would attack white girls, lower property values, or start racial violence. Whenever the people gave the black soldiers a chance and treated them decently, there was no trouble. The raid at Brownsville, whether committed by soldiers or civilians, points out what would happen when there was hatred, segregation, and discrimination. Other reactions by Blacks to local discrimination involved the smashing of beer glasses by soldiers objecting to higher prices for Blacks and a riot protesting Jim Crow streetcars in San Antonio. The army automatically assumed that the soldiers were guilty if violence occurred as a result of discrimination. One example of this treatment occurred after the raid at Brownsville, when the military made no effort to prove otherwise or to understand the causes of the event and punished the Blacks harshly. General Garlington's justification for his theory of a conspiracy of silence and his refusal to believe the Blacks no matter what they said were also based upon racial stereotypes. Blacks were guilty and never could be proven innocent. The Brownsville incident also triggered several more reactions. Texas Congressmen introduced the first two of the elimination bills in Congress in late 1906, and they continued in a steady stream until 1917. Sen. Benjamin Tillman's diatribe against the black soldiers attacking Filipinos was a result of the Brownsville incident. Many people suggested that the transfer of the Ninth and Tenth cavalry regiments and the Twenty-fifth Infantry to the Philippine Islands came as a consequence of the affray. The army tried to deny the charge but did not convince many Blacks.

There was one other factor that also affected the status of the black soldier—black militancy among soldiers and civilians. Black civilians thought very highly of black soldiers. Many homes contained lithographs of the Ninth and Tenth Cavalry charging up San Juan Hill. Black newspapers featured stories about the soldiers in Mexico and the career of Charles Young. They also felt protective about them and objected to discrimination, as the deluge of letters after Brownsville attests. At the same time a growing segment within the black community was unwilling to accept the racial status quo and the philosophy of Booker T. Washington. This discontent led to the rise of protest organizations and organized campaigns to change things. This new feeling, which extended to Blacks in the army, combined with others to increase friction. The blacks in the military felt a responsibility to uphold the position accorded them by the black public. They disliked the army's prejudicial actions and the deterioration in their position. Their protests took many forms, some refused to reenlist, others pressured the army for changes, while still others used violence. They objected to minstrel shows as degrading, and they bombarded theaters that showed antiblack movies. Charges that they were cowards or could not get along with whites peaceably drew quick rebuttals. Not only did this reaction have little effect in stopping the deterioration but it also added to the racial pressures within the service.

Given this increase in tensions it is strange that there were no real efforts to make Blacks ineligible to join the army. In fact the War Department worked to defeat attempts in Congress to do so. There are a number of possible reasons for this. First of all, the proportion of Blacks in the service continually decreased. No new black regiment was created after 1869, while many white ones were. Consequently the Blacks really represented only a small and shrinking part of the service and could be generally ignored, if necessary. Secondly, had there been a strong drive for removal, the black population and a few white sympathizers would have raised a great fuss against it. It was always easier for the War Department to avoid any struggle and continue to accept the black regiments. However, this attitude did not help those who wanted more black officers. Educational handicaps made it very difficult for a black man to become an officer. The army just maintained this situation by doing nothing. This certainly was the way most white officers wanted it, since they did not desire to be commanded by or to have to serve with a black officer. Thus while keeping the status quo helped maintain the four black regiments and probably prevented their ouster, it also hindered the expansion of the black officer corps.

In the period after 1890 the negative influence of racism overcame the positive force of the needs for defending the nation. It was a force that built up slowly in the last decade of the nineteenth century but grew quickly in the first years of the twentieth. New currents, such as colonialism, proximity to cities, increased black militancy, and greater awareness of the racial situation, all worked to destroy the good life for the black soldier and officer. The black soldiers continued to perform the daily routine, but for the most part the general public ignored them. They no longer could feel that the army highly prized them. The discrimination, segregation, and antipathy toward black soldiers and officers that occurred during World War I should have been no surprise to any one familiar with the events of the previous twenty-five years. By 1917 the first golden age of the black soldier had ended.

Appendixes

APPENDIX A

Black Federal Volunteer Regiments in the Spanish-American War

Regiment	Muster In	Officers	Enlisted Men	Dates of Service in Foreign Countries	Muster Out
Seventh U.S.V.I.	6 July– 23 July 1898	58	985	. . . .	28 February 1899
Eighth U.S.V.I.	22 June– 24 July 1898	50	1,128	. . . .	6 March 1899
Ninth U.S.V.I.	18 June– 16 July 1898	72	1,047	Cuba 22 August 1898– 26 April 1899	25 May 1899
Tenth U.S.V.I.	2 July– 22 July 1898	48	999	. . . .	8 March 1899

APPENDIX B

Information Concerning Questionnaires

In order to obtain information about the life of the black soldier, I sent questionnaires to officers who had served in the black regiments. To obtain a list of every officer who had been assigned to one or more of the black units between 1891 and 1916, I consulted the *Official Army Register*. The next step was to consult the *Register of Graduates, United States Military Academy* for 1966 and 1967 for the addresses of those surviving officers or their descendants who had been cadets. About 10 per cent of the officers on the list were located this way, and Questionnaire A was mailed to them.

The list of officers was then compared with the *Official Army Register* of 1967 to see if any other officers were still alive. Several additional names were obtained, and this second group was sent Questionnaire B. The percentage of officers' responses to these questionnaires was very high.

The names of a few enlisted men were obtained by writing the Ninth and Tenth Cavalry Regimental Association. Because the number involved was small, I sent these men Questionnaire A, and in this case the response was even smaller. In an additional effort to gather the names of more enlisted men, the Veterans of Foreign Wars, the Defense Department, the Veterans' Administration, and the newspaper, *The Stars and Stripes-National Tribune*, were contacted but with little result.

While generally the answers did not provide specific information, they did enable the author to gain a general impression of the officers' attitudes and activities toward their black regiments.

Covering Letter—Questionnaire A

August 12, 1966

Dear_____,

I am a graduate student in American History at the University of Wisconsin in Madison. The subject area for my doctoral dissertation is the Negro Soldier and his activities during the years 1891–1917.

Through my research I have learned that you [your father, your grandfather]* (name of officer) served with the _____ Regiment from_____to_____.

In an effort to gather information about the activities and experiences of the Negro soldier I have prepared the enclosed questionnaire. [Although the questions are phrased as though they were being put to your father (or grandfather) personally, I would appreciate it if on the basis of letters and/or personal reminiscences you or other members of your family would answer them as you think your father (or grandfather) would have.]* It is not necessary to answer all of the questions, but please try to answer all those which you feel you can answer *accurately.* If you wish the source of the information to remain confidential, please indicate this on the last page of the questionnaire.

Your participation and any information which you can contribute to this project will be greatly appreciated.

*This phrase was omitted when the questionnaire was sent to the officer himself.

Sincerely,

Marvin Fletcher

P.S. If you have any letters, manuscripts or post newspapers which you might care to lend me, I will be glad to Xerox them and return them to you immediately.

Appendix B

Questionnaire A

If the space provided for your answer is not sufficient, please feel free to write on the back of the page or on another piece of paper.

1. Name_____ 2. Regiment served with__

3. Dates of service with this regiment:__

4. (a) Was your assignment to a Negro regiment voluntary? Yes__No__If yes, why did you choose a Negro regiment?

(b) If you had a choice again, would you pick a Negro regiment over a white regiment? Yes__No__Why?

5. Briefly outline the daily schedule of your unit during peacetime, giving time of day and the type of activity performed (i.e., 5 A.M. - Reveille).

6. (a) Were the Negro soldiers under your command generally careful about their personal appearance and personal cleanliness? Yes__No__

(b) Were they cooperative in cleaning their barracks? Yes__No__

(c) Were they careful about the condition of their uniforms, equipment and horses? Yes__No__

7. (a) What type of training did the Negro troops under your command receive? (e.g., marksmanship)

(b) Did they dislike any particular drill? Yes__No__If Yes, which one?

8. Were the Negro non-coms capable leaders? Yes__No__Comments:

9. Did the Negro troops prefer to take orders from their Negro NCO's rather than from white officers? Yes__No__ Comments:

10. (a) Were there any Negro commissioned officers on any post at which you served? Yes__No__ If yes, how did the Negro officers get along with the white officers?

(b) Were these Negro officers able to command Negro troops as well as the white officers? Yes__No__ Comments:

11. (a) How much off-duty time per week did the Negro soldiers have? 1–5 hrs.__, 5–10__, 10–20__

(b) How did they spend their off-duty time on the post?

(c) If they left the post during their off-duty time, where did they go?

(d) If they went to a near-by town, how did the citizens react?

12. (a) How much off-duty time did you have? 1–5 hrs.__, 5–10__, 10–20__, 20–30__

(b) How was your off-duty time spent?

13. (a) How many of the Negro soldiers in your unit were married before they joined the army?

(b) How many of the married men had their wives with them on the post at which they were stationed?

(c) Where did the wives live?

(d) What did the wives do to earn a living?

(e) Did the Negroes without wives marry while they were on duty at the post? Yes__No__

(f) Of the Negroes who married while on the post, how many married home-town girls?__ local girls?__

14. How many of the Negroes in your unit could read and write?

15. Generally, did the Negro soldiers receive letters? Yes__No__

16. (a) Were there any nonmilitary educational opportunities (i.e., reading, writing) for the Negroes on the post? Yes__No__ If yes, what kind of activities?

(b) Who was in charge of this education program?

(c) How many of the Negroes took advantage of the program?

17. Did the Negroes who got this education get promotion as NCOs? Yes__No__ Comments:

18. (a) Did the Negroes want the opportunity to be promoted to the rank of second lieutenant? Yes__No__ Comments:

(b) If yes, how did the white officers view this desire of the Negro soldiers?

19. (a) Were the Negroes of your regiment ever stationed at the same post as

white soldiers? Yes__No__ If yes, was there ever any trouble between the two groups of soldiers? Yes__No__ Comments:

(b) Were the white and Negro troops housed in the same barracks? Yes__ No__

(c) Was there segregation of eating facilities? Yes__No__ If yes, what type? (e.g., separate dining rooms, etc.)

20. (a) Was your regiment, company or troop ever detached to a fair or to an exhibition? Yes__No__ If yes, which one?

(b) How did the Negroes conduct themselves on these occasions?

(c) What was the reaction of the citizens to the Negro soldiers?

21. (a) How did your unit do in interregimental athletic competition?

(b) Did it ever win any trophies?

22. (a) Was your unit ever in an interregimental rifle competition? Yes__No__ If yes, how did it do?

(b) Did it ever win any trophies?

23. (a) Was your regiment in any other type of interregimental competition? Yes__No__ If yes, what kind?

(b) How did it do?

24. (a) Did your regiment have a band? Yes__No__ If yes, on what occasions did it perform?

(b) Did the band ever perform off the post? Yes__No__ If yes, please describe.

(c) Did the musicians get any special privileges? Yes__No__ If yes, please describe.

25. (a) Was your troop ever stationed at Fort Myer? Yes__No__ If yes, how did your troops behave?

(b) Did they fraternize with the Negro civilians of the area?

26. (a) Did many of the Negroes reenlist? Yes__No__ If yes, how many?

(b) For how long?

27. (a) Were you ever detailed for recruiting duty? Yes__No__ If yes, where and when?

28. (a) How many Negroes applied to you for enlistment?

(b) Did they seem as intelligent as those already in your regiment? Yes__ No__ Comments:

(c) Did the Negroes applying for the army give any preference for assignment to either infantry or cavalry? Yes__No__ If yes, which branch?

(d) What reasons did they give for their preference?

29. (a) Was there any interest among the soldiers in your regiment in the activities of Lt. James Moss and the Bicycle Corps? Yes__No__

(b) Did any of your soldiers participate in the Bicycle Corps? Yes__No__ If yes, what if anything did they tell you about their participation?

30. (a) Were there any religious services at your post? Yes__No__

(b) Did many of the Negro troops attend? Yes__No__ How many?

(c) Did the Negro troops sing any spirituals at these services? Yes__No__

31. (a) Did your unit ever participate in breaking up a strike? Yes__No__ If yes, when and where?

(b) What was the attitude of the troops toward this duty?

(c) What was your attitude?

(d) What was the attitude of the strikers toward the Negro troops?

32. Did you ever serve with your regiment in combat? Yes__No__ If yes, when and where?

33. How did your unit reach the battle area?

34. If you went by ship, were there any white troops also on board? Yes__No__ If yes, was there any trouble between the two groups of soldiers?

35. (a) Did your unit perform well under fire? Yes__No__ Comments?

(b) Did the NCOs lead their men well in combat? Yes__No__ Comments:

36. Is there any particular incident of heroism on the part of a Negro soldier which you remember? If so, please describe it:

37. Is there any particular incident of cowardice on the part of a Negro soldier which you remember? If so, please describe it:

38. Would you have rather commanded a white regiment or a Negro regiment in combat? Negro___White___ Why?

39. If you served in a foreign country (i.e., Cuba, Mexico, Philippines), how were the relations between the Negroes and the natives?

40. Did the Negroes regard the natives as equals or inferiors?

41. Are there any memories of post life with the Negro soldiers that you can recall? Yes___No___ If yes, would you please relate some of them.

42. If you desire to keep your name confidential, please check Yes here. Yes___ No___

43. If you know of anyone who might be able to supply more information about the Negro troops, I would appreciate your putting their name and address below.

Persons to whom Questionnaire A Was Sent

Name	Relationship of Person Answering Questionnaire if Other than Soldier	Returned
A. Officers		
Adams, Sterling P.		No
Armstrong, Frank S.	Son	Yes
Augur, Ammon A.		No
Babcock, Conrad S.		No
Balsam, Alfred S.		No
Barnum, Malvern Hill	Grandson	Yes
Barzynski, Joseph E.		No
Bingham, Sidney V.		No
Bluemel, Clifford		Yes
Boone, Abbott		Yes
Boyd, Charles T.	Wife	Yes
Bradburn, Clarence E.	Wife	Yes
Brant, Gerald C.	Son	Yes
Budd, Arthur D.		No
Bullard, Robert L.		No
Burt, James D.		No
Burt, Reynolds J.		No
Cabell, De Rosy C.	Daughter	Yes
Carter, William V.		Yes
Chandler, Clark P.	Son	Yes
Chaney James E.		Yes
Chapman, William H.	Son	Yes
Chilton, Alexander		Yes
Crane, Charles	Son	Yes
Cummings, Richard E.	Son	Yes
Davis, Arthur J.	Son	Yes
Davis, Benjamin O., Sr.		No
Denson, Eley P.		No
Deuel, Thorne, Jr.		Yes
Dockery, Albert B.		Yes
Dodd, George A.		No
Dusenbury, Ralph W.		No
Edwards, William W.	Daughter	Yes
Elliott, J. Duncan		Yes
Elser, Max A.		No
Erwin, James B.	Daughter	Yes
Evans, William P.	Son	Yes
Farnum, Francis H.		Yes
Finley, Walter L.		No
Fleming, Robert J.	Son	Yes
Foster, Herbert S., Jr.		No
Frank, Walter H.		No

Freeman, Samuel D.	Grandson	Yes
French, Charles G.	Grandson	Yes
Fuller, Horace H.		No
Ganoe, William A.		No
Garrard, Joseph	Grandson	Yes
Glenn, Edwin		No
Gose, Ernest B.		No
Graham, Ephraim F.	Son	Yes
Green, James O.		No
Greene, James S.		No
Ham, Samuel V.	Grandson	Yes
Hamilton, George F.	Son	Yes
Hammond, Thomas W.		No
Harbold, Robert P.		No
Harrison, George R.	Son	Yes
Haskell, William N.		No
Hatch, Everard	Son	Yes
Henry, Guy V., Sr.	Son	Yes
Hester, John H.		Yes
Hoge, Benjamin F.		Yes
Holbrook, Willard A.		No
Holderness, Arthur	Son	Yes
Hubbard, Eustis L.		No
Jacob, Richard H.		No
Johnson, Ronald D.		No
Kernan, Francis J.		No
King, Joseph C.		Yes
Kromer, Leon B.		No
Ladd, Jesse A.		No
Leitch, Joseph D.		No
Lenihan, Michael J.		No
Lewis, Edson A.	Son	Yes
Lewis, John E.		No
Lindsey, Julian R.	Son	Yes
Lininger, Clarence		Yes
Lovell, George E., Jr.		No
Matile, George A.		Yes
Meals, Charles A.	Son	Yes
Miller, Alexander		No
Miller, Claude		No
Miller, Samuel W.		No
Mooney, James S.		Yes
Olmstead, Jerauld A.	Grandson	Yes
Palmer, John McA.	Prof. I. B. Holley	Yes
Pegram, John C.		Yes
Philoon, Wallace C.		Yes
Preston, Guy H.	Grandson	Yes
Reed, William A.		No

Riggs, Kerr T.	Son	Yes
Ryan, William O.		Yes
Saltzman, Charles M.	Son	Yes
Sands, George H.	Grandson	Yes
Schillerstrom, Merl P.		Yes
Shattuck, Amos B.		No
Shekerjian, Haig		Yes
Sneed, Albert L.		Yes
Spaatz, Carl		Yes
Stodter, Charles E.		Yes
Symmonds, Charles J.		No
Torrey, Zerah W.		No
Troxel, Orlando C.	Son	Yes
Van Deusen, Edwin R.		Yes
Wadsworth, Leland		Yes
Walsh, Robert D.	Son	Yes
Ward, Orlando		Yes
West, William W., Jr.	Son	Yes
Whitehead, Henry C.		No
Wilbourne, Arthur E.		Yes
Winfree, Stephen		Yes
Wise, Richard H.		No
Wuest, Jacob W.		Yes
Young, Charles	Son	Yes

B. Enlisted Men

Anderson, Robert E. [Tenth Cavalry]	No
Bowen, Reuben A. [Twenty-fifth Inf.]	Yes
Burton, George A. [Twenty-fifth Inf.]	Yes
Claborn, John [Tenth Cavalry]	No
Daniel, P. [Ninth Cavalry]	No
Hawkins, Thomas [Ninth Cavalry]	No
Lenton, Jalester [Tenth Cavalry]	No
Lynn, Albert A. [Tenth Cavalry]	No
Schuyler, George S. [Twenty-fifth Inf.]	Yes
Thomas, Frank [Tenth Cavalry]	No

Covering Letter—Questionnaire B

1 November 1967

Dear _____,

I am a graduate student in American History at the University of Wisconsin in Madison. The subject area for my doctoral dissertation is the Negro soldier and his activities during the years 1891–1917.

Through my research I learned that you [or your father] served as an officer in one of the four Negro regiments. Your address was furnished by The Adjutant General, Department of the Army.

In an effort to gather information about the life and experiences of the Negro soldier I have prepared the enclosed questionnaire. It is not necessary to answer all of the questions, but please try to answer all those which are applicable as fully and accurately as possible. While I realize that there was little race consciousness as we know it today in the early 1900s, I am interested in any manifestations of it in that period which you may recall. If you wish the source of the information to remain confidential please indicate this on the last page of the questionnaire.

Your participation and any information which you can contribute to this project will be greatly appreciated.

Sincerely,

Marvin Fletcher

P.S. If you have any letters, manuscripts, or post newspapers which you might care to lend me, I will be glad to Xerox them and return them to you immediately.

Questionnaire B

If the space provided for your answer is not sufficient please feel free to write on the back of the page or on another piece of paper.

1. Name of officer_____ 2. Regiment served with_____
3. Dates of service with this regiment_____
4. Your name, if different, and relationship to officer described _____
5. Did the Negro troops under your command prefer to take orders from their Negro NCOs rather than from white officers?
6. If there were any Negro officers on any post at which you served, how did they get along with the white officers?
7. In your opinion were these Negro officers able to command troops as well as white officers?
8. Did any Negro enlisted men under your command desire to take the examination for a commission in the Regular Army?
9. Did any enlisted men under your command desire to take the exam for a commission in the Philippine Scouts?
10. How did the white officers view the desire of the Negro soldiers to become officers?
11. How did the men in your command react to the Brownsville incident of 1906?
12. How did the men react to any instances of racial discrimination in the town near which they were stationed?
13. If you were ever in combat with a Negro unit, how did it perform?
14. Please describe any particular incident of heroism on the part of a Negro soldier which you remember.
15. Please describe any particular incident of cowardice on the part of a Negro soldier which you remember.
16. If you served in a foreign country with a Negro regiment how were the relations between the Negroes and the natives?
17. Please relate any memories of post life with the Negro soldiers that you can recall.
18. If you know of anyone who might be able to supply more information about the Negro troops, I would appreciate your putting their names and addresses below.
19. If you desire to keep your name confidential, please check Yes here. Yes__ No__

_____
Date

Appendix B

Persons to whom Questionnaire B Was Sent

Name	Relationship of Person Answering Questionnaire if Other than Soldier	Returned
A. Officers		
Adams, John P.	Son	Yes
Akin, Spencer B.		No
Baird, Raymond C.		No
Baluvelt, Xavier F.		Yes
Barker, Ray W.		No
Barzynski, Joseph E.		No
Boettcher, Arthur		Yes
Boone, Abbott		No
Carmody, Robert E.		No
Chilton, Alexander W.		Yes
Cocke, Alexander R.		No
Edgerly, John P.		Yes
Engel, Emil		No
Grieves, Loren C.		No
Gunner, Edwin		No
Halstead, Frank	Son	Yes
Hammond, Thomas W.		No
Herwig, Leopold		No
Hester, John H.		No
Howe, Jerome W.		Yes
Mallon, Francis B.		Yes
Mauborgne, Joseph O.		No
Mills, Willis E.		Yes
Pegram, John C.		No
Pope, William R.		Yes
Robinson, Eugene		Yes
Saunders, Oswald H.		Yes
Smith, Selwyn D.		No
Sykes, Horace R.	Son	Yes
Tillson, John C. F., Jr.		Yes
Van Way, Charles W.	Son	Yes
Wagner, Otto		No
Watrous, Livingston		No
White, William R.		No
Wyman, Charles L.		No

APPENDIX C

Chronological Listing of the Sources
of New Second Lieutenants for Black Regiments*

Year	Cavalry			Infantry		
	West Point	Army	Civil	West Point	Army	Civil
1891	3	1	1	3k	0	4
1892	2	0	1	2	1	0
1893	2	0	0	2	0	0
1894	2	0	0	1	1	0
1895	4	0	0	3	0	0
1896	6	1	0	1	2	0
1897	1	0	0	3	1	0
1898	0	0	0	2	3	10
1899	4	3	3	0	5	9
1900	1	6	0	0	7	0
1901	2	14	10	0	5	8
1902	3	2	0	0	6	1
1903	2	0	0	2	3	1
1904	5	0	0	4	6	2
1905	3	0	0	3	0	0
1906	1	1	0	1	0	0
1907	0	1	0	4	0	0
1908	3	0	0	3	0	2
1909	3	1	0	1	0	0
1910	3	0	0	0	0	3
1911	1	0	0	1	1	2
1912	5	0	1	0	0	1
1913	3	4	1	1	1	0
1914	5	1	0	3	0	0
1915	4	0	0	2	0	0

* The material for this table was derived from U.S.
Department of War, *Official Army Register, 1891–1916.*

APPENDIX D

Geographical Distribution of West Point
Classes and Appointees to the Black Regiments

The following table lists the geographical distribution of each graduating class and the appointees to the black regiments. The table was compiled in an effort to determine if the numbers of appointees to the black regiments from the various sections of the country were proportional to the total class composition. The percentages represent each section's proportion of the total number of graduates or appointees.

The states were divided into geographical categories: South—Kentucky, Missouri, Arkansas, Virginia, North Carolina, South Carolina, Georgia, Florida, Alabama, Mississippi, Louisiana, Texas, and Tennessee; North—Maine, District of Columbia, New Hampshire, Vermont, Massachusetts, Rhode Island, Connecticut, New York, Pennsylvania, New Jersey, Delaware, Maryland, West Virginia, and Ohio; Midwest—Indiana, Michigan, Illinois, Wisconsin, Minnesota, Iowa; Plains—North Dakota, South Dakota, Nebraska, Kansas, and Oklahoma; Others—the remaining states and any cadets from foreign countries.

Black Soldier and Officer

Year	South	North	Midwest	Plains	Others
1891	.246 (.250)*	.354 (.500)	.338 (.250)	.015	.046
1892	.371 (.667)	.419	.177 (.333)	.016	.016
1893	.314 (.500)	.373 (.250)	.157 (.250)	.020	.137
1894	.296 (.667)	.407 (.333)	.204	.019	.074
1895	.270 (.285)	.365 (.428)	.230 (.142)	.038	.096 (.142)
1896	.273 (.285)	.493 (.714)	.136	.054	.041
1897	.328 (.250)	.313	.223 (.500)	.059	.074 (.250)
1898	.338	.372 (.500)	.186 (.500)	.051	.051
1899	.264	.292 (.750)	.264	.028 (.250)	.153
1900	.259	.463 (1.000)	.204	.037	.037
1901	.338 (.500)	.378 (.500)	.243	.014	.027
1902	.370 (.333)	.370 (.333)	.204 (.333)	.019	.037
1903	.247 (.500)	.376 (.250)	.226 (.250)	.065	.086
1904	.323 (.111)	.363 (.333)	.129 (.111)	.056	.129 (.444)
1905	.307 (.167)	.298 (.333)	.211 (.333)	.044	.140 (.167)
1906	.256 (.500)	.285 (.500)	.218	.064	.077
1907	.306	.351 (.500)	.189 (.500)	.045	.108 (.500)
1908	.343 (.500)	.333 (.167)	.139	.102 (.333)	.083
1909	.233 (.400)	.320 (.400)	.175 (.200)	.097	.175
1910	.277 (.667)	.217	.277	.060	.169 (.333)
1911	.268	.366 (1.000)	.220	.037	.110
1912	.295	.421 (.250)	.105	.063 (.750)	.116
1913	.290 (.250)	.290 (.250)	.183 (.500)	.065	.172
1914	.290 (.375)	.336 (.500)	.206 (.125)	.047	.121
1915	.232 (.500)	.421 (.167)	.159 (.167)	.055	.134 (.167)

*Figures in parentheses represent the proportion of the total number of cadets from the area to the number of cadets appointed to black regiments.

APPENDIX E

Class-Rank Ratio Table for
Appointees to the Black Regiments

The ratio used in this table was derived by using the following formula:

$$\frac{\text{Total number in class} - \text{Individual rank of graduate}}{\text{Total number in class}}$$

This formula was used rather than the simple rank-total ratio because the latter would have yielded a high value for a low ranking graduate. In order to avoid the confusing situation of a high-ranking officer being assigned a low value, the individual's rank was first subtracted from the total number in the class and then divided by this figure.

For example, in 1894, James A. Moss graduated 54th in a class of 54. Had the rank-total ratio been used Moss' score would have been 1. However, by using the (Total − rank)/total formula the score for Lieutenant Moss then becomes .000, while the score for the highest-ranking member of the class becomes .981.

Appendix E

Class/Rank Ratio of Men Appointed to the Black Regiments

Year	Cavalry	Infantry
1891	.692, .523	.323, .061
1892	.432	.048, .032
1893	.352, .294	.058, .019
1894	.759, .296	.000
1895	.731, .480, .327, .288	.154, .135, .115
1896	.699, .658, .630, .027, .013 .000	.123
1897	.298	.657, .104, .047
1898		.118, .101
1899	.694, .680, .486, .472	
1900	.240	
1901	.297, .108	
1902	.148, .074, .000	
1903	.323, .311	.247, .236
1904	.484, .314, .234, .185, .177	.096, .089, .048, .008
1905	.421, .298, .280	.079, .052, .044
1906	.385	.051
1907		.261, .117, .063, .054
1908	.250, .231, .064	.167, .028, .009
1909	.291, .126, .038	.388, .068
1910	.241, .168, .108	
1911	.500	.195
1912	.526, .252, .242, .200	
1913	.580, .538, .376	.043
1914	.224, .196, .186, .159, .112	.467, .084, .009
1915	.299, .250, .219, .098, .091	.317

Bibliography

I. Public Manuscript Materials

A. National Archives

1. General Records of the Department of State, Record Group 59. Dispatches from United States Ministers to Haiti, 1862–1906. Records of the Department of State Relating to the Internal Affairs of Liberia, 1910–1929.

2. Records of The Adjutant General's Office, Record Group 94. Document File, 1890–1917.

Muster Rolls. Ninth Cavalry, 1891–1912.

"The Negro in the Military Service of the U.S., 1639–1886."

"Numbers of Enlistments and Reenlistments in the U.S. Army by Months; White, Colored, Indian; 1891–1914."

Organizational Returns. Ninth Cavalry, January 1894–December 1916.

———. Tenth Cavalry, January 1891–December 1916.

———. Twenty-fourth Infantry, January 1891–December 1916.

———. Twenty-fifth Infantry, January 1891–December 1916.

Regimental Records. Seventh United States Volunteer Infantry, 1898–1899.

———. Eighth United States Volunteer Infantry, 1898–1899.

———. Ninth United States Volunteer Infantry, 1898–1899.

———. Tenth United States Volunteer Infantry, 1898–1899.

———. Forty-eighth United States Volunteer Infantry, 1899–1901.

———. Forty-ninth United States Volunteer Infantry, 1899–1901.

Taylor, John M. "The Philippine Insurrection Against the United States." Unpublished manuscript in page proof.

3. Records of the American Expeditionary Forces (World War I), 1917–1923, Record Group 120.

Carrizal Encounter (Boxes 70–71).

4. Records of the Office of the Judge Advocate General, Record Group 153.

Document File #20754.

5. Records of the War Department General and Special Staffs, Army War College, Record Group 165.

File #4483.

File #6926.

File #9524–9.

6. Records of United States Regular Army Mobile Units, 1821–1942, Record Group 391.

Tenth United States Cavalry, Historical Sketch, 1866–1892, and Report of Operations, Spanish-American War, 1898.

Letters Sent. Ninth Cavalry, 1891–1917.

———. Tenth Cavalry, 1891–1917.

———. Twenty-fourth Infantry, 1891–1917.

———. Twenty-fifth Infantry, 1891–1917.

War Diaries, Tenth Cavalry, Punitive Expedition, 16 March 1916–3 February 1917.

7. Records of United States Army Continental Commands, 1821–1920, Record Group 393.

Letters Sent. Department of Arizona, 1891–1893.

———. Department of the Dakota, 1891–1898.

———. Department of the Platte, 1891–1898.

B. Library of Congress, Manuscript Division

Bullard, Robert L. Papers.

Burt, Andrew S., and Elizabeth. Papers.

Moseley, George V. H. Papers.

Perea, Beverly. Papers.

Pershing, John J. Papers.

Root, Elihu. Papers.

Taft, William H. Papers.

Washington, Booker T. Papers.

C. United States Army Military History Research Collection

Johnson, Jasper. Questionnaire, Spanish-American War Survey. Twenty-fourth Infantry Regimental Papers.

Johnson, Richard. "My Life in the U.S. Army, 1899 to 1922." Forty-eighth United States Volunteer Infantry Regimental Papers.

Paulding, Grace B. "Memoirs." William and Grace Paulding, Papers.

Young, Charles. "Handbook of Creole as Spoken in Hayti." Typescript.

D. Chicago Historical Society

Kendrick, John F. "The Midsummer Picnic of '98." Unpublished manuscript.

E. Montana Historical Society

"History of Fort Missoula." Unpublished manuscript.

II. Government Publications

A. Federal

Byers, Jean. *A Study of the Negro in the Military Service.* Washington, D.C., 1950.

Houston, James A. *The Sinews of War: Army Logistics, 1775–1953.* Washington, D.C., 1966.

Pride, Armistead. *Negro Newspapers on Microfilm; A Selected List.* Washington, D.C., 1953.

Register of the Department of State, 1892–1916. Washington, D.C., 1892–1917.

Regulations for the Army of the United States, 1895. Washington, D.C., 1895.

Reynolds, Alfred. *The Life of an Enlisted Soldier in the United States Army.* Washington, D.C., 1904.

Revised Statutes of the United States. Washington, D.C., 1875.

Thomas, Robert S., and Allen, Inez V. *The Mexican Punitive Expedition.* Washington, D.C., 1954. (The pages of this book are numbered consecutively within each chapter.)

U.S., Congress, House of Representatives. *Report of the Secretary of War, 1889.* House Executive Document 1, part 2, volume 1, 51st Congress, 1st session, 1889–1890.

———. *Report of the Secretary of War, 1892.* House Executive Document 1, part 2, volume 1, 52d Congress, 2d session, 1892–1893.

———. *Report of the Inspector-General, 1892.* House Executive Document 1, part 2, volume 4, 52d Congress, 2d session, 1892–1893.

———. *Report of the Secretary of War, 1893.* House Executive Document 1, part 2, volume 1, 53d Congress, 2d session, 1893–1894.

———. *Report of the Inspector-General, 1893.* House Executive Document 1, part 2, volume 4, 53d Congress, 2d session, 1893–1894.

———. *A Bill to Reorganize the Artillery and Infantry of the Army and Increase their Efficiency.* H.R. 6139, 53d Congress, 2d session, 1893–1894.

———. *A Bill to Reorganize and Increase the Efficiency of the Infantry Regiments, Army of the United States of America.* H.R. 7338, 53d Congress, 2d Session, 1893–1894.

———. *Report of the Secretary of War, 1894.* House Executive Document 1, part 2, volume 1, 53d Congress, 3d session, 1894–1895.

———. *A Bill to Reorganize the Line of the Army.* H.R. 8739, 53d Congress, 3d session, 1894–1895.

———. *Report of the Secretary of War, 1895.* House Document 2, volume 1, 54th Congress, 1st session, 1895–1896.

———. *Report of the Secretary of War, 1896.* House Document 2, volume 1, 54th Congress, 2d session, 1896–1897.

———. *A Bill to Provide for Temporarily Increasing the Military Establishment of the United States in Time of War, and for Other Purposes.* H.R. 10069, 55th Congress, 2d session, 1897–1898.

———. *A Bill to Authorize the Establishment of an Army of Colored Men for the Occupation and Defense of the Islands Taken or Controlled by the United States in the War with Spain.* H.R. 10526, 55th Congress, 2d session, 1897–1898.

———. *A Bill to Provide for the Organization of a Division of Colored Immune Volunteers.* H.R. 10765, 55th Congress, 2d session, 1897–1898.

———. *A Bill to Authorize the Raising of 40,000 Colored Troops.* H.R. 10888, 55th Congress, 2d session, 1897–1898.

———. *A Bill to Raise 25,000 Colored Troops from the Nation at Large.* H.R. 10904, 55th Congress, 2d session, 1897–1898.

————. *Congressional Record.* 55th Congress, 2d session, 1897–1898.

————. *Increasing the Military Establishment of the United States.* House Report 1232, 55th Congress, 2d session, 1897–1898.

————. *Report of the Secretary of War, 1897.* House Document 2, volume 1, 55th Congress, 2d session, 1897–1898.

————. *A Resolution to Provide for the Mustering into the United States Volunteer Army of One Regiment of Colored Troops.* House Joint Resolution 288, 55th Congress, 2d session, 1897–1898.

————. *Report of the Secretary of War, 1898.* House Document 2, volume 1, 55th Congress, 3d session, 1898–1899.

————. *Report of the Major General Commanding the Army, 1898.* House Document 2, volume 2, 55th Congress, 3d session, 1898–1899.

————. *A Bill for the Reorganization of the Army of the United States and for Other Purposes.* H.R. 11087, 55th Congress, 3d session, 1898–1899.

————. *A Bill to Amend an Act Entitled "An Act to Provide for a Volunteer Brigade of Engineers and an Additional Force of 10,000 Enlisted Men Specially Accustomed to Tropical Climates," Approved May 11, 1898.* H.R. 11092, 55th Congress, 3d session, 1898–1899.

————. *A Bill for the Reorganization of the Army of the United States, and for Other Purposes.* H.R. 11137, 55th Congress, 3d session, 1898–1899.

————. *A Bill for the Better Organization of the Cavalry of the Army of the United States.* H.R. 11267, 55th Congress, 3d session, 1898–1899.

————. *A Bill for Increasing the Efficiency of the Army of the United States, and for Other Purposes.* H.R. 12176, 55th Congress, 3d session, 1898–1899.

————. *A Bill for the Reorganization of the Army of the United States, and for Other Purposes.* H.R. 9705, 56th Congress, 1st session, 1899–1900.

————. *Reports of Bureau Chiefs, 1899.* House Document 2, volume 1, part 2, 56th Congress, 1st session, 1899–1900.

————. *Report of the Major General Commanding the Army, 1899.* House Document 2, volume 1, parts 3, 5, 56th Congress, 1st session, 1899–1900.

————. *Coeur D' Alene Labor Troubles.* House Report 1999, 56th Congress, 1st session, 1899–1900.

————. *Reports of Chiefs of Bureaus, 1900.* House Document 2, volume 1, part 2, 56th Congress, 2d session, 1900–1901.

————. *Report of Major General Elwell S. Otis, 1899–1900.* House Document 2, volume 1, part 4, 56th Congress, 2d session, 1900–1901.

————. *Report of Major General Arthur MacArthur, 1900.* House Document 2, volume 1, part 5, 56th Congress, 2d session, 1900–1901.

————. *Report of Major General Henry W. Lawton, 1899.* House Document 2, volume 1, part 6, 56th Congress, 2d session, 1900–1901.

————. *Report of Military Operations in the Philippine Islands, 1899–1900.* House Document 2, volume 1, part 7, 56th Congress, 2d session, 1900–1901.

————. *Report of Operations of Second Division, Eighth Army Corps, 1899–1900.* House Document 2, volume 1, part 8, 56th Congress, 2d session, 1900–1901.

————. *Report of the Secretary of War, 1901.* House Document 2, part 1, 57th Congress, 1st session, 1901–1902.

————. *Report of the Lieutenant General Commanding the Army, 1901.* House Document 2, part 3, 57th Congress, 1st session, 1901–1902.

————. *Report of the Secretary of War, 1902.* House Document 2, volume 1, 57th Congress, 2d session, 1902–1903.

————. *Report of the Lieutenant General Commanding the Army, 1902.* House Document 2, volume 9, 57th Congress, 2d session, 1902–1903.

————. *Reports of Division and Department Commanders, 1904.* House Document 2, volume 3, 58th Congress, 3d session, 1904–1905.

————. *Report of the Secretary of War, 1906.* House Document 2, volume 1, 59th Congress, 2d session, 1906–1907.

————. *A Bill to Discontinue the Enlistment and Appointment of Negroes in the Army of the United States.* H.R. 20989, 59th Congress, 2d session, 1906–1907.

————. *A Bill to Repeal Sections 1104 and 1108, Revised Statutes, Edition of 1878.* H.R. 20994, 59th Congress, 2d session, 1906–1907.

————. *A Bill to Repeal Sections 1104 and 1108, Revised Statutes, Edition of 1878.* H.R. 3888, 60th Congress, 1st session, 1907–1908.

————. *Congressional Record.* 60th Congress, 2d session, 1908–1909.

————. *A Bill Fixing the Number of Infantry Regiments in the United States Army, Providing for a Chief of Infantry, Etc.* H.R. 23469, 60th Congress, 2d session, 1908–1909.

————. *A Bill to Repeal Sections 1104 and 1108, Revised Statutes, Edition of 1878.* H.R. 12340, 61st Congress, 2d session, 1909–1910.

————. *A Bill to Repeal Sections 1104 and 1108, Revised Statutes, Edition of 1878.* H.R. 1262, 62d Congress, 1st session, 1911.

————. *A Bill to Make it Unlawful to Appoint as Commissioned or Non-Commissioned Officers in the Army or Navy of the United States Any Person of the Negro Race.* H.R. 17541, 63d Congress, 2d session, 1913–1914.

————. *A Bill to Increase the United States Army.* H.R. 20188, 63d Congress, 3d session, 1914–1915.

————. *Congressional Record.* 64th Congress, 1st session, 1915–1916.

————. *A Bill to Make it Unlawful to Appoint as Commissioned or Non-Commissioned Officers in the Army or Navy of the United States Any Person of the Negro Race.* H.R. 3573, 64th Congress, 1st session, 1915–1916.

————. *A Bill for Making Further and More Effectual Provision for the National Defense, and for Other Purposes.* H.R. 12037, 64th Congress, 1st session, 1915–1916.

————. *A Bill to Make It Unlawful to Appoint as Commissioned or Non-Commissioned Officers in the Army or Navy of the United States Any Person of the Negro Race.* H.R. 12840, 64th Congress, 1st session, 1915–1916.

————. *A Bill to Prevent the Enlistment of Negroes in the Military Service of the United States.* H.R. 17183, 64th Congress, 1st session, 1915–1916.

————. *A Bill to confer pensionable status on veterans involved in the Brownsville, Texas, incident of August 13, 1906, and to require the Administrator of Veterans' Affairs to make certain compensatory payments to such veterans and their heirs.* H.R. 4382. 93d Congress, 1st session, 1973.

————. *An Act to amend title 38 of the United States Code to increase the monthly rates of disability and death pensions, and dependency and indemnity compensation, and for other purposes.* H.R. 9474, 93d Congress, 1st session, 1973.

————. "Pending Non-Service-Connected Pension Legislation." *Hearings Before the Subcommittee on Compensation and Pension of the Committee on Veterans' Affairs.* 93d Congress, 1st session, 1973.

U.S., Congress, Senate. *Congressional Record.* 45th Congress, 2d session, 1878.

————. *A Bill to Reorganize the Line of the Army.* S.R. 1778, 52d Congress, 1st session, 1891–1892.

————. *A Bill to Reorganize the Artillery and Infantry of the Army, and to Increase its Efficiency.* S.R. 2170, 52d Congress, 1st session, 1891–1892.

————. *A Bill to Reorganize the Artillery and Infantry of the Army, and to Increase its Efficiency.* S.R. 546, 53d Congress, 1st session, 1893.

————. *A Bill for the Reorganization and Increase of the Army.* S.R. 2418, 53d Congress, 3d session, 1894–1895.

————. *A Bill to Increase the Efficiency of the Infantry and to Improve the Infantry Organization of the Army of the United States of America.* S.R. 2478, 53d Congress, 3d session, 1894–1895.

————. *A Bill to Increase the Efficiency of the Infantry Organization of the Army of the United States.* S.R. 2548, 53d Congress, 3d session, 1894–1895.

————. *A Bill to Provide a Modern Organization for the Line of the Army.* S.R. 538, 54th Congress, 1st session, 1895–1896.

————. *A Bill to Reorganize the Line of the Army.* S.R. 1472, 54th Congress, 1st session, 1895–1896.

————. *A Bill to Increase the Efficiency of the Infantry of the Army of the United States.* S.R. 2004, 54th Congress, 1st session, 1895–1896.

————. *A Bill to Provide for a Military Peace Establishment.* S.R. 2130, 54th Congress, 1st session. 1895–1896.

————. *A Bill to Provide for a Volunteer Division of Colored Troops in the United States Army Specially Adapted to Tropical Climates.* S.R. 4797, 55th Congress, 2d session, 1897–1898.

————. *A Bill to Provide for a Force of Colored Troops in the Volunteer Army of the United States.* S.R. 4840, 55th Congress, 2d session, 1897–1898.

————. *A Bill Providing for the Reorganization of the Army of the United States.* S.R. 4900, 55th Congress, 3d session, 1898–1899.

————. *A Bill for the Reorganization of the Army of the United States, and for Other Purposes.* S.R. 4938, 55th Congress, 3d session, 1898–1899.

————. *A Bill for the Reorganization of the Army of the United States, and for Other Purposes.* S.R. 5023, 55th Congress, 3d session, 1898–1899.

————. *A Bill to Provide for Raising, Organizing, and Maintaining the Volunteer Army of the United States.* S.R. 5118, 55th Congress, 3d session, 1898–1899.

————. *Coeur D' Alene Mining Troubles.* Senate Document 24, 56th Congress, 1st session, 1899–1900.

————. *Report of the Commission Appointed by the President to Investigate the Conduct of the War Department in the War with Spain.* Senate Document 221, 56th Congress, 1st session, 1899–1900.

————. *Journal of the Senate of the United States.* 56th Congress, 2d session, 1900–1901.

————. *Congressional Record.* 59th Congress, 2d session, 1906–1907.

————. *Summary Discharge or Mustering Out of Regiments or Companies.* Senate Document 155, parts 1–2, 59th Congress, 2d session, 1906–1907.

————. *Congressional Record.* 60th Congress, 1st session, 1907–1908.

————. *The Brownsville Affray.* Senate Document 389, 60th Congress, 1st session, 1907–1908.

————. *Proceedings of a General Court-Martial Convened at Headquarters, Department of Texas, San Antonio, Tex., February 4, 1907, in the Case of Maj. Charles W. Penrose, Twenty-fifth United States Infantry.* Senate Document 402, part 2, 60th Congress, 1st session, 1907–1908.

————. *Proceedings of a General Court-Martial Convened at Headquarters, Department of Texas, San Antonio, Tex., April 15, 1907 in the Case of Capt. Edgar A. Macklin, Twenty-fifth United States Infantry.* Senate Document 402, part 3, 60th Congress, 1st session, 1907–1908.

————. *Hearings Before the Committee on Military Affairs Concerning the Affray at Brownsville, Tex., on the Night of August 13 and 14, 1906.* Senate Document 402, parts 4–6, 60th Congress, 1st session, 1907–1908.

————. *Oscar W. Reid v. United States.* Senate Document 486, 60th Congress, 1st session, 1907–1908.

————. *Congressional Record.* 60th Congress, 2d session, 1908–1909.

————. *Special Message of the President of the United States Communicated to the Senate on December 14, 1908.* Senate Document 587, 60th Congress, 2d session, 1908–1909.

————. *Employment of Herbert J. Browne and W. G. Baldwin by the War Department at Brownsville.* Senate Document 626, 60th Congress, 2d session, 1908–1909.

————. *Affairs in Liberia.* Senate Document 457, 61st Congress, 2d session, 1909–1910.

————. *Companies B, C, and D, Twenty-fifth United States Infantry—Report of the Proceedings of the Court of Inquiry Relative to the Shooting Affray at Brownsville, Tex., August 13–14, 1906 by Soldiers of Companies B, C, and D, Twenty-fifth United States Infantry.* Senate Document 701, 61st Congress, 3d session, 1910–1911.

————. *Congressional Record.* 93d Congress, 1st Session, 1973.

————. *A Bill to confer pensionable status on veterans involved in the Brownsville, Texas, incident of August 13, 1906, and to require the Administrator of Veterans' Affairs to make certain compensatory payments to such veterans and their heirs.* S. 1999, 93d Congress, 1st session, 1973.

U.S. Department of the Army. *United States Army Register, 1967.* Washington, D.C., 1967.

U.S. Department of Commerce. Bureau of the Census. *Historical Statistics of the United States; Colonial Times to 1957.* Washington, D.C., 1960.

————. *Twelfth Census of the United States, 1910: Population.*

U.S. Department of the Interior. Bureau of the Census. *Tenth Census of the United States, 1890: Population.*

————. *Eleventh Census of the United States, 1900: Population.* U.S. Department of War. *General Orders, Series of 1898.*

————. *Annual Report of the Secretary of War, 1907.*

————. *Annual Report of the Secretary of War, 1908.*

————. *Annual Report of the Secretary of War, 1912.*

————. *Annual Report of the Secretary of War, 1916.*

————. *Official Army Register, 1891–1917.*

B. State

Biennial Report of the Adjutant General of Alabama, 1898. Montgomery, Alabama, 1898.

Biennial Report of the Adjutant General of Illinois, 1897–1898. Springfield, Illinois, 1899.

III. Periodicals

A. Articles

Alexander, Thomas G., and Arrington, Leonard J. "The Utah Military Frontier, 1872–1912: Forts Cameron, Thornburgh, and Duchesne." *Utah Historical Quarterly* 32:4 (Fall 1964):330–54.

Arnold, Paul T. "Negro Soldiers in the United States Army." *The Magazine of History* 11:3 (March 1910):119–25.

Bonsal, Stephen. "The Negro Soldier in War and Peace." *North American Review* 185:616 (7 June 1907):321–27.

Bowman, Larry G. "Virginia's Use of Blacks in the French and Indian War." *Western Pennsylvania Historical Magazine* 53:1 (January 1970):57–104.

Bullard, Robert L. "The Negro Volunteer: Some Characteristics." *Journal of the Military Service Institution of the United States* 29:62 (July 1901):27–35.

Coffman, Edward M. "Army Life on the Frontier, 1865–1898." *Military Affairs* 20:4 (Winter 1956):193–201.

————. "An Old Soldier's Story." *Louisville Courier Journal*, 2 December 1956.

Coleman, Rufus A. "Mark Twain in Montana, 1895." *Montana Magazine of History* 3:2 (Spring 1953):9–17.

Dunton, W. Herbert. "The Fair in the Cow Country." *Scribner's Magazine* 55:4 (April 1914):454–65.

Dwyer, Robert J. "The Negro in the United States Army." *Sociology and Social Research* 38:2 (November-December 1953):103–12.

Foote, Mary H. "Coeur D' Alene." *Century Magazine* 48:1 (May 1894):102–15.

Gatewood, Willard B., Jr. "Negro Troops in Florida, 1898." *Florida Historical Quarterly* 49:1 (July 1970):1–15.

Gianakos, Perry E. "The Spanish-American War and the Double Paradox of the Negro American." *Phylon* 26:1 (Spring 1965):34–49.

Head, William H. "The Negro as an American Soldier." *World Today* 12:3 (March 1907):322–24.

Langley, Harold D. "The Negro in the Navy and Merchant Service, 1798–1860." *Journal of Negro History* 52:4 (October 1967):273–86.

Maslowski, Pete. "National Policy Toward the Use of Black Troops in the Revolution." *South Carolina Historical Magazine* 73:1 (January 1972):1–17.

Murray, Robert A. "The United States Army in the Aftermath of the Johnson County Invasion." *Annals of Wyoming* 38:1 (April 1966):59–76.

Nelson, Henry L. "Davids Island: The Enlisted Man of the Army." *Harper's Weekly* 34:1749 (28 June 1890):509–12.

O'Connor, Richard. "Black Jack of the 10th." *American Heritage* 18:2 (February 1967):14–17, 102–7.

Ogden, George W. "A World Afire." *Everybody's Magazine* 23:6 (December 1910):764–66.

Parker, W. Thornton. "The Evolution of the Colored Soldier." *North American Review* 168:507 (February 1899):223–28.

Reddick, L. D. "The Negro Policy of the United States Army, 1775–1945." *The Journal of Negro History* 34:1 (January 1949):9–29.

Remington, Frederic. "Vagabonding with the Tenth Horse." *Cosmopolitan* 22:4 (February 1897):347–54.

Roosevelt, Theodore. "The Rough Riders." *Scribner's Magazine* 25:4 (April 1899):420–50.

Rudwick, Elliott M. "The Niagara Movement." *The Journal of Negro History* 43:3 (July 1957):177–200.

Ruhl, Arthur. "The Gallery at San Antonio." *Collier's Weekly* 47:6 (29 April 1911):13.

Schubert, Frank N. "Black Soldiers on the White Frontier: Some Factors Influencing Race Relations." *Phylon* 32:4 (Winter 1971):410–15.

———. "The Suggs Affray: The Black Cavalry in the Johnson County War." *The Western Historical Quarterly* 4:1 (January 1973):57–68.

Smythe, Donald. "John Pershing at Fort Assiniboine." *Montana* 18:1 (January 1968):19–23.

Steele, Matthew F. "The 'Color Line' in the Army." *North American Review* 183:605 (December 1906):1285–88.

Troxel, Orlando C. "The Tenth Cavalry in Mexico." *Journal of the United States Cavalry Association* 18:116 (October 1917):197–205.

Villard, Oswald G. "The Negro in the Regular Army." *The Atlantic Monthly* 91:548 (June 1903):721–29.

Wharfield, Harold B. "The Affair at Carrizal; Pershing's Punitive Expedition." *Montana* 18:4 (October 1968):24–39.

Bibliography

B. Newspapers and Magazines

The Afro-American Sentinel (Omaha, Nebraska).
The American Citizen (Kansas City, Kansas).
The Army and Navy Journal.
The Army and Navy Register.
The Bee (Washington, D. C.).
The Broad-ax (Salt Lake City, Utah, and Chicago, Illinois).
The Burlington Free Press (Vermont).
Cheyenne State Leader (Wyoming).
The Chicago Defender.
The Chicago Tribune.
The Colored American (Washington, D.C.).
Colored American Magazine.
The Colored Citizen (Topeka, Kansas).
The Crisis.
The Daily Palo Alto (Stanford, California).
The Enterprise (Omaha, Nebraska).
The Freeman (Indianapolis, Indiana).
The Gazette (Cleveland, Ohio).
Harper's Weekly.
The Illinois Record (Springfield, Illinois).
Journal of the Military Service Institution of the United States.
The Journal of Negro History.
Journal of the United States Cavalry Association.
Leslie's Weekly.
The Daily Missoulian (Missoula, Montana).
The Weekly Missoulian (Missoula, Montana).
The Nation.
New York Age.
New York Evening Journal.
The New York Times.
Portland New Age (Oregon).
The Recorder (Indianapolis, Indiana).
The Richmond Planet (Virginia).
The Rising Sun (Kansas City, Missouri).
San Francisco Examiner.
St. Louis Palladium.
St. Louis Post-Dispatch.
San Antonio Express (Texas).
The Savannah Tribune (Georgia).
The Searchlight (Wichita, Kansas).
The Seattle Post Intelligencer (Washington).
Southern Workman and Hampton School Record.
Spokane Daily Chronicle (Washington).
The State Ledger (Topeka, Kansas).

The Washington Post (District of Columbia).
The World (New York City).

IV. Books

Alexander, Charles. *Battles and Victories of Allen Allensworth.* Boston, 1914.
Alger, Russell A. *The Spanish-American War.* New York, 1901.
Anderson, Robert E. *Liberia: America's African Friend.* Chapel Hill, N. C., 1952.
Atkins, John B. *The War in Cuba: The Experiences of an Englishman with the United States Army.* London, 1899.
Bigelow, John, Jr. *Reminiscences of the Santiago Campaign.* New York, 1899.
Blount, James H. *The American Occupation of the Philippines, 1898–1912.* New York, 1912.
Bogue, Allan G., Phillips, Thomas D., and Wright, James E. *The West of the American People.* Itasca, Ill., 1970.
Bonsal, Stephen. *The Fight for Santiago: The Story of the Soldiers in the Cuban Campaign from Tampa to the Surrender.* New York, 1899.
Cashin, Herschel V. *Under Fire with the Tenth United States Cavalry.* New York, 1899.
Chew, Abraham. *A Biography of Colonel Charles Young.* Washington, D.C., 1923.
Clendenen, Clarence C. *Blood on the Border.* New York, 1969.
Cornish, Dudley T. *The Sable Arm: Negro Troops in the Union Army, 1861–1865.* New York, 1956.
Coston, William H. *The Spanish-American War Volunteer.* 2d ed. Middletown, Pa., 1899.
Crane, Charles J. *The Experiences of a Colonel of Infantry.* New York, 1923.
Curtis, Mary. *The Black Soldier: or, The Colored Boys of the United States Army.* Washington, D.C., 1915.
Dalfiume, Richard M. *Desegregation of the United States Armed Forces.* Columbia, Mo., 1969.
David, Jay, and Crane, Elaine. *The Black Soldier—From the American Revolution to Vietnam.* New York, 1971.
Davis, John P., ed. *The American Negro Reference Book.* Englewood Cliffs, N.J., 1966.
Davis, Richard H. *The Cuban and Porto Rican Campaigns.* New York, 1898.
Dixon, Thomas, Jr. *The Clansman: An Historical Romance of the Ku Klux Klan.* New York, 1907.
Downey, Fairfax D. *Indian-Fighting Army.* New York, 1941.
Edwards, Frank E. *The '98 Campaign of the 6th Massachusetts, U.S.V.* Boston, 1899.
Elkins, Stanley M. *Slavery.* New York, 1963.
Faust, Karl I. *Campaigning in the Philippines.* San Francisco, 1899.

Fishel, Leslie H., Jr., and Quarles, Benjamin. *The Black American, A Brief Documentary History*. Glenview, Ill., 1970.

Flipper, Henry O. *The Colored Cadet at West Point*. New York, 1878.

Foner, Jack D. *The United States Soldier Between Two Wars: Army Life and Reforms, 1865–1898*. New York, 1970.

Foraker, Joseph B. *Notes of a Busy Life*. 2 vols. Cincinnati, 1916.

Franklin, John H. *From Slavery to Freedom*. 3d ed. New York, 1967.

Frazier, Thomas R., ed. *Afro-American History: Primary Sources*. New York, 1970.

Freidel, Frank. *The Splendid Little War*. Boston, 1958.

Gatewood, Willard B., Jr. *"Smoked Yankees" and the Struggle for Empire: Letters From Negro Soldiers, 1898–1902*. Urbana, Ill., 1971.

———. *Theodore Roosevelt and the Art of Controversy: Episodes of the White House Years*. Baton Rouge, La., 1970.

Glass, Edward L. *History of the Tenth Cavalry, 1866–1921*. Tucson, Ariz., 1921.

Goode, W. T. *The 8th Illinois*. Chicago, 1899.

Gossett, Thomas F. *Race: The History of an Idea in America*. Dallas, 1963.

Hemment, John C. *Cannon and Camera: Sea and Land Battles of the Spanish-American War in Cuba; Camp Life and the Return of the Soldiers*. New York, 1898.

Johnson, Edward A. *History of Negro Soldiers in the Spanish-American War, and Other Items of Interest*. Raleigh, N.C., 1899.

Kellogg, Charles F. *NAACP: A History of the National Association for the Advancement of Colored People*. Baltimore, 1967.

Kennan, George. *Campaigning in Cuba*. New York, 1899.

Key, Vladimir O., Jr. *Southern Politics in State and Nation*. New York, 1949.

Lane, Ann J. *The Brownsville Affair: National Crisis and Black Reaction*. Port Washington, N.Y., 1971.

Leckie, William H. *The Buffalo Soldiers: A Narrative of the Negro Cavalry in the West*. Norman, Okla., 1967.

Lee, Irvin H. *Negro Medal of Honor Men*. New York, 1967.

LeRoy, James A. *The Americans in the Philippines*. 2 vols. Boston, 1914.

Link, Arthur S. *Woodrow Wilson and the Progressive Era, 1910–1917*. New York, 1954.

Logan, Rayford W. *The Betrayal of the Negro*. New York, 1965.

Lynk, Miles V. *The Black Troopers, or, The Daring Heroism of the Negro Soldiers in the Spanish-American War*. Jackson, Tenn., 1899.

McCard, Henry S., and Turnley, Henry. *A History of the Eighth Illinois United States Volunteers*. Chicago, 1899.

McClure, Nathaniel F., ed. *Class of 1887, United States Military Academy; A Biographical Volume to Commemorate the 50th Anniversary of Graduation at West Point, New York, June, 1937*. Washington, D.C., 1938.

McConnell, Roland C. *Negro Troops of Antebellum Louisiana: A History of the Battalion of Free Men of Color*. Baton Rouge, La., 1968.

Marszalek, John F., Jr. *Court-Martial: A Black Man in America.* New York, 1972.

Mercer, Asa S. *The Banditti of the Plains: or, The Cattleman's Invasion of Wyoming in 1892.* Cheyenne, Wyo., 1894.

Merrill, James M. *Spurs to Glory: The Story of the United States Cavalry.* Chicago, 1966.

Miley, John D. *In Cuba with Shafter.* New York, 1899.

Millis, Walter. *The Martial Spirit.* New York, 1959.

Montague, Ludwell L. *Haiti and the United States: 1714–1938.* New York, 1966.

Morison, Elting E., ed. *The Letters of Theodore Roosevelt.* 8 vols. Cambridge, Mass., 1951–1954.

Moss, James A. *Memories of the Campaign of Santiago.* San Francisco, 1899.
———. *Military Cycling in the Rocky Mountains.* New York, 1897.

Muller, William G. *The 24th Infantry, Past and Present.* N.p., 1924.

Nankivell, John H. *History of the Twenty-Fifth Regiment of United States Infantry, 1869–1926.* Denver, 1927.

Nelson, Dennis D. *The Integration of the Negro into the U.S. Navy.* New York, 1951.

O'Connor, Richard. *Black Jack Pershing.* Garden City, N.Y., 1961.

The Official Roster of Ohio Soldiers in the War with Spain, 1898–1899. Columbus, Ohio, 1916.

Ottley, Roi, ed. *Sketch and History of the Constitution League of the United States.* N.p., 1939.

Parker, John H. *History of the Gatling Gun Detachment, Fifth Army Corps, At Santiago.* Kansas City, Mo., 1898.

Post, Charles J. *The Little War of Private Post.* Boston, 1960.

Quarles, Benjamin. *The Negro in the American Revolution.* Chapel Hill, N.C., 1961.

Rickey, Don, Jr. *Forty Miles a Day on Beans and Hay: The Enlisted Soldier Fighting the Indian Wars.* Norman, Okla., 1963.

Rodenbough, Theodore F., and Hasken, William L., eds. *The Army of the United States.* New York, 1896.

Roosevelt, Theodore. *The Rough Riders.* New York, 1961.

Sargent, Herbert H. *The Campaign of Santiago de Cuba.* 3 vols. Chicago, 1907.

Schuyler, George. *Black and Conservative: The Autobiography of George S. Schuyler.* New Rochelle, N.Y., 1966.

Sexton, William T. *Soldiers in the Sun: An Adventure in Imperialism.* Harrisburg, Pa., 1939.

Smith, Robert W. *The Coeur D' Alene Mining War of 1892: A Case Study of an Industrial Dispute.* Corvallis, Oreg., 1961.

The Spanish-American War: The Events of the War Described by Eye Witnesses. Chicago, 1899.

Steward, Theophilus G. *The Colored Regulars in the United States Army.* Philadelphia, 1904.

Thweatt, Hiram M. *What the Newspapers Say of the Negro Soldier in the Spanish-American War.* Thomasville, Ga., n.d.

Tompkins, Frank. *Chasing Villa.* Harrisburg, Pa., 1934.

Truman, Benjamin C. *History of the World's Fair.* Chicago, 1893.

Weaver, John D. *The Brownsville Raid.* New York, 1970.

Werner, Herman. *On the Western Frontier with the United States Cavalry Fifty Years Ago.* N.p., 1934.

West Point Graduates Association. *Register of Graduates, United States Military Academy, 1966.* West Point, N.Y., 1966.

————. *Register of Graduates, United States Military Academy, 1967.* West Point, N.Y., 1967.

Wharfield, Harold B. *Tenth Cavalry and Border Fights.* N.p., 1965.

Wilkes, Laura E. *Missing Pages in American History, Revealing the Services of Negroes in the Early Wars of the United States of America, 1641–1815.* Boston, 1861.

Wilson, James H. *Under the Old Flag: Recollections of Military Operations in the War for the Union, the Spanish War, the Boxer Rebellion, etc.* 2 vols. New York, 1912.

Woodward, C. Vann. *Origins of the New South: 1877–1913.* Baton Rouge, La., 1966.

————. *The Strange Career of Jim Crow.* 2d rev. ed. New York, 1966.

Work, Monroe N. *A Bibliography of the Negro in Africa and America.* New York, 1928.

Wormser, Richard E. *The Yellowlegs: The Story of the United States Cavalry.* Garden City, N.Y., 1966.

Young, Charles. *Military Morale of Nations and Races.* Kansas City, Mo., 1912.

Young, James R., and Moore, J. Hampton, ed. *Reminiscences and Thrilling Stories of the War by Returned Heroes.* Springfield, Mass., 1899.

V. Unpublished Materials

Allen, John H. Letters to author, 7 December 1966, 24 January 1967.

Armstrong, Frank. "Memoir." (Manuscript in possession of the Armstrong family.)

Brown, Richard C. "Social Attitudes of American Generals, 1898–1940." Ph.D. diss., University of Wisconsin, 1951.

Cook, Lawrence C. "The Brownsville Affray of 1906." M.A. thesis, University of Colorado, 1942.

Davis, Benjamin O., Sr. Interview with Edward M. Coffman and author, 2 June 1968.

————. Papers. (In possession of Mr. and Mrs. James McLendon.)

Ehrbar, Judson, Registrar, Juilliard School of Music. Letter to author, 16 January 1969.

Fletcher, Marvin E. "The Blacks in Blue: Negro Volunteers in Reconstruction." M.A. thesis, University of Wisconsin, 1964.

————. "The Negro Soldier and the United States Army, 1891–1917." Ph.D. diss., University of Wisconsin, 1968.

Foner, Jack D. "The United States Soldier Between Two Wars: Army Life and Reforms, 1865–1898." Ph.D. diss., Columbia University, 1968.

Fowler, Arlen L. "The Negro Infantry in the West, 1869–1891." Ph.D. diss., Washington State University, 1968.

Hay, Thomas. Interview with Alan C. Roochvarg, 28 August 1966.

Hay, William W. Interview with Earl Stover, 17 February 1967.

Henry, Guy V., Jr. Letter to author, 21 August 1966.

Johnson, Robert B. "The Punitive Expedition: A Military, Diplomatic and Political History of Pershing's Chase after Pancho Villa, 1916–1917." Ph.D. diss., University of Southern California, 1964.

Lane, Ann J. "The Brownsville Affray." Ph.D. diss., Columbia University, 1968.

Phillips, Thomas D. "The Negro Regulars: Negro Soldiers in the United States Army, 1866–1890." Ph.D. diss., University of Wisconsin, 1970.

————. Letter to author, 24 January 1969.

Schuyler, George S. Letter to author, 29 May 1967.

Tinsley, James A. "The Brownsville Affray." M.A. thesis, University of North Carolina, 1948.

Young, Charles. "Extracts-Colonel Young's Record." Mimeographed, in possession of author.

Abbreviations and
Shortened Expressions in Footnotes

AGO—Records of The Adjutant General's Office

ANJ—The Army and Navy Journal

ANR—The Army and Navy Register

AWC File—Army War College File

BOD, Papers—Benjamin O. Davis, Sr., Papers

BTW, Papers—Booker T. Washington, Papers

Burt, Papers—Andrew S. and Elizabeth Burt, Papers

Court of Inquiry—U.S. Congress, Senate, *Companies B, C, and D, Twenty-fifth United States Infantry—Report of the Proceedings of the Court of Inquiry Relative to the Shooting Affray at Brownsville, Tex., August 13–14, 1906 By Soldiers of Companies B, C, and D, Twenty-fifth United States Infantry,* Senate Document 701, 61st Cong., 3d sess., 1910–1911

JJP, Papers—John J. Pershing, Papers

Lawton Report—U.S., Congress, House of Representatives, *Report of Major General Henry W. Lawton, 1899,* House Document 2, vol. 1, pt. 6, 56th Cong., 2d sess., 1900–1901

LS, 9th Cav—Letters Sent, Ninth Cavalry, 1891–1917. Records of the United States Regular Army Mobile Units, 1821–1942

LS, 10th Cav—Letters Sent, Tenth Cavalry, 1891–1917. Records of the United States Regular Army Mobile Units, 1821–1942

LS, 24th Inf—Letters Sent, Twenty-fourth Infantry, 1891–1917. Records of the United States Regular Army Mobile Units, 1821–1942

LS, 25th Inf—Letters Sent, Twenty-fifth Infantry, 1891–1917. Records of the United States Regular Army Mobile Units, 1821–1942

Macklin Court-Martial—U.S., Congress, Senate, *Proceedings of a General Court-Martial Convened at Headquarters, Department of Texas, San Antonio, Tex., April 15, 1907 in the Case of Capt. Edgar A. Macklin, Twenty-fifth United States Infantry,* Senate Document 402, pt. 3, 60th Cong., 1st sess., 1907–1908

Maj Gen 1898—U.S., Congress, House of Representatives, *Report of the Major General Commanding the Army, 1898,* House Document 2, vol. 2, 55th Cong., 3d sess., 1898–1899

Maj Gen 1899—U.S., Congress, House of Representatives, *Report of the Major General Commanding the Army, 1899,* House Document 2, vol. 1, pts. 3 and 5, 56th Cong., 1st sess., 1899–1900

NA, RG—National Archives, Record Group

NMS—U.S., War Department, The Adjutant General's Office, "The Negro in the Military Service of the U.S., 1639–1886"

Otis Report—U.S., Congress, House of Representatives, *Report of Major General Elwell S. Otis, 1899–1900,* House Document 2, vol. 1, pt. 4, 56th Cong., 2d sess., 1900–1901

Paulding, Papers—William and Grace Paulding, Papers

SAWar Invest—U.S., Congress, Senate, *Report of the Commission Appointed by the*

President to Investigate the Conduct of the War Department in the War with Spain, Senate Document 221, 56th Cong., 1st sess., 1899–1900

Sec War 1892—U.S., Congress, House of Representatives, *Report of the Secretary of War, 1892,* House Executive Document 1, vol. 1, pt. 2, 52d Cong., 2d sess., 1892–1893

Sec War 1893—U.S., Congress, House of Representatives, *Report of the Secretary of War, 1893,* House Executive Document 1, vol. 1, pt. 2, 53d Cong., 2d sess., 1893–1894

Sec War 1898—U.S., Congress, House of Representatives, *Report of the Secretary of War, 1898,* House Document 2, vol. 1, 55th Cong., 3d sess., 1898–1899

Sec War 1906—U.S., Congress, House of Representatives, *Annual Report of the Secretary of War, 1906,* House Document 2, vol. 1, 59th Cong., 2d sess., 1906–1907.

Senate Hearings—U.S., Congress, Senate, *Hearings Before the Committee on Military Affairs Concerning the Affray at Brownsville, Tex. on the Night of August 13 and 14, 1906,* Senate Document 402, pts. 4–6, 60th Cong., 1st sess., 1907–1908

Southern Workman—Southern Workman and Hampton School Record

Special Message—U.S., Congress, Senate, *Special Message of the President of the United States Communicated to the Senate on December 14, 1908,* Senate Document 587, 60th Cong., 2d sess., 1908–1909

Summary Discharge—U.S., Congress, Senate, *Summary Discharge or Mustering Out of Regiments or Companies,* Senate Document 155, pts. 1–2, 59th Cong., 2d sess., 1906–1907

10th Cav Org Ret—Organizational Returns, Tenth Cavalry, January 1891–December 1916. Records of The Adjutant General's Office

10th Cav War Diary—Tenth Cavalry War Diary. Records of the U.S. Regular Army Mobile Units, 1821–1942

25th Inf Org Ret—Organizational Returns, Twenty-fifth Infantry, January 1891–December 1916. Records of The Adjutant General's Office

U.S.-Liberia Records—General Records of the Department of State Relating to the Internal Affairs of Liberia, 1910–1929. General Records of the Department of State

INDEX